W9-AZL-578

Praise for *The Yoga of Leadership*

The Yoga of Leadership is an informative and thought-provoking complement to books on leadership. Oriented toward individual transformation, Tarra Mitchell shares a morally deep and timely message empowering leaders to raise consciousness through what she calls holistic wellbeing. With the integrity of an insider, she intelligently weaves together the elements necessary to become inspiring leaders in today's fast paced work environment and offers a convincing case leveraging ancient wisdom, science, and stories. This book has profound implications for how we manage our days, weeks, teams, and organizations.

John Mackey, Co-Founder and CEO, Whole Foods Market, Co-Author,
Conscious Capitalism: Liberating the Heroic Spirit of Business

In our 30 years of working with clients on personal finance, we at Edelman Financial know that personal finance is more personal than finance. There is a necessary human element in *all* business endeavors. Tarra and I share the same language. *The Yoga of Leadership* teaches us how to tap into our inner self so we can be the best leader and person we can be. Brava, Tarra!

Jean Edelman, Co-Founder, Edelman Financial Services, and Author, *The Other Side of Money*

The Yoga of Leadership is a deep and meaningful resource with real world applicability. Tarra Mitchell brings the ancient wisdom of yoga into leadership in a way that will easily resonate. Tarra committed to me many years back that she would bring yoga to the business world in some way and here it is!

Rolf Gates, Teacher and Author, *Meditations from the Mat: Daily Reflections on the Path of Yoga,*
Meditations on Intention and Being: Daily Reflections on the Path of Yoga, Mindfulness and Compassion

You have to be happy, healthy, have a sense of calm and a ton of energy first before you can fully engage your teams. I know when my mind is stressed, there is no way I can be there for my team in a way that my team really needs me – to listen to them patiently, be available to brainstorm with them objectively and to coach them through tough situations. Tarra's book, *The Yoga of Leadership,* is one of a kind and shows you how to be your personal best while have fun along the way and building a longer and more fulfilling life for yourself. It is a must read for every business leader who is putting in long hours both at work and home and feeling tapped out!

Anurag Bairathi, SVP U.S. Consumer Markets, Liberty Mutual Insurance

In *The Yoga of Leadership,* Tarra Mitchell takes us beneath the surface of the popular physical practice to reveal the practical value of yoga's esoteric teachings. By drawing out the relevant details of an ancient system of self-realization, Mitchell offers readers a unique and elegantly structured approach to personal wellness, team empowerment, and inspirational leadership.

Hari-kirtana das, author of *In Search of the Highest Truth: Adventures in Yoga Philosophy*

This is one of those books that profoundly changes the way we think about life, work, and leadership. I have had the pleasure of convening hundreds of the most powerful female leaders in the private equity industry each year for the past ten years, and it is very clear that success in a demanding career is linked to personal wellbeing. All of us can benefit from Tarra's road map for caring for ourselves in a holistic way – for our own health and the health of our organizations. Tarra is a pioneer whose ideas and teachings on how to be a better leader should be embraced.

Beth Falk, Founder & Managing Director, Women's Private Equity Summit; Founder & CEO, Falk Marques Group LLC

This book tightly connects the theory of yoga, to the theory of leadership in such a way that they are interwoven. The author also makes the practices accessible in a reassuring way. A wonderful resource!

Candida Brush, F.W. Olin Distinguished Professor of Entrepreneurship, Vice Provost of Global Entrepreneurial Leadership, Babson College

At a time when every one of us are being called to lead in new ways, *The Yoga of Leadership* is a practical and inspiring guidebook for today's rising wave of leaders from all walks of life. Too often I find that when I read teachings on how to become a great leader - it just seems stressful and hard. Not so in this book. Step by step Tarra uncovers a pathway so you can increase the impact of your own unique leadership while experiencing how restorative, sustainable and deeply nourishing it can be at the same time. This is a fundamental shift in leadership mindset that is required to create a new world that works better for all people.

Jensine Larsen, Founder and CEO, World Pulse

I cannot claim to know that much about yoga, but as an international educator and business professional I know how important and vital it is to stay in balance and ensure that both mind and body are operating at maximum efficiency. Tarra's business career has taken her around the world and provided her the perfect canvas upon which to test and refine her knowledge of yoga, and I have no doubt that the benefits which flow from what she writes about in *The Yoga of Leadership* will prove invaluable to all who read the book.

Dr. Peter Brews, Dean, Darla Moore School of Business, University of South Carolina

Tarra Mitchell's *The Yoga of Leadership* is a must read for both yoga practitioners and business leaders alike. The author eloquently harnesses years of experience in both disciplines to provide a hands-on understanding of how yoga can improve leadership skills. Timely, important, and well-written, *The Yoga of Leadership* deserves a spot on everyone's bookshelf.

Mark Gilleo, three-time national bestselling author, *Sweat, Love thy Neighbor, Favors and Lies*

I deeply appreciate how this book offers practices and simple ways to incorporate ideas central to Yoga into effective Leadership style. Tarra has a gift in taking what many consider esoteric knowledge and sharing it in a way that educates and empowers. A must read for anyone looking for a way to utilize the ancient philosophy of Yoga to self-empower, self-transform and self-heal and for those in Leadership roles who want to challenge themselves to see their "whole self" and to see others from that same perspective!

Maryam Ovissi, Founder/Director/Visionary, BelovedYoga, Author, *Pilgrimage Through Patanjali's Yoga Sutras: Guidebook for 200 Hour Yoga Travelers*

A must read for business leaders who want to develop and maximize teams.

Sarah N. A. Camougis, Partner, Choate, Hall & Stewart LLP

Tarra Mitchell has combined her extensive experience in business and her intensive study of the science of yoga to create a guide for everyone interested in becoming a more effective and fulfilled leader. Her innovative use of the Pancha Maya Koshas creates a template to guide anyone seeking a healthier, happier lifestyle. From the heads of households to the heads of businesses and even to the heads of governments, *The Yoga of Leadership* will inspire all to live and to lead more holistically in a way that strengthens the entire team.

Mercedes von Deck, Orthopaedic Surgeon, Cambridge Health Alliance, RYT 500 hour

If we are to be happier while addressing the stressful challenges faced by our species and our planet, then we need to cultivate, fortify and train our internal selves to be the kinds of leaders needed in the outside world. *The Yoga of Leadership* is an essential, beautifully composed and distilled, guide to how we can elegantly bring thousands of years of scientifically proven Eastern wisdom into our very busy, modern, Western lives. How timely! Well done, Tarra Mitchell.

Nicholas R. Parker, Managing Partner and Co-Founder, Global Acceleration Partners, Founding Chairman of Cleantech Group

The light goes on! After practicing yoga for eleven years, *The Yoga of Leadership* helps me understand more about me and my path as a parent and as a leader running a 200 employee organization. I once thought of yoga as a way to round out my exercise regimen and as a stress reducer, but I now see the importance of yoga in my wellbeing and how everything - empathy, compassion, understanding, patience - starts within me. For those who are into perpetual improvement, this is a must read!

Michael Kamio, Founder, Anna's Taqueria

We are all physical, energetic, emotional, intellectual and spiritual beings. This approach in *The Yoga of Leadership*, not only cultivates self awareness and equanimity in the workplace, but transcends from the workplace into our lives as a whole. As an Integrative Physician, long time yoga practitioner and teacher, I am thrilled to see these concepts brought so eloquently into contemporary life. The melding of wise ancient principles with the present, using the Pancha Maya model and other yogic teachings, is just brilliant. This isn't only about being strong, productive, compassionate corporate leaders. Tarra lays out a thorough, practical and inspiring guide to live our lives with integrity, gratitude and discernment.

Lisa Lilienfield, MD, Kaplan Center for Integrative Medicine, RYT (registered yoga teacher) 500 hour

Tarra drills home the relationship between holistic health and leadership in an eye-opening way. As an entrepreneur running a global business and a family of five, my days are jammed full but it turned out that I have already been doing many of the things she suggests for health and stress management like exercise, yoga, healthy diet, and massage. Yet, I've never considered how these measures affect my leadership in the way she discusses in the book. A must read for all business owners with busy lives.

Krassen Draganov, Founder and CEO, Dynamo Software, Inc.

THE
YOGA
OF
LEADERSHIP

A Practical Guide to Health,
Happiness, and Inspiring
Total Team Engagement.

TARRA
MITCHELL

The Yoga of Leadership
by Tarra Mitchell

Copyright © 2017 Tarra Mitchell

All rights reserved. No part of this book may be used or reproduced by any means, graphic,
electronic, or mechanical, including photocopying, recording, taping, scanning or by any
information storage retrieval system without prior written permission of the author (Tarra Mitchell).
The exception would be in the case of brief quotations embodied in critical articles and reviews
and pages where permission is specifically granted by the author. Requests for permission to
make copies of any part of this work should be submitted to the author. Please do not participate
in or encourage piracy of copyrighted materials in violation of the author's rights. Purchase
only authorized editions. For permission requests, contact the publisher at address below.

TarraYoga LLC
PO Box 81427
Wellesley, MA 02481
info@tarramitchell.com
www.tarramitchell.com

A NOTE TO THE READER

The information in this book is not intended as a substitute for the advice of physicians or
other qualified health professionals. The author of this book does not dispense medical advice
or prescribe the use of any technique as a form of treatment for physical, emotional, or medical
problems. The reader is advised to consult with his or her physician before undertaking any of the
practices contained in this book. The intent of the author is only to offer information of a general
nature to help you in your quest for personal growth, success, and life satisfaction via physical,
emotional, mental, and spiritual well-being. Although every precaution has been taken to verify
the accuracy of the information contained herein, the author assumes no responsibility for any
errors or omissions. Neither the author nor the publisher shall be liable or responsible for any loss,
injury, or damage allegedly arising from the use of any information contained in this book.

Because of the dynamic nature of the Internet, any web addresses or links
contained in this book may have changed since publication and may no longer
be valid. The views expressed in this work are solely those of the author.

ORDERING INFORMATION

Individual books may be ordered through most booksellers including online
retailers. Books can also be purchased through the authors website www.
tarramitchell.com or by contacting the author at info@tarramitchell.com.

Books may be purchased in quantity and/or special sales by
contacting the author info@tarramitchell.com.

Certain stock imagery © iStock.

LCCN: 2017915662
ISBN: 978-0-9995082-1-3 (paperback)
ISBN: 978-0-9995082-0-6 (hardcover)
ISBN: 978-0-9995082-3-7 (ebook)

Leadership 2) Yoga 3) Health 4) Success 5) Motivational

First edition.

Printed in The United States of America

Developmental Edit by Yoga:edit
Illustrations by Bryson Maynard

To my husband, Matthew Mitchell, thank you for your patience, love, and support. You have helped me validate many of the teachings in this book by your own good example and for that I will be forever grateful.

To my children, Ethan and Maia, I adore you. You are everything beautiful in this life. May you live inspired lives in a world filled with love and kindness.

Contents

Acknowledgments

Remembering and acknowledging all of the amazing people who influenced and supported me along this journey is a very satisfying exercise. I am particularly grateful to all the leaders I've met along this writing adventure. Their expressions of interest in this work have been humbling and continue to fuel my belief that it is the right book at the right time.

I would first like to thank my editor Lori Snyder of Yoga:edit who meaningfully reorganized and cutback the manuscript. I would also like to extend a special word of gratitude to Bryson Maynard whose artistry resulted in an outstanding set of illustrations.

I would like to express deep appreciation to Ronnie Taylor, Scott Hopkins, Annette Cardullo, Mark Gilleo, Carolyn Weininger, Hari-kirtana das, and Matthew Mitchell who read and offered valuable feedback on early copies of the manuscript. Their guidance was a critical part of shaping the material and sharing what I know in a way that is meaningful to leaders.

With honor and respect I would like to thank Hari-kirtana das. His mastery of yoga philosophy and the ancient texts helped this book gain the heightened yogic integrity and accuracy that I so desired. I owe the completion of this work to him. His support and years of mentorship were essential to helping me to clarify yoga as a way of being in everyday life—including leadership—and to put that into words. All translations of the Bhagavad Gita verses used in the book are his.

I would like to thank Rolf Gates. Rolf ignited this path of yoga in a real way for me in my life. His wise and authentic teachings continue to inform my everyday. I wish to express sincere appreciation to Maryam Ovissi. She is the spark that fueled this wild ride. Maryam initially exposed me to many of the yoga frameworks, tools, and techniques used in the book. Her mentorship and her belief in me, her belief that I would see this project through, helped me remain committed to the work.

I am particularly grateful to the host of gifted yoga teachers who have inspired me through their words over the years. Their words are like poetry, a ballad for thirsty hearts and souls: Jacqui Bonwell, Jafar Alexander, Marni Sclaroff, Coelli Marsh, and Masaaki Okamura. I also wish to thank the many knowledgeable yoga teachers who spent time helping me with parts of the book: Carolyn Weininger, Karen Cutone, Kerry Weleko, Vinaya Saunders,

Loretta Arcangeli, and Rheema Garrett. I would finally like to thank the teachers who, through their own amazing physical practices, have helped my practice over the years: Andrea Fotopoulos, Renata Loree, Meaghan Kennedy Townsend, and Roman Szpond. Finally, thank you to all yogis continuing to honor the tradition and supporting communities around the world.

Thank you, Dr. Joe Esposito, who reviewed the accuracy of the physical aspects of the yoga practice and Dan Gooder Richard of Gooder Group whose candid advice helped me navigate the publishing world. I am finally grateful to all the researchers, scientists, doctors, and authors whose good works allowed me to substantiate the aspects and importance of holistic health and well-being.

I would like to acknowledge with gratitude and love the support of family and friends, far too many to name, you give my life meaning. Thank you for always being there, no matter what. A very special word of thanks to my mother, Cathy Guerriero, and to my father, Bill Bohr. Their unconditional *love* has always served to give my fragile spirit the strength needed to break convention and try new things. I would also like to honor the late Anastasia Kirby Lundquist. An author and a friend, Anastasia inspired me to write by her encouragement and through her own example as a centenarian who never stopped writing and publishing. I am very grateful for the love and support of: Charlene Mitchell, Bob Guerriero, Richard Mitchell Jr., Teresa Mitchell, Rachel and Kevin Wisniewski, Carolyn and Jeff Adams, Richard Mitchell, Laurie and Brian Mitchell, and Julie Lehman.

Last but certainly not least I would like to extend huge gratitude and appreciation to my husband, Matthew Mitchell, who supported this very long effort and to my children, Ethan and Maia, whose enormous stores of love and joy fuel me every day.

Introduction

Old Maxim
Being a leader is a title one earns.

New Maxim
Being a leader is an embodied state.

The Yoga of Leadership elucidates the aspects of yoga that can help you develop qualities and skills essential to leaders, which will help you become a happier and healthier leader who is able to connect with and fully engage your team. Embodying these qualities will allow your truest expression of an inspiring and powerful leader to emerge. While some people possess leadership qualities more naturally than others, in our fast-paced world it is likely that every leader could use a little help from time to time. If you are already inspiring the masses, you will discover insights into reasons *why* you are so engaging and learn ways to teach others what comes so naturally to you.

Let me paint a vision. Wouldn't it be great if we all woke up every morning feeling energized, excited to go to work, and enthusiastic about the day? We kiss our happy spouses and kids goodbye and commute to the office, content and relaxed. Our team welcomes us with smiles, eager to work hard. When the day is done, we go home, eat dinner, and have some non-work fun. Before our eyes close that evening, we reflect upon the abundance in our lives and sleep soundly.

Sound crazy? From today's perspective, it might, but this scene does not have to be a dream. It is possible for each one of us to enjoy this reality most of our days if we choose to. But we've forgotten that our bodies and minds are meant to live this way to be healthy and well. And we aren't sure how to get there from the frenzy of our current reality.

Included in *The Yoga of Leadership* are practical steps to maintain holistic health and foster team growth and engagement. With a base of vibrant leaders serving as examples to their teams, an enterprise will have the foundation that affords it the opportunity to optimize productivity, enhance team engagement, attract and retain top talent, boost morale, and improve results—all while decreasing healthcare costs.

Given my work in the investment industry and driving organizational change as a consultant, I understand. Like you, my days were full. I wanted to perform, to make a difference, to succeed. But somewhere along the way, I realized that my perspectives and desire for achievement were, in certain ways, contradicting my ability to be the effective and inspiring leader I wanted to be. I began to look for a way to improve, and I found it in a surprising place: the philosophies and techniques of the ancient practice of yoga.

In writing this book, it has often felt like a paradox to marry leadership and yoga, as the nature of these two things is witnessed today as quite incompatible. Yet I love to defy convention, to envision new possibilities, and to make people think. To me, there was a practical and pragmatic union between the two seeming opposites. This program synthesizes Eastern and Western thinking and practice into a new paradigm that offers engaging and inspiring leadership as an *embodied* state, one that is not separable from the health and well-being of the leader.

In the last two decades, more and more research has been done around holistic well-being, and the ancient wisdom of yoga is now complemented by the most current evidence-based findings that validate the efficacy of its tools and techniques. Modern science is proving over and over how the methodology and tools of yoga help us control emotions and manage stress, focus and concentrate better, think more clearly and decisively, and make more conscious decisions. And the principles of yoga mitigate risk while enhancing connection, positivity, and happiness.

The program outlined in the *The Yoga of Leadership* uses a holistic model for well-being inspired by a yoga framework called the *Pancha Maya Kosha model*. The model is based on teachings from ancient Sanskrit texts called the *Upanishads*, which are believed to be over three thousand years old and are collectively considered some of the most influential books ever written. The *Taittiriya Upanishad* introduces the five interlocking dimensions, or layers, of holistic well-being: physical, energy, mind, knowledge, and bliss.

We all have bodies with lots of parts; we are living, breathing, energetic beings. We have minds that think; we have intellects that discern, and at our innermost depths, we have the capacity for great joy. You can't take our bodies, minds, and spirits apart; they don't detach very comfortably! They must be considered as a unit, as an integrated whole. Research clearly demonstrates that the health of all these parts of ourselves directly impacts my ability to see clearly my unique value and to be empowered by my value. In my mind, I just didn't have time to take a breath, pause, and be more thoughtful about my choices and perspective while still continuing to achieve at work; nor did I appreciate its importance. So, I doggedly powered on. Really I was afraid of the consequences of not overachieving and letting my guard down. At the first annual Women's Private Equity Summit at Half Moon Bay, I was discussing yoga with another attendee. She had never tried it, and she asked me why I liked it so much. At a loss for words I paused and said I liked it because it was "the answer." She asked, "To what?" I said, "To so many things."

And so a seed was planted. It dawned on me that yoga had become a necessary complement to my fitness and nutrition regimen. Since that day, I've been on a search for a more rational answer to what I then intuitively felt to be true: yoga offers tools, techniques, and philosophy we can implement in our lives and at the workplace to support our holistic well-being and become the kinds of leaders we want to be. What I now know is that yoga, including the meditation and self-awareness (mindfulness) aspects, is infinitely rich in its benefits—traversing fitness, stress management, pain management, psychology, philosophy, and conscious living. The most desirable aspect of yoga for leaders taught in this text lies in its ability to help a person control the mind and senses. I now realize that I need to practice yoga because it helps me control my mind and senses and accordingly reactions to ordinary stressors, which allows me to maintain a clear and open-mind. Control of the mind and senses is necessary to possess or to cultivate the skills essential to inspiring leadership. It is not possible to be a rational and discerning leader without control of the mind and senses.

Back in my work world in early 2009, the markets were bleeding all over the globe. I called it quits on an ill-timed investment company I'd founded, had my son, and decided to weather the financial storm in a state of Zen by training to become a yoga teacher. I started to write about life and living. I began to teach and study a lot of yoga and meditation. In fact, I *immersed* myself in yoga and meditation and became a yoga philosophy junkie. Slowly—this took some time and investigation—an understanding began to emerge.

Looking back, if I practiced then what I practice now, work would certainly have been easier and less stressful. I would have been a more engaging, mentally strong, resilient, confident, and principle-led leader and a more courageous and calm person. This writing stems out of a long interplay of work, family life, extensive international travel, and years of research and instruction.

The first two chapters of *The Yoga of Leadership* summarize the state of our health and well-being and introduce the key frameworks used throughout the book. The text then illuminates seven yogi secrets, including each of the five layers of holistic well-being, one in each chapter, taking you on a path to personal transformation. By connecting to each of your layers you will learn how to make choices along the way that lead to a healthy body, an untroubled mind, and a renewed sense of meaning and purpose in your work. In the ninth chapter, you will be guided to create a practical and possible holistic well-being action plan for your life, so that you can to show up each day with essential leadership qualities like authenticity, vitality, strength, equipoise, and discernment. Through your own holistic well-being you transform your ability to engage and inspire others improving every imaginable business outcome.

It is an honor to be put in a position of leadership, one that involves responsibility to yourself and to others. The state of *being* a leader is an *embodied* state, not merely a title on a business card. It does not matter whether you are a leader with a team of ten thousand or a leader with no direct reports. If you are in a position to influence others toward a goal, you are a leader and you have an opportunity to lead by example. You have an opportunity to serve as a catalyst for positive change through your own efforts toward holistic well-being. We function better when all of our dimensions are healthy and well.

Be a vanguard. Be the change. Be the leader you are meant to be.

Section 1
Holistic Well-Being and Leadership

The actions of a great leader will surely be emulated by others; the exemplary acts of such leaders set the standard by which all others are measured.

—Bhagavad Gita 3.21

Chapter 1
Leadership and Well-Being

Old Maxim
I am my body.

New Maxim
I am a complex, holistic being.

Resolve: I will think about my well-being in terms of the interconnected layers of my being. I will honor my dimensions by giving each balanced attention.

Holistic well-being allows me to establish a framework for developing personal qualities inherent in great leaders who are happy, healthy, and able to connect with and inspire their teams.

Being a leader brings with it a responsibility to do something of significance that makes families, communities, work organizations, nations, the environment, and the world better places than they are today.
—*A Leader's Legacy*, James M. Kouzes and Barry Z. Posner

Definition of a Leader

A leader by conventional definition is a person of influence who guides others toward the attainment of objectives. There are two types of people we refer to as *leaders*. First are those who lead by example. We choose to follow this type of leader not because we have been recruited or paid but because they are great at what they do, and on some level, they make us feel safe, secure, and supported. At a fundamental level, we want to feel safe, secure, and supported in all areas of our lives, and certainly at work.[1]

In contrast, the other kind of person we have come to call a leader is someone who has been given a leadership role but does not lead by example. They are neither role models nor mentors. We do what these people say simply because someone pays us to do so. These are not true leaders; they are merely people in positions of power. But because our society has empowered so many of these kinds of leaders, we look primarily to them as examples of what it means to lead. As a result, the very idea of the word *leader* has been distorted. We don't simply need more leaders; we need great leaders who are awake, aware, and inspiring. We need leaders who have control of their mind and senses and can see life at a deeper level. Consider this definition.

A great leader is one who *inspires* the *highest* level of work that teams can reasonably aspire to for the satisfaction of the organizations mission. To *inspire* others, this great leader must do his or her personal best to serve as a positive example by taking care of his or her physical health, controlling his or her mind and senses, cultivating mental strength and resilience, and operating with principle and purpose. At work this great leader must foster a healthy and supportive work environment, build strong connections with the team, and take responsibility for all stakeholders in the ecosystem in which the organization operates. To inspire the *highest* level of work, with humility this great leader must orient all actions toward the highest good and consider all possibilities by expanding his or her usual ways of thinking.

Great leaders lead from a place of principle and holistic well-being; they know themselves and have figured out, consciously or unconsciously, how to take care of themselves holistically.

Some of the challenges and misconceptions that prevent great leaders from emerging involve the following:

1. A distorted definition of a leader reinforced by unprincipled behaviors we witness by others in highly visible leadership roles.
2. Organizational cultures and leaders that place a sense of urgency on all work products and tasks, including those that are not urgent.
3. A model of healthcare that focuses fundamentally on the physical body, limiting us from learning about and understanding ourselves holistically.
4. A lack of education concerning how measures of holistic self-care, including the control of our mind and senses, directly benefit our ability to lead and function optimally.
5. Organizational cultures and leaders apathetic toward the well-being of their teams.
6. A lack of motivation to place self-care on our priority list when there are countless other seemingly more important things to do.
7. A lack of compelling reasons and ideas around what we can do to fit well-being into our busy schedules every day.
8. A disconnection from our internal selves, i.e. our feelings, emotions, sense of self, sense of being centered and balanced often resulting in a degradation of meaning and purpose in our work and our lives.

It is sad that so many of us see ourselves as so flawed and *choose to numb* with lifestyle drugs, instead of considering that small shifts of the external aspects of our lives and a little self-care may be sufficient to tend to our needs. Tending to your holistic well-being *is* self-care.

Self-Care

In his classic best seller *The Relaxation Response*, Herbert Benson, MD, Associate Professor of Medicine at Harvard Medical School and founder of the Mind-Body Medical Institute at Massachusetts General Hospital, refers to certain self-care measures as "the third leg of the stool."[25] These self-care measures involve alternative approaches to healing. Within the Western healthcare model, alternative merely refers to that which is outside of established systems. Yet, according to Dr. Benson, for the vast majority of doctor's visits, *only* the third leg of the stool is necessary. It's important to remember that what is considered outside of established systems is merely that which is not completely understood today—or, more likely, that which has not even been considered, given current systemic restraints. But for certain, today's alternative is tomorrow's conventional.

The Office Effect

Our need to maintain a connection to ourselves and support our holistic well-being in life does not stop at the office door; in fact it begins there, for the office is where much of the degradation happens. The *office effect* leads to physical and mental imbalances.

Physical Imbalance

Over time, too much sitting causes our physical bodies to weaken and compensate in an imbalanced way. Our muscles become atrophied, and our skeleton becomes arthritic. We develop adhesions and knots in our muscles as our joints stiffen and our bodies grow weak. We develop back pain, neck pain, eye pain, forearm pain, hand pain, and other pain, which we usually remedy with prescription drugs or costly surgery.

We often eat unmindfully at our desks while we continue to work, leading to weight gain and taxing our cardiovascular, immune, and digestive systems. Extra bulk on some of us strains our cardiovascular system, making more work for our heart to move us. Our diet for many of us doesn't nourish us properly to keep our immune system functioning well and maintain a healthy inflammatory response, so when we get sick it takes longer for our body's natural protection to kick it. Unmindful eating or skipping meals slows down our digestive system and, combined with our poor diet, we may find that we now have digestive distress. We become sluggish, lose energy, and are less vibrant, which directly impairs our capacity for managing stressors creating an internal environment for dis-*ease*. We eventually develop conditions of the heart and kidneys, requiring costly medical care, pharmaceutical drugs, and/or surgery.

The costs of these progressive conditions represent the bulk of employers' direct healthcare costs. Absenteeism and presenteeism increase. Vitality wanes. Healthcare costs surmount.

Mental Imbalance

Too many of us race around with our teams to keep up with short-term results motivated to earn more money, to build up our résumés, to feel worthy or proud. At a point we begin to wonder why we are doing what we are doing and wonder whether we are making a difference. We go about our day in a robotic disconnected way. Or we may overwork and feel stressed impacting our decisions and our principles. This pressure- cooker lifestyle can make us feel discontent and often unhappy, leading to issues of the mind like chronic stress, anxiety, and depression. With such a busy pace we can easily lose connection with others, replacing speech with written forms of communication or becoming overly reliant on technology. We can become detached from others, as we are absorbed in and distracted by our work and our gadgets. We then may also begin to lose connection with our spouses, children, friends, nature, and any life outside of work. We can become disconnected from ourselves, from our unique value and the purpose of our work. We may find that we have high blood pressure, sleeping disorders, panic attacks, and anxiety or depression. We become more tired and less energized. We too often medicate ourselves to cope. Absenteeism and presenteeism increase. Vitality wanes. Healthcare costs surmount. Dis-*ease* in the mind leads to dis-*ease* in the body.

Reclaim Control

Are you noticing a trend? As the leader, you can stop this cycle. It's your choice. Every day, you make choices in consideration of the health and well-being of yourself and your team, or not. Every day, you take measures to connect to meaning and purpose in your work, or not. You decide whether the urgency and number of work tasks are reasonable and appropriate. You manage the negotiations and establish the deadlines. You have the opportunity to help your teams prioritize work tasks and to offer them your full support. You choose whether to honor requests for flexibility, or not. This really comes down to whether you believe as a leader that you have a *personal responsibility* to your team. If you do, strongly align yourself with your team. Orient yourself toward supporting, guiding, and helping them, with the understanding that a well team will function more productively than an unwell team.

Concluding Statement

The most effective way to have your team members tend to their well-being—improving their productivity, engagement and mitigating healthcare costs—is for you to embody this message first. When organizational leaders actively participate in supporting their own holistic well-being, it can become part of the culture, not just an externally run and managed program. As you reflect upon this multidimensional program for holistic well-being, you will see how it can also serve to improve upon the pool of contenders for leadership roles by helping the pipeline of talent develop qualities essential to effective and inspiring leadership. As you contemplate the ideas suggested, you will come to appreciate the wide variety of mutually reinforcing ways there are to support holistic well-being in the workplace. You have the opportunity to lead movements of change beginning with your own efforts. Become the healthy, happy, and inspiring leader that you've always wanted to be. Commit to it. Tackle your holistic well-being for yourself, your family, and your team.

Chapter 2
Yoga: The Science of Consciousness

Old Maxim
I work my body and mind separately.

New Maxim
I address the needs of the body and the mind in
an integrated manner seeking balance.

Resolve: I will reflect upon the needs of my body and my mind in
consideration of my life and how I am feeling each day. My choices
will be oriented toward what I uniquely need to maintain balance.

Considering my unique daily needs to maintain balance
will allow me to function effectively in a fast-paced life and
attend fully to the needs of my team and my family.

The trouble with having an open mind, of course, is that people
will insist on coming along and trying to put things in it.
— *Diggers,* Terry Pratchett

It is true, as the late Mr. Pratchett's quote indicates, this chapter continues to invite *your* open mind to consider different ways of thinking about yourself and your leadership. This chapter highlights the depth and breath of yoga and lays the groundwork for the tools and practices shared throughout the book. A brief history of yoga in the context of its ancient roots clears up misconceptions and dispels myths that circulate as the practice continues to take on its own western evolution. In the end you will have a much clearer sense of the depth of this increasingly popular practice and you will see how you can choose different aspects of the practice to support your own holistic well-being.

The Practice

Many of us today are first introduced to yoga by moving from pose to pose on a rubber mat in a group exercise class led by a teacher. I initially used group yoga classes as a way to supplement my weekly exercise routine with stretching. This is how a lot of people initially find their way into a yoga class. Then, for many years, I sought out the most physically intense and hot yoga classes I could find. I wanted to sweat and accomplish. I also have a history of low back pain leading me to visit six chiropractors and physical therapists in four states. I found my yoga movement practice to be a necessary way to keep me out of pain, off pain medication, and out of surgery. In time, I started to come upon teachers whose words made me think. And then, I kept going back, because practicing yoga made me feel better, more connected and grounded. I was becoming more aware of my thoughts and emotions and began to see my life in a different way. My path is the path of many a yogi. Now I know that while the practice on the mat is extraordinarily helpful and absolutely necessary for most of us, one never has to step onto a mat to practice yoga because *yoga is a way of life.*

Yoga and the Mind–Body

Yoga is a mind–body practice, but some folks think it's a stretch class. The word *yoga* is often defined to mean *to yoke* or *to unite.* It refers to joining the mind, the body, and the senses, so you can focus inward, cultivating an inner serenity. Traditional yoga was not a physical practice at all but a path to finding serenity of mind through self-awareness, meditation, and life lessons guided by a master teacher and taught one-on-one. Tao Porchon-Lynch, the oldest yoga teacher on the planet, once referred to yoga as the inner dance of life. Today's yoga looks different from the traditional practice, but the focus on principle, breathing practices, awareness training, and meditation integrated into the movement class continue to offer the mind–body connection.

Movement: Asana

For those unfamiliar with a yoga class, it involves a sequence of poses done on a mat. It now typically represents the *asana* part of the yoga practice and stems from the movement-oriented Hatha yoga tradition. The asana practice involves a series of movements including forward bends, back bends, twists, and side-lengthening poses. Group classes are held in a yoga studio or a gym typically for sixty to ninety minutes. As yoga has expanded around the world, so too have the various styles of yoga. Practitioners often work privately with a teacher to learn appropriate alignment of poses for their bodies and to incorporate other layers of the yoga practice into their lives.

A yoga movement (asana) class is terrific for the physical body, helping stiff people become limber and offering all-over strength and flexibility training. Yoga asana offers a fabulous way to lengthen and release bodily tension, so we can be fully mobile and exist without discomfort and pain. It requires no flexibility, none whatsoever, because you start from where you are and grow from there. And although it may look like it from the outside, it's not about trying to perfect a bunch of poses. Rather, the poses act as a springboard to the non-physical aspects of the yoga practice. They allow us to release tension so that we can relax and do the other work. If your yoga experience is not relaxing and you feel that you are moving unconsciously in a fast way that may leave you susceptible to injury, look for a new teacher or a new yoga studio.

The Deeper Purpose

Movement has become a focal point of yoga practice, a key to unlocking yoga in your life. The complexities and pace of the modern world have necessitated the physical practice of yoga as a way to help us release tension, improve balance, and relax before we can even begin to become still, conscious, and aware. The practice releases tension including emotion, thus shaking things up and making us notice and feel. It also allows us to manipulate and harness our energy in life-serving (helpful) ways. By moving the body in unfamiliar ways, we create new patterns and, as we say in yoga, plant new seeds to take root and sprout. Ultimately, the movement piece of yoga is a tool that supports relaxation, calms the nervous system, and accesses the mind through conscious efforts of breathing and observation. When we release tension in our bodies, they relax. Through the self-awareness part of the asana practice, overtime we learn to concentrate better, focus better, and become better listeners, and even nicer people. We make decisions from a clear place. With an improved capacity to relax, concentrate, focus, and listen, we become better leaders too.

Is Yoga a Religion?

Perhaps because yoga focuses on the mind and living in a principle-centric manner some confuse yoga for a religion. Yoga is not a religion, although it can complement a practitioner's religion. In fact, I have had amazing and thoughtful yoga teachers who leveraged passages from ancient books of various religions in their classes to support a point they were making. Since yoga teaches a practitioner to pay better attention to what s/he says and thinks, many yoga practitioners find that their yoga practice actually deepens their religious faith in a meaningful way. Yoga's principles of non-judgment and acceptance foster yoga communities that are diverse and supportive.

Popularity

Because it works so well, yoga movement practice has become exceedingly popular. The "2016 Yoga in America Study" commissioned by certifying body Yoga Alliance and *Yoga Journal* magazine reported that over 36 million Americans actively practice yoga, an 85 percent increase over the 2012 study, and practitioners spent a whopping $16 billion in the past year on yoga services and products.[26] Like no other health and wellness modality, the full practice of yoga combines the intelligence of the mind with the intelligence of the body and is established in morality. Through your yoga practice, you may begin to understand the subtle nuances of what makes you *you,* growing better able to use your unique abilities to self-actualize. Through self-awareness and self-reflection, yoga allows us to observe and better understand why we do what we do, affording us the opportunity to break habits that don't serve us and adopt those that do. Yogic tools, techniques, and philosophy help good leaders become even better in all areas of their lives.

Yoga's Introduction to the West

While yoga's origins are many thousands of years old and varied, modern yoga hit the world stage when the charismatic and young Swami Vivekananda introduced yoga and Hinduism to the Parliament of the World's Religions in Chicago in 1893. He became an immediate sensation and subsequently participated in a national speaking tour. On the heels of that popularity, Vivekananda published *Raja Yoga,* a well-received book that introduced the American public to yoga as a meditation-based practice. Vivekananda also democratized yoga's dominant teachings, moving away from the ancient belief that yoga was something to be studied and understood by only a few wisdom teachers by insisting that yoga was a *science of consciousness* that should be taught, studied widely, and made accessible to all human beings.[27] Vivekananda's successes led to a resurgence of yoga in India and paved the way for Sri Krishnamacharya to profoundly influence the modernization and popularization of the practice in the early twentieth century. Krishnamacharya further democratized the practice by teaching yoga to women for the first time in history, and his teachings continue to influence most contemporary yoga teachers today.

The History

The Origin of Classical Yoga: The Ancient Texts

Yoga is an ancient discipline, with vast and varied roots that bear allegiance to historical texts, which continue to be interpreted by scholars and practitioners. Dating of these texts continues to be debated. The origins of yoga are found in the *Upanishads*, philosophical compositions that conclude each of the *Vedas*, which are considered to be among the world's oldest sacred texts. The Vedas contain rites and rituals of ancient civilizations and are believed to have originated around five thousand BCE, surviving in the oral tradition until being written down, approximately two thousand five hundred BCE. Seals found in archeological sites depicting figures seated in yoga meditation postures are taken as evidence that yoga was practiced in the Indus Valley as early as four thousand BCE.[28] Many divergent schools of thought having different beliefs emerged from ancient yoga and so we also find yoga full of contradiction and paradoxes.

The *Bhagavad Gita*, a summary of the *Upanishads*, is a poetic scripture that integrates the various schools of yogic thought through an epic poem involving the mental challenges of a warrior tasked with leading his troops to battle. Surviving the oral tradition, the *Bhagavad Gita* was written into the middle of the longest epic poem in the world (one hundred thousand verses), the *Mahabharata*.[29] Dates vary appreciably but the origin of the *Mahabharata* is suggested by scholars to fall somewhere between the ninth and fourth centuries BCE. Rutgers University professor Edwin Bryant, PhD, shares in his translation and commentary of *The Yoga Sutras of Patanjali* (to be discussed next) that the *Mahabharata* makes reference to yoga nearly nine hundred times.[30]

A scholar named Patanjali interpreted and codified the yoga teachings of the time into 195 short statements or *threads* of knowledge, in a book called *The Yoga Sutras of Patanjali ("Yoga Sutras")*; *sutra* means *thread*. The *Yoga Sutras* were written before the fifth century BCE and compiled in a manner intended for memorization and sharing in an oral tradition. This emerged as a seminal text in classical yoga as a system to elevate consciousness. Yet Patanjali's yoga was merely his own interpretation of a tradition with many versions and nuances that were richly practiced and debated even at the time of his writing.[31] The cryptic style of his writing is understood to mean that the text was designed to be taught by a teacher to a student and to this day the *Yoga Sutras* are taught through interpretation and commentary.[32] The original

Sanskrit text continues to be translated and interpreted by scholars around the world.

Origin of the Movement Practice (asana)

Hatha yoga—sun (*ha*) and moon (*tha*), a union of opposites—on which most modern Western movement oriented yoga is based, was formed around nine hundred CE. It combines the mental practices described in Patanjali's classic text, the *Yoga Sutras* with structured postures (asana). The postures are intended to manipulate our life energy and awaken our internal power. Hatha yoga is centered on the body and movement, helpful to today's increasingly sedentary society. The classic surviving manual on hatha yoga is the *Hatha Yoga Pradipika*. Hatha also means *force*, which implies that the practice requires *effort*. You will find that many yoga classes offered in the West are movement based and involve strength and endurance.

While the exact dates of these ancient works are disputable, it's important to understand that yoga has been around for a long, long time. It has morphed somewhat overtime to serve the needs of the culture using it. However, the very important thread that makes yoga *yoga* is that it remains *a science of consciousness*. A science that helps a practitioner cultivate serenity of mind and clear perception. Yoga scholar, philosopher, and theologian Hari-kirtana das describes yoga as a science that holds as an intention the development of an inner condition that supports direct perception of the true nature of the world and our own true nature.[33] Important to leaders, the practice of yoga helps us to cultivate mental strength and resilience allowing us to lead happy, healthy, and connected lives.

The books themselves are influential and continue to serve as important teaching tools. Many yoga teachers commonly use the *Yoga Sutras,* the *Bhagavad Gita,* and/or the *Hatha Yoga Pradipika* as guides to their own yoga practice and their teaching. Given the many translations and interpretations that exist, yoga teachers may have multiple copies in their libraries from which to refer at a given time. The majority of classes taught today are directed toward moving the body making one teacher's path relatively indistinguishable from another's. Further most teachers are taught a patchwork of the yogic schools of thought and may not be dedicated to a specific path. This text references and is likewise inspired by more than one path and school of thought.

The Methodology and Philosophy

Classical Yoga's Eight-Limbed Path

The Eight Limbs of Yoga

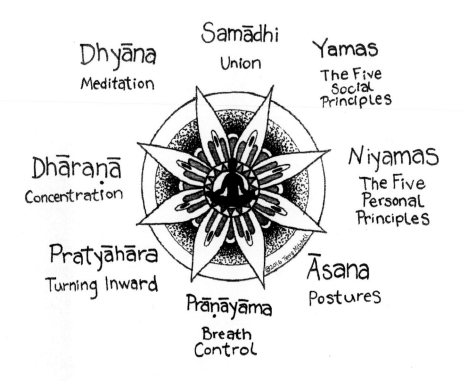

Dhyāna
Meditation

Samādhi
Union

Yamas
The Five
Social
Principles

Dhāraṇā
Concentration

Niyamas
The Five
Personal
Principles

Pratyāhāra
Turning Inward

Āsana
Postures

Prāṇāyāma
Breath
Control

In his seminal text, the *Yoga Sutras,* Patanjali offered a systematic approach to expanding consciousness through what is called *ashtanga* yoga, meaning *eight-limbs* and sometimes called *the eight-limbed path.* Different from the modern physical practice of yoga, this systemic approach focuses on psychological techniques[34] that can lead to serenity of mind. The limbs are discussed further in association with the various dimensions of our holistic well-being. The eight-limbed path does not have a chronology; rather, all of the limbs are to be practiced as part of daily life. One must not perfect the previous limb before practicing subsequent ones; they happen concurrently.

The Eight Limbs of Yoga

1. **The Five Social Principles *(Yamas)*:** Five principles, disciplines, or restraints with regard to how you act in relationship to others. Your personal responsibility to others. (*Yamas*, Sutras II.35–II.39)

2. **The Five Personal Principles *(Niyamas)*:** Five principles or observances with regard to how you care for and maintain your own inner resources in a manner that is beneficial. Your personal responsibility to yourself. (*Niyamas*, Sutras II.40–II.45)

3. **Postures *(Asana)*:** In the ancient context, asana refers to your seat and, in particular, finding a steady and comfortable seat or posture from which one can breathe and meditate. Asana can also be considered with regard to how one is seated in one's life, as the steadiness and ease of posture that one chooses to uphold. It has now come to be known as the movement part of the practice as one moves through forms called yoga poses. (*Asana*, Sutras II.46–II.48)

4. **Breath regulation *(Pranayama)*:** Intentional breathing in an effort to manage the energy of the body including our emotions through the breath. The breath offers the mind–body connection. This practice involves the awareness and intelligent control of our life force energy as we move through cycles, seasons, and changes in our everyday lives. (*Pranayama*, Sutras II.49 – II.51)

5. **Turning Inward *(Pratyahara)*:** Withdrawing from distractions by not being affected by them and by making choices that are not distracting. We do this by ignoring distractions—or deliberately noticing distractions and allowing them to fade into the background—so we can learn to concentrate. We can also make more choices in life that are not distracting to allow space for clearing our minds. The ability to turn inward when we choose to and not be affected by sense distractions (things we see, hear, smell, taste, or touch) is a prerequisite to concentration. (*Pratyahara*, Sutras II.54–II.55)

6. **Concentration *(Dharana)*:** Concentrating our attention on a single object and continuing to draw our mind back to that object when the mind wanders. This prepares us for meditation. Concentration is a prerequisite to meditation. (*Dharana*, Sutra III.1)

7. **Meditation *(Dhyana)*:** Existing in undisturbed states of meditation for longer periods of time to attain steadiness of mind. (*Dhyana*, Sutra III.2)

8. **Absorption *(Samadhi)*:** In the ancient context, this internal experience is accessed when, through sustained concentration (meditation), we become absorbed in our object of meditation. This is an esoteric ideal and challenging to grasp intellectually. I encourage you to consider instead a reflection of Samadhi, an *everyday Samadhi*, which can be accessed when the elements of our lives are in good shape, cultivated through the practice of the other limbs and tending to the needs of our holistic self. We then experience wonderful moments where we feel absorbed in our life, extremely contented, joyful, and happy; I refer to those as *Samadhi moments*. (*Samadhi*, Sutra III.3)

Oldies but Goodies: Ancient Principles

Life pulls us in directions that aren't always helpful, and having a set of principles helps to keep me from being drawn in directions that don't serve me quite as often. They serve as useful guides for parenting my children too. Principles can be referred to as codes, tenets, edicts, observances, abstentions, morals, vows, or ethics; they are all of these things. Most religious and political orders have some set of grounding principles. Since ancient times we have established some basic understandings of what it means to be *human*. Because of this, we find that the principles amongst most systems—political, religious, or otherwise—are quite similar. Organizations sometimes call them values. Patanjali's yoga is a uniquely principle-centric, yet non-dogmatic science. The yoga principles—and, in fact, all philosophy shared in the book—is introduced as a guide, as a way for you to consider the importance of principle in your leadership and in your life. The intention is not to impose yoga-specific philosophy rather to offer ideas so that you may create your own. We adopt principles into our lives in an effort to purify our consciousness and our instruments of perception (our senses). In this way we can experience more freedom from afflicted thoughts that cause us to suffer and find more serenity in our days.

In yoga, we practice ten basic principles comprised of both social principles (*yamas*) and personal principles (*niyamas*). The five social principles help us lead happy and healthy lives and foster a deep connection to the world around us. They are: non-harming, truth, non-stealing, temperance, and non-possessiveness. Embodying the yamas involves a conscious practice of self-restraint and self-containment. The five personal principles support our well-being in life through a deep connection to ourselves. They are: purity, contentment, discipline, self-study, and aligning life toward meaning and purpose. Embodying the niyamas involves intention and ongoing practice.

Yogis choose to follow these principles. Leading from your own set of principles is internally satisfying and allows you to live in a more contented and connected way at the office and at home.

Yoga's Social and Personal Principles

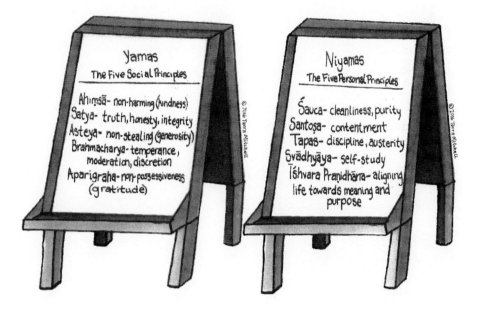

A Principled Office

Leading through Your Principles

As humans and as leaders, we require a set of principles, so we can think and act with conviction and without damaging our health. It is hard to feel balanced and happy when we operate from a questionable or unclear place. It doesn't feel good. Compromising our principles adds stress and strain, which drains us of vitality and breaks down our physical and mental systems. A directionless place void of principles gives us no parameters by which to operate.

Principles are not answers; nor are they rooted in stone. They simply offer important guideposts and point us in the right direction. Nestled somewhere between a vacillating mind and a tranquil mind reside principles. It is a matter of doing your best to find truth and do the right thing. Take care to make sure that your principles are objective, unbiased, pure, and that they arise from a calm and helpful place.

Standing Strong

Principles are our ethical foundation and a vital component of a life where we do our best to exist in harmony and thrive—while naturally being wildly successful and inspirational! Many of you may have stories of leaders who lead through principle, even when it put them at personal or professional risk. Most of the time, our principles will help us with common everyday decisions and behaviors that are not so sensational. But, at times, it may require great courage to go against the grain. To embody your principles, you may at times need to be armed with an unwavering resolve. Leading from principle requires courage. It is not for the faint of heart to share what may be a bold or contradictory view. Take care not to confuse principled with self-righteous, which is close-minded and led by the false ego. Leading through principle should make your interactions with others much better, not worse.

Think About Your Principles

You have typically been exposed to principles, values, ethics, and morals at various times in your life. Initially, it might have been from your parents, teachers, or place of worship. Later, in college ethics class, you may have discussed them again. While you may have an embodied sense about certain principles, you may not think about them very often. In your busy life, you may not even realize that you are acting outside of your core principles. When our lives are so full, we can get into the mode of reacting, saying, and doing things quickly and impulsively without regard to the consequences to ourselves and to those around us. This place of discomfort damages our health and well-being and affects our decisions and relationships.

Write Down Your Principles

Choose a set of principles that resonates with you, and employ them. Define them in detail for yourself. Be thoughtful about what they mean as they extend beyond the office into your home and from the home into the office. Principled leaders are principled people *all the time*. Principles do not stop at the office door; nor should they stop in front of the home.

Creating and writing your list of principles is an important intellectual exercise. Leading from principle involves paying attention and consciously choosing behaviors (thoughts, words, and actions) consistent with the principles you choose until the behaviors become habits. Habits become part of your being, part of your embodied self, and part of your character. When we establish these principle-led habits, doing things in principle becomes embodied thus part of our subconscious.

Principle-Centric Leadership

Principles embodied by the leadership will pervade the organizational culture, thus mitigating the risk of both small and large violations. Openly and immediately addressing small violations of communication or other behaviors in a non-threatening manner will quickly result in overall compliance and a more pleasurable place to work. If small offenses are permitted over a long period of time, they inevitably escalate into serious issues. For example, if psychological abuse or bullying—a behavior of blatant disrespect directed toward another person—is permitted at an organization, it can easily lead to something more serious, such as harassment. Instead of dealing with a relatively minor violation in behavior, you have to deal with a serious one that may cost an organization significant time and money. Acting out of principle is also an important corollary to returns and performance. In the not-so-distant past, we have again and again witnessed massive losses, company implosions, and other tragedies causing great harm to employees, clients, customers, and investors the world over. Possess an attitude of conviction with regard to principle-led leadership.

Clearing the Murky Water

Decisions are often not clear-cut and simple; there is a lot of murky water we must tread through first. Crystalizing your own set of principles and working toward keeping them current and relevant for you will influence, affirm, and help you make decisions. Our principles offer a framework by which to guide our lives. The ruminating stops, making us more decisive and discerning. Leading through principle allows the sediment to fall away and the waters to clear. We sleep better when we make principle-based decisions in our days. We feel better when we act from a place of clarity, and so do our teams. As a leader, it is appropriate to guide your life from principle every moment of every day. It supports the health of your spirit. When we move away from principle, we diminish our bliss and imbalance the mind. To be truly well and functioning optimally, we need to experience joy, foster contentment in the everyday, and maintain healthy relationships with our team. This is attained through a life lived from principle.

Observe Principles in Action

Different principles are introduced in each chapter. As you move through this program, reflect upon the social and personal principles, and consider rewriting them for your workplace. Consider keeping a copy of yours in your briefcase or purse, hang a version on your office wall, or have a copy on your smartphone or tablet. This way you have them available to refer to when you inevitably come upon a difficult situation that you know you would like to resolve in a manner that honors your principles. Spend time observing yourself and the interactions of others at work in an effort to identify principled actions and word choices that can be used as models to follow. Begin to notice the unprincipled actions and word choices that can serve as teaching moments, and reflect upon the full consequences of unprincipled behaviors. In putting our principles first and foremost, we have the opportunity to foster healthy and non-hostile work environments that support the well-being and productivity of our teams.

Philosophy: Manifesting Happiness and Connection

Social Principle 1: Non-harming—Kindness (ahimsa)

Of the five social principles, *ahimsa* or non-harming (showing kindness) is the most important. It is the pinnacle principle. At work, this requires a conscious commitment toward not harming others in word choices, actions, or decisions. The positive equivalent of non-harming is being supportive, kind, and respectful. The easiest way to connect with other people is through kindness and support. It is essential that leaders foster a connection with their teams in order to motivate and inspire them. Micromanaging and constantly playing the devils advocate are not supportive and do not build trust. Connection and growth happen by giving the team the freedom to try and the freedom to fail while supporting them all the time. Be considerate of the team's basic need for success and let them know that you are supporting them along the way.

> If you are a taskmaster with yourself, others will feel your whip. If you are critical of yourself, others will feel your high expectations of themselves as well. If you are lighthearted and forgiving with yourself, others will feel the ease and joy of being with you. –Deborah Adele, *The Yamas & Niyamas*

Central to yoga is the idea that we are all part of a universal consciousness. Accordingly, we practice yoga for ourselves *and* for others. When thinking about principles, it is as important to consider the effect on us, as it is to consider the effect on others. Respecting and being kind to ourselves are imperatives to naturally being respectful and kind toward others. This is further addressed under the principle of self-study, svadhyaya.

Empathy at the Office

A meaningful part of the principle of non-harming or showing kindness involves practicing standards of behavior involving respect and empathy. Empathy at work requires you to assess and work skillfully with other people. Empathy is a soft skill that is increasingly looked upon as a critical asset for a leader. It allows leaders to be attuned to and consider the feelings, wants, and needs of their team members as part of their decision-making process.[35] Working effectively with a wide variety of individuals and guiding their success requires a degree of adaptability. Leaders who can read other people really well easily tune into their feelings, wants, or needs. They can leverage this kind of information to keep their team happy and engaged, to circumvent personnel issues, to satisfy a client or stakeholder, or to forge new business relationships.

An empathetic environment is safe and open. It allows freedom of expression and allows people to operate in a less-guarded manner. When this happens, creativity flourishes, productivity increases, and innovation is possible. Empathetic leaders are very approachable. They welcome new ideas from staff and encourage contribution by offering mechanisms for collaboration and sharing. When top leaders adhere to such practices themselves, the practices will trickle down through the corporate culture. Empathy-building teaches solution-based approaches to problems in consideration of others. Every industry could benefit from creativity and innovation in order to evolve in the global marketplace and solve great problems. Creating a work environment that promotes empathetic behavior is one way to foster upstanding behavior.

Bad behavior breeds bad behavior. In many companies, the corporate culture is so damaged by poor examples of leadership at all levels that employees are effectively silenced. They do not feel they have a voice; either they are in fear of losing their jobs or do not feel that what they say will be heard anyway. Such closed environments teeter along a fine line that does not differentiate appropriate decisions from inappropriate decisions, thus posing risk to the enterprise ranging from illegal activity that harms customers in some way to, more commonly, psychological abuse of employees, dramatically hindering productivity and disenfranchising employees.

Communications at the Office

As a leader, non-harming at the office includes reflecting upon whether communications and actions support your well-being, that of your employees, and that of the enterprise's ecosystem members. Are your communications in person and in writing respectful, considerate, constructive, and kind? Constructive criticisms—criticism coupled with thoughtful alternatives presented openly for debate and stated in a supportive manner—are appropriate, but ridicule, judgment, and gossip are not. As leaders, when we conduct ourselves in a defensive or overly contradictory manner, it puts our team on guard. It makes them feel violated, leading them to become guarded and defensive, making it difficult for our team members to be open and to maintain their own values and principles. Words matter. Tone matters. Facial expressions matter. We have a profound opportunity to perpetuate positive and productive behaviors amongst the team through our own example.

With courage, conviction, and a strong inner sense of self, stand firm and fully support your team along their path of learning and growth. Supporting carries with it a dose of compassion and patience and allows each person to learn through his or her own path. One never absolutely knows the needs of another. Living life free of fear and open to the broader world and its nuances liberates our ability to be kind. From an open, fear-free place, we can better appreciate the unique differences, perfections, and imperfections that go along with being human. We can choose to be kind to ourselves and to others. Being kind to yourself includes taking care of yourself by orienting your life toward holistic well-being. Then you can help your team members show themselves kindness.

Non-violence

The yogic definition of ahimsa would importantly involve non-violence. While most (but not all) organizations are inherently non-violent, the societies in which we operate support different levels of violence. The cycle of violence in a society and around the world is perpetuated through the ways we stimulate and feed the mind. The more that we feed our minds violent media, programming, and other images the more tolerant we become to violence. The more we accept violence toward other humans and even other creatures, the more we perpetuate the cycle. When we support violence, most Eastern philosophies including yoga would say that we perpetuate the karmic cycle of violence toward ourselves. How can you promote non-violence and kindness into your life and leadership?

Questions for Leaders: Kindness and Non-Harming

1. Are your meetings places for bantering, raised voices, and finger pointing?
2. Are people friendly at the office? Do they laugh from time to time? How can you foster a better rapport?
3. Are there a lot of water cooler discussions and gossip at the office?
4. Do people communicate in a productive yet kind manner via e-mail, on the phone, and in person?
5. Are you aware of discontentment or unresolved issues at the office that haven't been addressed?

6. Is there too much e-mailing and texting at the loss of connection and interpersonal relations?
7. Are word choices in office communications appropriate?
8. Does the team support and appreciate one another?
9. Are the rules of behavior clearly stated and openly discussed? Are violations in behavior immediately reprimanded and addressed?
10. Have you considered the effect of cultural nuances in the office environment to be sure that all team members including the leaders understand and are held accountable to the same code of conduct?
11. Are team members eager to help one another with high-priority work projects?
12. Do you have big personalities at the office that are offensive to others? Do you employ bullies?
13. Do team members feel safe sharing their ideas and opinions? How is the team encouraged to participate?
14. In internal communications, are customers, owners, and competitors communicated about respectfully and with appreciation? Are they ever mocked?
15. Are possible consequences to stakeholders and to the broader ecosystem a subject of discussion before organizational decisions are made?

Yoga: Natural Order and Psychology

The Yoga of Balanced Living

The yoga teachings are attentive to the natural, universal order that continually seeks balance and considers holistic well-being in recognition of this natural order. At the atomic level, yoga is attentive to the fact that everything in our lives is interconnected, in constant movement and exchange. Accordingly, as biological organisms, our physiology continually seeks homeostasis, which is affected by our habits and the world around us.

Yoga philosophy considers that all matter emerges from a fundamental substrate called *prakriti* from which three aspects of nature emerge, called *gunas*. The three gunas in nature are activity, balance, and inactivity—called *rajas, sattva,* and *tamas* respectively. These aspects are represented in everything in nature. From our bodily composition to our state of mind the gunas are represented in differing proportions. We can consciously make choices that serve to make one of these aspects of nature more present; you can think of this as stronger or more influential. Hari-kirtana das has a practical way of explaining the qualities of nature in the context of how we make choices in our lives. We either make choices in the mode of passion (an active, *rajasic,* choice), in the mode of goodness (a balanced, *sattvic,* choice), or in the mode of inactivity also referred to as the mode of ignorance (an inactive, *tamasic,* choice). In this text we consider the gunas in the context of creating clarity around our everyday choices and how those choices affect our biology, our minds, and our everyday life experiences that influence our well-being and our leadership.

The Three Qualities of Nature: Gunas

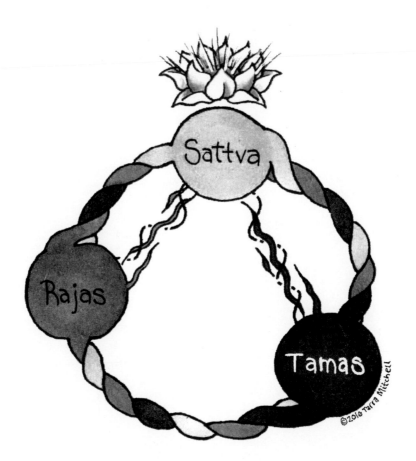

Rajas is a state of passion, energy, and activity that can easily manifest as overdoing and excess in our lives. When we make rajasic choices, they are choices made in the mode of passion. Tamas is a state of inactivity or ignorance that can easily manifest as darkness, heaviness, lethargy, and fear. When we make tamasic choices, they are made in the mode of ignorance. Sattva is a state of balance, harmony, and intelligence. Sattvic choices are in made in the mode of goodness. Sattvic can also refer to a state of mind where it is steady, clear, and serene. From this place, we can think, say, and do things that are intelligent, discerning, kind, and wise. We cultivate sattva by moving toward more sattvic choices in our lives and by reducing both our unhelpful rajasic tendencies, those that stem from selfishness and greed, and our unhelpful tamasic tendencies, which are often, at their root, reckless and delusional.

Personal Attributes and Associations

The qualities of nature can be applied to everything you do. All three are always represented, but our goal is to seek a proportion that serves us in the moment and serves our well-being overall. Helpful tamasic choices keep us grounded, supported, and stable yet easily tip toward delusion. Helpful rajasic choices motivate us toward our goals yet easily turn to excess. Sattvic choices allow us to live consciously and intelligently and exist in communion with life. Life is already very full of rajas, activity, and often we tend toward tamas, inactivity, in an imbalanced and unhealthy way. So efforts in our lives most of the time are to keep a healthy mix by actively trying to make more sattvic choices. The way life reflects the qualities of nature will be expounded upon at various points in the text. The ongoing daily practice toward balance is a fundamental intention of a yogic lifestyle to support happiness, health, and connection with humanity.

Our diet, lifestyle, choices, behaviors, and basically everything we choose to do and think can be considered in terms of the qualities of nature. Some examples of personal attributes and associations that will bring further clarity to these qualities of nature are listed in the next table. The list is crafted in a way that is symbolic of life today. Go through the list and highlight all of those that you feel describe you and the choices you make in general. If your answers are different at work versus home, for example, make multiple passes. Reflect upon your answers, and consider the meaning of balance, equilibrium, and homeostasis accordingly. How do your attributes and associations impact your ability to connect with and engage your team? Do they help you motivate your team? How do your attributes and associations impact your ability to maintain your health and well-being? What is a better mix for various times in your life, so you feel motivated, secure, and balanced? How can you move toward a more balanced lifestyle overall?

Gunas: Attributes and Associations

	Rajas (Activity)		Sattva (Balance)			Tamas (Inactivity)		
motivation	drive	tenacity	intelligence	harmony	serene	pessimistic	doubt	lazy
excess	overdoing	movement	discerning	calm	light	ignorance	fear	reckless
anxious	activity	forceful	self-control	clean	steady	careless	laziness	obstructing
impatient	energy	erratic	peaceful	open/receptive	purity	immoral	materiality	grudges
restless	change	cravings	objective	happy	pragmatic	lethargic	stale	damaged
hankering	agitated	disorganized	innovative	discerning	positive	ignorant	dark	denial
passionate	manic	projects	inspiring	thoughtful	pleasure	indifferent	heavy	depressed
unreasonable	obsessive	stressed	balanced	content	flexible	delusional	inert	disturbed
workaholic	addicted	scattered	knowledgeable	clear perception	truthful	procrastinating	neglect	pain
ambitious	greed	unfocused	balanced movement	resilient	empathetic	unaspiring	denial	demonic
over-exercise	selfish	uncooperative	quality sleep	focused	confident	inactive	repressed	slow
lack of sleep	desire	fast	small portions	courageous	forgiving	oversleeping	hiding/veiling	dull
speed eating	intense	reactionary	light and fresh food	adaptable	equanimity	overeating	impure	monotone
very spicy food	argumentative	unsustainable	herbal tea	cooperative	meticulous	processed food	destructive	unhygienic
caffeine	challenging	imbalanced	emotional control	lucid	engaging	alcohol	disengaging	messy
dynamic	self-centered	egoist	supported	stable	safe	old food	violent	impure

Expanding Consciousness

Yoga is a practice in becoming conscious. Yoga is not a practice in becoming *perfect*. Don't make an exploration of the qualities of nature into an opportunity to harass or be critical of yourself. For example, I like to drink wine. Drinking alcohol in general is a numbing agent, and as such is considered in this model to be in the mode of ignorance. Even though I know this, it hasn't stopped me from enjoying wine more than I should, but I am fully aware of this choice. I also know that I'm disciplined about my well-being in other ways and continue to seek to improve. Paying attention to the choices we make and their quality is a practice of awareness, clarity, and insight that will have an influence on your choices.

We can all work to be better; however, yoga philosophy includes practicing compassion and non-judgment, even as you look for balance. We are working toward well-being that will allow for inspiring leadership, not perfection. Consider how raising your own consciousness through the choices you make in your day will support your ability to engage your team. As an enlightened leader with an expanded consciousness, you become a catalyst, driving change and leading enterprise in a health-enhancing manner. Through your example you can allow the positive benefits to spread far and wide.

Finding Balance

Balance might be something you think is impossible to maintain. It seems an arcane word that doesn't belong in our society. But the necessary daily shifts are smaller than you might think. A sense of balance comes from within; we cultivate a sattvic life though the choices we make, including the actions we take, the words we speak, and even the thoughts we think.

Take inventory of your life, and become more aware of the places you may need to adjust to allow for the right balance *for you*. Again, this is a personal choice. First, lay a broad foundation for discovery by completing this table. Begin by ranking the items on the list in order of importance to you. Next, rate each category according to what percentage of your total energy you feel you expend toward each activity. The percentages should add up to 100 percent. This is a personal energetic response and not the actual amount of time you spend in a day at a job. Clearly, during the week everyone who works full-time spends more time at work than they do at home (awake). Finally, place in the *preferred* column the percentage of your total energy that you would want to funnel toward that activity.

Your ratings give you a clue as to the things you might want to focus on first to feel more balanced. Comparing how you feel you spend your time relative to where you prefer you spend your time can indicate how satisfied you are with your balance and the quality of your time spent. Our goal is to have the contents of our lives feeling as though they are at or near balance and spending our time in *high quality* ways. Quality time is time spent deeply connected to and fully immersed in what we are doing. We are neither distracted nor thinking about what we must do next when time spent is high quality. Reflecting upon your ratings allows you to consider whether your life is generally in a balanced and satisfying place or not. When our self-selected priorities are meaningful to us and in line with what we are actually doing, we feel great. We feel energized and happy. We are highly productive and fully engaged. When there are gaps between our priorities and actual energy spent, we feel disconnected. We feel depleted and disengaged, in work and in life.

This is a point-in-time exercise. Your assessment may change if you were to complete this table again following a major life change, next year, or even with the changing of each season. What can you do to move toward a better balance?

My Energy Expenditure

Rank		Current	Preferred
	Work		
	Education, networking, reading, skills-development, and research related to work		
	Family duties		
	Attending to physical health (diet, cooking, meal planning and preparation, and movement/exercise)		
	Self-study and self-awareness (reflecting upon principles, observing habits, reflecting upon vitality, practicing being present)		
	Contemplative time (quiet, relaxation, meditation)		
	Connecting to meaning in life. Refining and understanding your personal vision, mission, and purpose. Setting goals and holding yourself accountable.		
	Cultivating relationships with immediate family		

Maintaining connections to others (extended family, friends, and community)		
Enjoyment and pleasure (personal, social, and spiritual)		

The Obstacles to Growth

The Five Obstacles: Kleshas

In yoga we are taught that we have a natural tendency toward five mental blocks called *kleshas* (Sutras II.3–II.9). The kleshas are defined as afflictions that cause suffering and distress, such as afflicted thoughts, or hindered thinking and are obstacles to our growth. These can be likened to veils on our persona, covering or obscuring reality or truth, like seeing life through glasses that distort reality. According to the *Yoga Sutras,* the kleshas are: root misconception of reality called ignorance (*avidya*), misidentification with our self-image called the false ego[36] (*asmita*), attachment (*raga*), aversion (*dvesa*), and fear of death or what modern interpretation refers to as fear of loss (*abhinivesa*). When we begin to overcome these natural tendencies, we begin to clearly see the truth in life and in our own true nature—lightening our mental load, releasing burdens, and awakening to new possibilities. Patanjali suggests that through clear-seeing, discrimination, and meditation we can overcome these obstacles.

In a leadership context, these mental obstacles are limiting and block our growth as a leader. As obstacles they prevent us from seeing things clearly and from leveraging our powers of discernment. They lesson our ability to cultivate an open-mind, prevent us from having vision, and limit our imagination. These hindrances block us from finding our authenticity and our inner strength, through which others find inspiration. Yogic techniques discussed throughout the text, including practices in self-awareness, self-reflection, and meditation, help us become aware of and transcend these mental blocks allowing us to develop qualities essential to leadership success. The first obstacle, avidya, is introduced below and the others are shared in subsequent chapters.

Mistaken Reality

© 2016 Tarra Mitchell

The primary obstacle to growth is avidya. Avidya is a false belief, a mistaken reality, a fundamental misunderstanding of what is; it is a base misconception. The words *ignorance* and *delusion* are often used as translations. It is the root mental block, the obstacle from which the other obstacles extend. Directly translated, avidya means (*a*) without or lacking and (*vidya*) vision, knowledge, or illumination. Under this veil we are engulfed in darkness, empty of knowledge and insight, unable to see things as they really are and who we are. A common analogy involves walking into a darkened room and mistaking a rope for a snake. Yoga philosophy explains this as mistaking the *self* as the body and mind. We are neither our temporary material bodies nor our ever-changing minds; we are all spiritual sparks of consciousness. We enter the womb of a particular mother at the time of conception and a temporary material body begins to form around us.[37] We all wear this veil. Other translations refer to this veil as lacking self-awareness or intellect.[38]

Using our worldview and beliefs as our guide, we give great weight to the transient and impermanent aspects of our lives, and we often believe that we have control over everything. We develop a perspective on specific things in our lives according to a worldview and beliefs shaped by our lives, and we often tend to believe this perspective is an absolute and clear picture. This perspective can be quite powerful shaping our attitude and governing everything we say and do. Yet our worldview itself, the starting point, is a mirage, an illusion with blurred edges that morph and change. We seek out our view of the world as we move along life's journey and our view shifts and changes. We see everything in our lives through the prism of the different people, events, and circumstances we have uniquely experienced and learned from, and then we mistake it for truth. This is a mistaken reality that causes division, disappointment, and suffering. It is only a perspective, not *truth*. Avidya is when we mistake our worldview, beliefs, and perspectives for objective truth.

When Reality Disappoints

Being fixated on our worldview—blindly believing it is truth and our perspectives are reality—sets us up for disappointment and suffering, because we in turn establish a lot of expectations and maintain a sense of entitlement to support our worldview. We then measure life according to results and outcomes and résumés and track records, and we put a great deal of effort into making certain we are moving toward our worldview and our expectations are met. Or we may simply expect everyone else to treat us a certain way, to behave in a certain way, and to think a certain way—and we put a great deal of energy into forcing our worldview and perspectives upon others. Focused intently on either scenario, we put ourselves in one bucket and others in another. We create separation and division between ourselves and other people, creating conditions ripe for judgment, disconnection, and even fear. Standing on our own *side*, we lose sight of the moments of connection that are necessary as humans to find satisfaction and joy in our lives.

If we have a strongly held expectation of a certain outcome that is not realized, for example, we typically get upset, place blame on ourselves or on others, and set another expectation. Each time we approach life with the expectation, the belief that we are entitled to a result, we immediately set ourselves up for disappointment if/when our worldview does not pan out. Important to leaders, when we operate thinking our *perspectives* are actually *truths* and carry all of these expectations and entitlements with us and it affects our reasoning abilities, we are taken further away from self-awareness, open-mindedness, and discernment. We mistake our perspective for truth, instead of humbly seeking to understand through a process of reasoning. Reasoning in yoga is neither exclusively self-identified nor authoritarian; rather, it involves a triad of inquiry, direct perception, and guidance from others in the know. In fact, self-identified reasoning with no other efforts to validate the reasoning is considered speculation and conjecture based on incomplete information, a mere guess. When you cling to your perspectives—instead of revisiting them and testing them through reasoning in the current time—you operate in an uninformed way, taking actions and making decisions based on guesses and speculation. When we all do this, as the cliché goes, this is the blind leading the blind.

The Seeds in our Minds

We have so very many impressions planted in our minds that we cannot begin to know where they all came from, and often these seeds get planted in the most innocent of ways at the youngest of ages. Then they sprout and grow into something more. To be amusing, some of my dearest business school friends from the southern states nicknamed me "the fast-talkin' Yankee" and spoke of the "War of Northern Aggression." I was a northerner in a southern university. I came to understand that they learned about this "war" in school. I learned about this war for the first time at age twenty-five—from them. We clearly possessed parts of our worldviews and perspectives based upon what we had been taught at a young age in school. And we had been taught very different things.

Both and It Depends

While wearing this veil that shrouds our ability to see the truth, we may move into self-righteousness, believing fully that there is a right and there is a wrong. If we strongly feel our worldview (beliefs, perspectives) is right, this causes others to suffer and causes us to suffer, as we are in constant debate and strife over whose worldview is right. Most of the time, the answer to who is right is *both* and *it depends*, and the rest of the time it is simply *I don't know*.

Ambitious leaders, for example, often think that if they accomplish a set of established objectives, then they deserve and expect a promotion or a raise. That is their view of how the world should operate. I believe in meritocracy too, and I certainly have tended to set such expectations in my life. Given that there are only so many promotions and so much excess cash to go around, though, you can see how setting such an expectation immediately establishes a scenario for disappointment. This is not to say that we did not deserve the promotion, but note that when we cling less tightly, we get less disappointed. Strongly held expectations turn into self-righteousness and immediately create scenarios for deep disappointment, division, and warring factions. In the wise words of the yoga teacher and author Rolf Gates, "Expectations are pre-meditated resentments and not good traveling companions." In a yoga movement class there are many opportunities for expectation; we invite the students to instead move out of judgment, to create space to allow what happens to happen, and to find peace in that place.

Therein lies our work. We cannot predict the future with certainty. At the office, we often set goals and objectives for our team members that create expectations in their minds. Now that we see the scenarios we create, we can proceed with caution. As a leader, you must get the team rowing in the same direction through goal setting, but take care and make the goals clear, reasonable, establish buy-in, and write them down. Revisit them and make sure they remain clear and reasonable and be willing to adjust them over time—so instead of being set in stone they can become markers. It's also important to have an honest, objective, and open evaluation process, so all of the team members know how they are performing along the way and have a clear sense in advance about what they will receive in return for their efforts. The work for the leader becomes how to not cling to any outcome (goal, objective) so strongly that a failure derails the culture and disengages the team. Work to enact a compensation and feedback process that *your team* believes is open and fair. We want to handle what comes our way in a manner that makes us better able to operate with clear vision and discernment, importantly in a way brings people *together* and does not create separation and division. Connection and engagement are the antithesis of division and separation.

If you want to be a healthier, happier leader who can better connect with and engage your team, you can also learn to ask more questions. Get information directly from the source where possible, and seek guidance from other people whom you find discerning, open-minded, objective, and unbiased. Consider how responding with *both* and *it depends,* immediately creates a more open environment. Practice trusting and connecting more. Of course we all want to perform but use this discussion to inform your usual way of thinking so you may show up, do your best, and be happy, no matter how you or your team performs.

Concluding Statement

To move from unconscious living to conscious living—where we find ourselves happy, healthy, and better able to connect and engage our teams—our work is to move from *avidya,* ignorance, to *vidya,* clear seeing and knowledge. When we see things clearly, we are fully conscious of our thoughts, words, and actions in the present moment. This self-awareness combined with a requisite dose of humility helps us become more open-minded and clear. With self-awareness and discipline we can make everyday choices that allow us to live in a more balanced way necessary for cultivating essential leadership qualities. As you move through the dimensions in subsequent chapters, you will see how orienting your life to support your own holistic well-being requires intention, discipline, and planning. This program will, over time, illuminate the way you see your life and allow you to become clear on the things you can do to enhance your well-being and your leadership. You will also begin to observe how certain leaders in your organization seem to take care of their holistic well-being and how others clearly have not. Upon reflection, you will observe that leaders who appear happy, healthy, humble, self-controlled, and principled are more effective, engaging, and inspiring to others.

Section 2
Seven Yogi Secrets for Leadership Success

Chapter 3
Yogi Secret #1: Aligned Intention

Old Maxim
Happiness, health, and inspiring leadership happen to lucky people.

New Maxim
Happiness, health, and inspiring leadership happen when
clear intentions are purposefully aligned with life.

Resolve: I will set the intention to be happy, healthy,
and inspire total team engagement and arrange my life
in a manner that will support this intention.

Setting intentions that support my well-being—and working
strongly toward them by arranging my life in a manner that
supports my intentions—will allow me to develop personal
qualities inherent in great leaders who are happy, healthy,
and able to connect with and inspire their teams.

Freedom is not the absence of commitments, but the ability
to choose - and commit myself to - what is best for me.
—*The Zahir,* Paulo Coelho

Inspired Lives

Your intention is your commitment to yourself. Yogis and great leaders both know that setting an intention influences everything. In yoga, *sankalpa* is defined as your strong intention or resolve, something you fully intend to do.[39] The world is filled with the ails of good intentions hoping to fix the lives of *others* in accordance with ones own conceptions. The intention you set here is personal, current, and involves bettering yourself and your life in some way. Ask yourself, what is your commitment to yourself?

Setting an intention before you begin will help you hone in on the tools that serve your intention best in each moment. This necessitates that the intention be high level and the actions you take to satisfy your intention change and flex in accordance with your needs. Your intention will guide you to what kind of balance feels best at any period in time. It will be a reminder of why you are doing this at times when you feel frustrated or overwhelmed. Everything we need is already within us. We are simply offering ourselves the space to invite what we need to resurface. Borrowing from the late spiritual leader and author Dr. Wayne Dyer—we are infinite and divine just as we are. As spiritual beings living human lives, we are meant to lead *inspired* lives.

Setting Your Intention

In keeping with the definition of a great leader, consider that your simplified version of that intention can be: *to be an inspiring and principled leader who is both happy and healthy and serves as a great example.* We can do whatever we choose to set our minds to. We don't have to re-educate ourselves or try to be someone else. We merely have to align our lives toward our intentions and show up again and again, in all areas of our lives, to manifest that reality. To believe anything else is limiting. To be inspirational for example, look for inspiration again and again and again. Study inspiration in all its forms. If you believe strongly in your intention, you will automatically look out for opportunities to work toward that intention. You will look for signs and clues that validate the intention and then opportunities will present themselves. Obstacles will not deter you; you will see them instead as teachers who serve your intention and strengthen your resolve. Bit by bit, we change our habits of thought and our habits of action that do not serve what we want to those that do. When we better ourselves, we are also helping everyone around us.

The Future

It may be helpful to start with visualization, another yogic tool, to further clarify how your life might appear if you were to satisfy your intention. Visualize how you want to be as a leader. What does that look like? We are painting an ideal picture while recognizing that we do not live in an ideal world and so we strive to do our very best directed toward the higher ideal. You might rewrite the vision below in a way you feel is appropriate using words that sound like your voice:

I wake up every morning feeling energized, excited to go to work and enthusiastic about all that's in store for me. I move my body, eat a healthy breakfast, kiss my happy spouse and kid(s) goodbye and drive to the office, feeling relaxed and content. My team welcomes me with smiles, eager to work hard. I focus on being supportive and kind to my team and make efforts to connect with each one of them. I look for inspiration in the everyday. I am conscious of my thoughts, words, and actions. I try to observe and improve upon the e-mails I write, the conversations I have, the decisions I make, and even my thoughts. When the day is done, I spend quality time with my family and have some non-work fun. I do a few things to wind down and relax and go to bed early. Before my eyes close that evening I reflect upon the abundance in my life and sleep soundly.

Include how you would like to see yourself acting as a leader who inspires others and what goes along with that. What precedes and succeeds your life at work that serves as a good alignment toward your intention? Consider the words you would want others to use as they describe your leadership. Be specific. Write it down in a journal. Once clear on your intention and what that looks like, with resolve begin to align your life toward manifesting it using ideas shared throughout the book.

A Base of Support

Establish a trusted base of support. Identify the people who believe in what you want to do, and allow that community to have a central role in your life to help you along your journey. Empower your intention by seeing how it will help improve aspects of your life and work that you do not find satisfying. Write those improvements down. Armed with a clear, strong intention, and a base of support, any resistance will fade.

Use your intention to help choose which tools from this program to implement when. If you are in agreement, from this point forward include in your intention that you will initiate this path by finding a way to carve out an average of *thirty minutes* each day of the work week, not necessarily at the same time, and an hour including preparatory time on days off, to start to do what it takes to transform your journey and your leadership. The goal is to start small, cement habits, and build from there. By the final chapter you will be fully informed and prepared to choose how to spend those thirty minutes.

Philosophy: Manifesting Your Intention

In yoga, the last three *niyamas* or personal principles (*tapas, svadhyaya,* and *ishvara-pranidhana*) are called as a unit, *kriya* yoga. Kriya yoga can serve as a foundation from which to build your life of holistic well-being; it represents the work or action in the yoga practice that supports your intention. This work involves discipline (tapas) and ongoing self-study (svadhyaya) that is oriented toward a higher purpose and meaning in life (ishvara-pranidhana). Practicing kriya yoga will help you keep you focused and moving in alignment with your intention. This foundation will be used throughout the book.

Personal Principle 3: Discipline—Austerity (tapas)

> The inner fire is the most important thing mankind possesses.
> —Edith Södergran

The principle of discipline involves aligning yourself, with a measure of austerity, with what you want to manifest. This represents the willpower to continue to change habits that are not helpful to those that are. Tapas, the fire inside that lights us up, presents outwardly as steadfast enthusiasm, will, and zeal. Tapas

> How you do anything is how you do everything.

is the effort and the tenacity with which you approach every aspect of your life as oriented toward what you want in keeping with the highest of ideals. It is our motivation, our drive. When we operate all aspects of our daily lives with discipline and intention, we show up that way at work, too.

The Art of Paying Attention

Tapas can also be thought of as the art of paying attention, striving to be conscious of every thought, every word, every action, and putting all of yourself into everything. Cultivating tapas helps you show up *wholeheartedly* in both your personal life and work life. Wholeheartedness involves a complete, sincere, earnest, and full commitment to whatever we are doing in our lives. Tapas further involves self-control through conscious observation or *being present*. It involves a dedication and commitment to observing yourself all the time and acting purposefully to manifest what you want. Examples of habits that support tapas include setting an intention, establishing goals, creating a plan, and revisiting progress along the way. These markers give you something to align your life toward and discipline your efforts. Consider sharing your intentions and goals with your team, along with the ways you have aligned your life toward achieving them.

Passion and Attachment

We want to sustain the embers and the heat of tapas, even when life or work seems to want to drown out the flames completely. Even our closest friends can feed us beliefs that limit our potential and can deter us from our intention. With sustained heat, though, our efforts become easier and more natural to maintain. And as momentum builds, our efforts continue to gain strength and resilience and serve to fuel our motivation and drive even more. With sustained tapas, we show up fully and do our best in all areas of our lives.

> With sustained tapas we show up fully, do our best in all areas of our lives, and can let the results go because we know we've done our best.

As with anything that we put a lot of ourselves into, we can tend to overdo this, or be too passionate. Motivation and drive are good and necessary—it means that our heart is in something. But when they become simply passion it *can* also be bad. When motivation and drive become simply passion, our actions can become disruptive and maligned. Because if our heart is really in something and so we are very passionate about it, then we are really *attached* to it. For example, at work we may get attached to the way we want things done, and our passion for that might blur reality and mask an even better way. The heat of passion can be way too hot, particularly in a work environment where we become jaded by our passion, unable to be discerning and clear. We've all seen people who are so passionate about a subject that they have absolutely no capacity to even consider a different point of view. They are fixated on their *attachments*, their beliefs. An environment of too much passion sets us up for stress, exhaustion, and a lack of emotional control, too. As a leader, you can see how this would impact your ability to remain open, discerning, and reasonable.

Motivation and Drive

Healthy motivation and drive are linked to tapas and involve your ability to channel all of your emotional energy toward whatever you do while finding enjoyment in the process. That last part is important; the best leaders are motivated and driven by more than money or power. They are consummate learners, curious, highly productive, and always working toward mastery and innovation.[40] Healthy motivation and drive necessitate that a leader do his or her very best, reflect upon his or her actions, and orient his or her efforts toward higher ideals. Healthy motivation and drive is fostered through a deep connection to your work.

In the leadership context motivation and drive stem from a person's *inner* condition. A leader's job is to establish the existential condition that allows for the motivation and drive of our team to emerge. The right existential condition helps each member of the team access his or her own stores of motivation and drive. This existential condition is the human condition that requires safety, security, support, and connection. The opposite conditions demoralize, and serve to squander motivation and drive.

Do It Just Because

It's important to reiterate that tapas does not involve results or outcomes. It is about wholehearted action and intention, our strength and our staying power that allow us to lean into discomfort and move through challenge when times get really rough. Tapas comes in the form of the power and courage we harness to stand by our convictions. We strive to conduct ourselves in a disciplined manner in all ways possible, all the time, as best we can with our whole heart. A line from the classic holiday song "Santa Claus is Coming to Town" has Santa saying to the children, "Be good, for goodness sake." Likewise, "Be disciplined for discipline's sake." This frees us, because we can then let go of the results, since we know we've done our very best and that is all we can do. We can let go of the results because there comes a point when we must accept that our very best is what we have to offer and that it is enough. Only when we are healthy in body and mind can we offer our very best. Further, seeking a result from the act of discipline would have us focused on the future, taking us out of the present moment. Tapas also requires a belief in oneself. When one believes in oneself each outcome and result becomes less significant. This is not to say that we don't aspire to good outcomes. We always aspire to good outcomes and continually seek to better ourselves to achieve them. But we will not always achieve a desired result because we are not entirely in control of the result. So it is often said that we practice detachment from results. This principle has us trying our best all the time in everything we do with the highest intent yet being okay with whatever happens and accepting and being kind toward ourselves along the way. This describes a concurrent yogic practice that pairs compassion and detachment, which serves as an important focus in my life.

Team Tapas

In order for the team to maintain team engagement, which can be thought of like *team tapas*, we need to make efforts to cultivate a sense of value in every aspect of every person's role. Everyone's role should be openly recognized as important, valued, appreciated, and taken seriously. Even mundane activities should be treated as being as important to organizational success as complex ones. Every team member should be encouraged to approach every activity with wholehearted attention and a clear understanding of how his or her work contributes to the broader mission.

Tending to Your Sacred Fire

As a leader, people look to you for guidance and direction. True discipline is pervasive. Good leaders tend to be disciplined and passionate about their work, so you are likely to already adhere to this principle at work, but perhaps it is not balanced across all areas of your life. A leader who works like a workhorse yet has terrible eating habits or can *never* make it to his or her kids sporting events is not practicing a measure of discipline in all areas of life.

We adhere to a disciplined awareness so that we can create a life that respects our holistic well-being. Through disciplined awareness practice, we make choices that are nourishing and avoid those that deplete our well-being. This allows us to align our lives in a manner that keeps the inner fire going and affords us opportunities for growth and expansion. Our efforts at discipline will ebb and flow, but our work as leaders is to stay the course, nourishing our well-being and honoring the impact we have on others. Tend to your sacred fire within to keep it burning brightly, and help to stoke, not squander, that fire in others.

Questions for Leaders: Discipline and Austerity

1. Do you set intentions or goals each year? What leadership attributes are you trying to cultivate? Do you know what you really want? Do you set quarterly and annual goals and review them regularly with your team?
2. Do you make healthy food choices? Are healthy food choices made available to your team?
3. Do you move your body? Does your team? Do you support your team accordingly?
4. Do you sleep well? Do you attend to your appearance appropriately?
5. Do you prioritize the needs of your family and allow your team to do the same?
6. Are you enthusiastic about your work? Is your team? Are you full of energy and vitality? Are you able to approach the most mundane parts of your job with enthusiasm?
7. Is the team sufficiently challenged? Are individual skill sets wisely and fully utilized? Do you know the unique capabilities of each of your team members? Do you develop their talents? Are *you* challenged at work?
8. Do you courageously lean into uncomfortable situations and resolve problems?
9. Do you reflect on and lead from a set of principles that have meaning to you? Do you speak up when your convictions and principles are challenged?

10. Do you smile at work? Are you punctual? Do you communicate consciously? Are you thoughtful?
11. Does each team member understand how his or her role fits into the function of the broader enterprise? Have you made the full scope of responsibilities and expectations clear to every member of the team?
12. Do you hold your team accountable? Do you have a mechanism so that you are aware of progress and able to offer support and feedback along the way?
13. Do you give the team members autonomy, affording them the opportunity to do their jobs independently? Do you allow them to make mistakes and constructively learn from them?
14. Are codes of conduct and rules discussed as a group and individually? Are violations quickly remedied?
15. Where in your life do you lack discipline? How does that impact your well-being, your relationship with others, and your ability to lead?

Personal Principle 4: Self-study (svadhyaya)

The principle of self-study, or *svadhyaya*, is a key to personal growth and transformation. Interesting and nuanced, self-study includes an ongoing commitment to self-observation and self-reflection with an intention toward self-betterment directed toward something greater than oneself. Always striving to do better, svadhyaya involves turning inward, spending quiet time in contemplation to figure out what is real and true for you. Through self-observation, we come to understand our authentic selves and how we are or are not aligning ourselves toward our intention. In the classical sense, svadhyaya involves leveraging the wisdom of ancient teachings in an effort to understand your true nature and to orient your efforts toward a noble intention by seeking guidance from those further along.

Be Kind to Yourself

You can consider this principle in your life by studying how you treat yourself. It's not easy to stop working yourself over if you've been doing it for a long time. I am often critical of myself. I tend to examine what I have done wrong, to a fault. I tend to be quick to judge myself, and I do this out of habit, so I don't always realize when it's happening. While working on early drafts of this book, I gave a series of questions to initial readers. When I received group feedback based upon the set of questions I had given them, I felt a bit deflated. Upon reflection, I found that I'd asked them only to offer criticism for my work, things that needed to be fixed. I hadn't asked them what they liked, what resonated. Upon this realization, I targeted individual discussions trying to balance likes and dislikes and, in the end, restored my faith in the project. My work is to be more kind to and forgiving of myself and to resist the part of me that wants to give myself a hard time. When I am too hard on myself, I have come to appreciate the great weight this bears on others. When I live in fear of being wrong, looking bad, or being criticized, or not being good enough, the conversations I have with others become heavier. Observation of svadhyaya involves taking very good care of yourself so that you are best able to serve. This includes being kind toward yourself. Self-ridicule is a self-defeating behavior and isn't kind. Nor is engaging in activities that are harmful to your body and imbalance the mind.

Balanced Living

Everyone will have a unique sense of what *balance* means. Imbalance caused by lack of sleep and overbooked schedules creates disharmony and leads to a life ripe for outbursts, missed appointments, tardiness, unreliability, and a lot of apologies. There is a point of diminishing returns at work when we need to stop and call it a day. When we keep working beyond such point, our work degrades, as does our health and well-being. Imbalance on an ongoing basis aggravates the body and mind having a cumulative effect, ensuring mediocre work performance and productivity losses. Everything deteriorates when you are chronically imbalanced, including the ability to think, process, reason, regulate behavior, and control emotion. Feeling imbalanced on a consistent basis is not respectful of your own health and well-being. It neither serves the enterprise or your family nor sets a good example as a leader. Take seriously measures like getting enough sleep, eating healthy, and relaxing to support and restore the body and mind.

Reflective Leadership

There is a leadership term that complements svadhyaya (self-study) called reflective leadership. The principle of svadhyaya has a reflective quality, as though we carry around a mirror and observe our own selves as we move through life. What we are giving out to the world around us gets reflected right back to us too. What we see in others that we dislike, for example, is often a reflection of what we dislike about ourselves and are fearful of being seen as having those qualities. Or how we feel we are being treated is often a reflection of the energy we are giving out. If we assume someone is judging us in a negative way, which doesn't feel good, instead of practicing forgiveness, we may create thoughts and labels regarding the accused judger thus judging them. We have evolved brains so we judge all the time but this is an emotionally charged judgment, not derived from discernment and intelligence. We have judged them, possibly even now impacting our mood and affecting our entire day. Furthermore, what we feel about what we are being judged on could actually be what we tend to question about our own selves, stemming from our own fears and insecurities. We just don't want to hear it from another person. The reverse is also true. What we are drawn to in others can be precisely the parts of our own selves that we really like or want more of. If we see someone as inspiring and intelligent, well guess what? We see that as a superior quality that we try to cultivate in ourselves. If we admire someone's positivity and good nature, we again see ourselves as trying to be positive and good-natured and find working toward those qualities important. The latter statements are also judgments, positive judgments. There is one neutral place in all this and one simple question to ask as you self-reflect. The neutral place is grounded in kindness, fostering connection. In the leadership context you could ask yourself whether you are engaging your team in a way that *serves* everyone. It is only through engagement and connection that you can begin to motivate and inspire your team.

Svadhyaya (self-study) can balance tapas (discipline) if tapas gets out of hand. The reverse is also true: too much self-reflection and we might find ourselves in a sea of wondering without actually experiencing things firsthand. If we get stuck in this rut of wandering, a variety of fears come up, and then we rely on our discipline and drive to pull us back into the realm of taking a risk and trying things again, when fear may otherwise hold us back. We should take care to not allow the process of self-reflection to taint our belief in ourselves so that we become afraid of leading, of trying something new, of taking a stand.

The most advanced way to practice svadhyaya is in the present moment. The principle of self-study requires a healthy dose of humility and a beginner's mind, where you approach every situation with a fresh outlook independent of past experiences. Svadhyaya has an enduring quality too. It stays with us. We are always in a mode of self-reflection where we always aspire to better ourselves, while being rooted in the knowing that the next time we make a mess of things we will again aspire to do better because that's what we always do.

Self-Study and Self-Control

Constant study and review of the choices you make is a healthy process undertaken by some of the most successful leaders in the world. Leading graduate schools are routinely teaching emotional and contextual intelligence. We now recognize that knowing and having control of every part of ourselves is an essential quality of leadership, as knowing ourselves well allows us to more effectively develop and manage relationships with a wide variety of stakeholders all over the world.

A good time to practice this principle is with your word choices during hot-tempered times at the office, reflecting upon what causes you and others to become upset. E-mail communication is a great source of self-study. Word choices, length, and punctuation all set the tone and send an indirect message. E-mails often get misconstrued and then emotions arise. Importantly, when people feel supported and there is a culture of mutual trust and respect, communications are less likely to be misunderstood. In the words of Maryam Ovissi, "Our emotions are our teachers." As teachers, they show up and have something to share. We will learn from emotions, if we are willing to be a witness to them and listen. When we understand what emotions are there to tell us, we can use that information to intelligently guide us toward the next moment. Understanding our own emotions will help us better relate to the emotions of others as well.

Self-Study and Better Leadership

Begin to pay attention to your thoughts, self-talk, verbal and written word choices, and the rationale behind your decisions. As a leader, you can direct your efforts in self-study toward developing or enhancing a number of essential leadership qualities and skills discussed throughout the text, including:

- adaptability and resilience
- building trust
- clear and focused communications
- clear intentions and goals
- confidence and self-esteem
- connecting to meaning in work
- creating a shared purpose
- discernment and objectivity
- discipline, motivation, and letting go
- emotion-awareness and control
- empathy, compassion, and detachment
- energy and vitality
- focus, concentration, and memory
- good listening skills
- healthy personal relationships
- influencing others through support and respect
- inner strength and courage
- integrity

- open-mindedness and pragmatism
- positivity
- self-awareness
- team engagement and collaboration

When we learn how to observe ourselves and the world around us, we also naturally become better able to help our team members incorporate self-observation into their lives. Let them know what you are working on to support your well-being and your leadership. Include in your team's annual or quarterly reviews a discussion on self-study with the setting of developmental goals.

Questions for Leaders: Self-Study

1. Do you take the quiet time necessary to self-reflect and determine what you want out of your work and life?
2. In what areas in your life are you seeking to better yourself to achieve what you want? Do you have a path to align your life toward achieving those goals?
3. How do you share your goals with your team to inspire them?
4. Do you pause for a moment to contemplate your word choices, thoughts, emotions, and decisions, to begin to understand yourself better?
5. What self-care measures do you do to support the health of your body and mind?
6. Do you have your team set their own individual goals toward self-betterment and help them identify a plan to accomplish them?
7. Do you encourage the team to self-reflect and communicate about how they could better work together?
8. Do you feel that communication is consistent with the maintenance of principle at an enterprise?
9. Do you offer adequate training programs to allow your team members to advance their skills?
10. Do you participate in ongoing education programs? How are you advancing your skills?

Personal Principle 5: Orientation (ishvara-pranidhana)

This principle connects us to our lives and our work and offers it meaning. It involves an orientation toward something greater, something *higher*. In the traditional context, Patanjali's yoga as previously introduced is non-dogmatic having one orienting his or her efforts toward any conception of the highest truth that resonates. It is sometimes referred to as your teacher within, the teacher who is there with you all the time. This orientation toward higher purpose stems from the awareness that your efforts as a leader, and the efforts of the enterprise, are part of—and not independent from—something more. It only takes a mere moment to ask yourself whether your very next work decision is in the highest good at that moment. It takes little time to reflect upon the ecosystem in which the enterprise operates and consider whether decisions would improve upon the ecosystem. It is honorable to mitigate necessary harm that comes as a consequence of doing business while offering appropriate and adequate remedies. Making it a habit to always ask yourself *what is the highest good* in your every thought, word, and action is one way to consider this principle at work. Setting an intention and goals with an orientation toward a higher good is also a way to embody this principle. But to be clear, this exercise isn't about saving the world or working for organizations that think they are saving the world. This principle, and yoga, is about the inner experience and how you are *being* in your current life and how you could do better. Consider that the highest good could simply be a leader's ability to honor the well-being of his or her team while generating the greatest outcomes for stakeholders and respecting the ecosystem in which the organization operates.

Orientation can importantly be understood as accepting the grace of the moment and resisting less. It can be witnessed as a surrendering to the flow of the forces at work and in our lives. Noticing and feeling when you are seamlessly functioning *in-the-flow* rather than struggling against it is a moment of pure awareness. While in-the-flow, things feel seamless, and the day moves freely. Visualize a leaf floating down a stream, lightly bouncing about with the ripples and around small rocks without being deterred in its path. Functioning against-the-flow feels like you are tackling one obstacle after another, constantly impeded by abutting boulders and unraveling in the process. Obstacles will always arise at work, but can you find a way to function more often in the flow? With compassion, can you allow more and accept more? It is unrealistic to think we can operate in perfect circumstances. How can you do your best to orient *your* efforts toward a higher purpose while functioning in the flow?

If a newly set goal for example seamlessly begins to flow well in your life, then it is probably in your highest interest to go for it. If everything seems to challenge or go against your goal, leaving you exhausted, then perhaps you need to revisit the goal. Perhaps you need to think about it a different way, from a different angle, shifting it subtly, releasing any stubborn tendencies. Is there another way you can orient your days and moments toward something higher? Perhaps the timing isn't right and this specific goal can be set aside and resumed at a later date. Or perhaps that goal isn't meant for you. We've all experienced the challenge in trying to force things through and in the process resisting other things. To work in the flow of life involves *softening* into it and letting go of any resistance as it comes. Examine the resistance that appears, and seek to understand precisely where it is coming from. If you are certain about your goals but they are simply not working in your life, and you discover there is an obvious obstacle blocking your path, then perhaps you are in need of a meaningful life change and realignment. Pay close attention to yourself during those in-the-flow moments to discern what makes these periods unique from others.

Rather than waging war against our lives, this principle has us surrendering to, releasing into, and accepting our lives. Connection to a higher purpose becomes clarified when the mind is quiet. Time spent in contemplation and meditation will allow opportunities for harmony and connection to reveal themselves. As you become more open to the idea of finding the higher purpose in your own leadership and life, you will naturally think of more ways to align yourself and your team accordingly.

Questions for Leaders: Orientation

1. At the end of the day, do you reflect upon the higher purpose of the things you are doing in your life? Do you set goals that embody a higher purpose? Are they working in your life?
2. Is there a dedicated block of time for enterprise goals to be revisited annually by leadership? Are they established in consideration of the ecosystem in which it operates?
3. Do you regularly review the vision, mission, and principles with the team so they feel a connection to the organization that is deeper than a paycheck?
4. Are all members of the team rowing in the same direction, or are opposing energetics at play?
5. Are all leaders connected to and in adherence of company principles?
6. Do you have space for quiet contemplation and connection throughout the office or outside the office? Is it used?
7. Do you tend to function in your life in the flow or against the flow? Does this change certain times of the year or in certain seasons? What takes you out of the flow?
8. How can you, your team, and the enterprise function in the flow? What does that mean to you?

Concluding Statement

It may be hard work at first to maintain an intention to support your holistic well-being and consequently inspiring leadership. It requires a constant, everyday effort. Success comes with the triad of discipline, ongoing self-reflection, and an orientation that recognizes your holistic well-being as an integral component of happiness, health, and cultivating the qualities essential to effective and inspiring leadership. The amount of effort will decrease over time as unhelpful habits fade and helpful ones emerge. Then it no longer becomes work; it becomes life.

Chapter 4
Yogi Secret #2: Physical

Old Maxim
Feeling exhausted is normal.

New Maxim
Feeling refreshed is normal.

Resolve: I nourish my physical body with food, movement, quality sleep, and cleanliness. I am aware of tension held in my body and take measures to release tension and to free energy for helpful purposes.

Yogi Secret #2 allows me to develop or maintain personal qualities inherent in inspiring leaders, including: healthy body ~ increased energy ~ personal pride

The state of yoga is never attained by one who eats too much or abstains from eating, nor for one who sleeps too much or remains ever awake. But for one who appropriately balances their eating, action, recreation, sleeping and wakefulness, linking all such activities to the practice of yoga, all miseries are vanquished.
—Bhagavad Gita 6.16–17

The first layer is the physical dimension called the *annamaya kosha* and is fueled by food. This dimension is tangible, a form of matter including our cells, blood, muscles, organs, bones, tissues, fluids, etc. *Anna* means food; we are literally composed of what we eat. In addition to diet, we care for our physical bodies through movement, quality sleep, and good habits of self-care. Everything that goes into our bodies (including through the skin) either supports the function of our bodies or it doesn't. This includes clean air and pure water.

When you maintain your physical self, you keep your weight in check, your body mobile and strong, and you take efforts to release tension and alleviate pain. When you take care of your body, more feel-good hormones rush through it and you consequently experience more pleasurable feelings and positive emotions. You also have more energy and accordingly are more productive, engaged, and have a more positive outlook. And you are less likely to get sick or injured and miss work.

Annamaya Kosha (Physical)

Our *Too*-Full Lives

Our lifestyles have changed dramatically since the information and telecommunications revolutions starting in the mid-1980s. We are in the Information Age. If we so choose, we can be connected twenty-four hours a day to a variety of devices. As leaders, many—if not most—of our jobs now expect a certain amount of connection outside of traditional working hours, blurring the once clear distinction between *at work* and *not at work*. It's only been in the last fifteen or twenty years, with the appearance of mobile devices, that we have been so connected to work. As a point of comparison, the length of the industrial revolution in America was eighty years. We have gone through a lot of change in a relatively short period of time.

Our family construct has changed appreciably as well. Dual-income families have become the norm, with the overall result being a much more eventful and hectic life. As evidenced by the state of our health, perhaps our lives are too event-*full*. Our lifestyles are more full of hustle than our bodies and our minds seem able to handle and still be well.

Full Lives and Our Nervous System

Our full lives can impact the levels of hormones in our body and cause our nervous systems to shift. We have two opposing parts to our autonomic nervous systems. The first part is our maintenance mode, the parasympathetic nervous system, which is meant to be the everyday, default state. In this state, the mind is calm and clear, and the body is in the mode of healing and growth. Tension releases from the body and regeneration, digestion, and restoration can take place. Our mind is calm, too, and this is when our best thinking and learning take place. This system is sometimes referred to as our rest-and-digest or rest-and-relax system.

The second part of our autonomic nervous system, the sympathetic nervous system, is aroused when we experience any form of stress. Then, our system increases production of the fight or flight stress hormones epinephrine, norepinephrine, and cortisol. This is our emergency response system. We tap into this system when we need to move and think quickly. It is intended for emergency situations—like lunging out of the way of a careening vehicle or running out of a house on fire. When our sympathetic nervous systems are active, our blood pressure increases, our rate of respiration increases, blood is shunted to the major muscle groups, white blood cells mobilize to fight possible infection, and energy sources are readied.[41] Brain activity also increases. This is a state of the big S word: *stress*. Many of us live in a persistent state of stress; so living in our sympathetic nervous systems becomes our *new normal*. At the office, we do not have lions running around looking for a meal or cars about to ram us as we sit at our desks, yet our minds are in a hectic state of reaction and survival. In this state, we are neither thinking straight nor are we learning or creating. Yet many of us don't even know we are in this state because it feels normal to us. All this urgency is man-made; how we *react* to the urgency is self-made.

Some level of stress, called *eustress*, is beneficial. Eustress is the stress enjoyed by athletes, stage performers, and all kinds of high achievers. It gives us a helpful, positive boost to jump-start our day. It gives us energy and motivates us and enhances our ability to think quickly and focus. When working to win a really big deal or client or finalizing a large project or initiative, one feels the benefits of good stress.

Getting Control of Your Nerves

Many of us may move into our sympathetic nervous system to get a job done on deadline. A healthy stress response would mean that our bodies return to the rest-and-relax state after the threat (the deadline) is over. This healthy stress response is a sign that we are in control. When we are chronically aroused and heightened, though, we don't give our bodies a chance to rest and regenerate, which damages our bodies and our minds. In fact, board certified internist and author Timothy McCall, MD, writes in *Yoga as Medicine*, "All told, it could be argued that stress is the number one killer in the Western world today."[42] It is important to your health to learn to feel the sensations in your body, so you can begin to notice when you are heightened for no good reason and take efforts like moving, breathing, centering, or expanding perspective (discussed in subsequent chapters) to return to the rest-and-relax side of your nervous system. Mentally strong leaders have this kind of control, they are relatively unaffected by setbacks seeing them instead as opportunities for self-improvement. Noticing the sensations associated with our nervous system is a self-awareness practice that can be done all the time.

The Cost of Stress
Stress and Dis-function

Ongoing stress manifests as muscular, emotional, or mental tension that becomes part of our everyday existence. This at first leads to relatively minor conditions, like aches and pains, migraine headaches, anxiety, hypertension, poor sleep, or chest pain. Eventually, when left uncontrolled, ongoing stress leads to serious cardiac conditions like heart disease and heart attack and serious mental conditions including violence and suicide.[43] Empirical evidence is showing a direct relationship between stress and many serious illnesses as well, including Type 2 diabetes, heart attacks, strokes, depression, and autoimmune diseases.[44]

> The CDC reports on their website that seven million Americans (31 percent) have high blood pressure and another 30 percent have prehypertension, with numbers that are higher than normal and trending toward high. High blood pressure costs the nation $47.5 billion in direct medical expenses annually and $3.5 billion in lost productivity.–Centers for Disease Control and Prevention

Stress in the Workplace

A 2013 survey of American workers conducted by Harris Interactive indicated that 83 percent of American workers were negatively stressed by something at work. Among the top reasons cited by high earners (household income greater than $100,000) were unreasonable workload and commute time.[45] The American Institute of Stress reports that American businesses lose

$300 billion annually to absenteeism, losses in productivity, employee turnover, healthcare costs, and workman's compensation claims stemming from stress.[46] Other situations that cause stress include: unreasonable expectations, layoffs, ridicule, back-stabbing behaviors, deadlines, marginalizing efforts, crucial meetings, harassment, poor communication, upcoming presentations, losing or winning a client, lack of feedback, shouting, and lack of support. As a leader, it is appropriate to find solutions to these workplace conditions in an effort toward improving team engagement and satisfaction, and mitigating organizational costs.

Stress Is a Contagion

As we are now beginning to realize, merely being party to colleagues who are stressed can affect us, too. Stress transfers from one person to the next. Diane Sawyer reported on ABC news in April of 2014 that studies have found stress to be contagious. We can catch it from others like a pox. We merely watch others who are showing signs of stress and our bodies react. As leaders, this makes it even more important to manage our stress, because we are like a workplace barometer for our teams. When we are stressed and anxious, we give our stress to everyone with whom we come in contact. Yet we often exhaust ourselves at work and have convinced ourselves that doing anything less would cause us to lose our standing, our clients, or our jobs. We seem to feel that taking time for our health and well-being is audacious when there is so much to be done.

Many leaders are overachievers and too often fall prone to the sort of ongoing stress that just *hangs around*. We may find ourselves short-tempered, anxious, and very concerned about efficiently managing time, and may at times have difficulty with interpersonal relationships. Some of us manage to show up at the office seemingly calm but are simply good at internalizing our stress. In this case, we may find that our organs and our bodily systems begin to degrade. Bottling up our stress simply harnesses it *inside* to linger and cause damage to our *insides*. And we may think we are keeping it all in, but its quite unlikely that we aren't energetically and negatively affecting others with our stress.

Developing qualities essential to leadership success comes with having an enhanced capacity to manage daily stressors in a way that supports your well-being and, consequently, that of others. If stress is a problem for you, you will discover throughout this book a wide variety of ways you can begin to decrease stress, mitigate stress, and enhance your capacity for handling stress in your life. The first step is in understanding your relationship to stress.

Your Relationship to Stress

Stress is a unique phenomenon, to be certain. We each have our own relationship to the contents of our lives and to what heightens our nervous system, what *revs us up*. Something that is very stressful to one person may not be stressful at all to another. I find two days alone with little kids far more stressful than traveling to Japan to pitch a billion dollar fund two dozen times with a translator in tow. But both heighten me in different ways. Pitching the fund in Japan is high-stress, but I find it rewarding and exciting and it has a set end-point. Parenting is also rewarding but (God-willing) does not end. It involves a lot of caretaking and duty, and even though I love my kids dearly, caring for them can at times feel overwhelming to *me*. What causes you stress?

The curious question though, is, what exactly is *stress*? After decades of research, the answer is that there is no common agreement as to its definition.[47] But we all know from experience that stress manifests in the body *and* mind. We know that it deposits itself in the body in the form of tension. When we sit at our desks all day, our physical bodies tense up, and we often feel that tension in our necks, shoulders, and backs. When our lives are too full, our minds race, and we may feel the tension in the form of headaches. Emotional tensions can occur in times of change or transition or when relationships in our lives are altered. We feel emotional strain, for example, when a loved one gets sick, and we consequently experience physical tension that arises from the emotional strain.

Physical workplace stressors involve hunching over desks and bending our necks to look at devices while simultaneously handling a variety of inputs. We must spend time doing the exact opposite to counteract these stressors like bending the opposite ways and spending time in places without any inputs. Our posture will evolve as depicted below if we let it, which will take time to unwind so we can again stand erect, breathe fully, and maintain our mobility. Can you function your best as a leader in a frazzled state?

Evolution of a Leader

Inertia and Our Food Addiction

> We are the most in debt, obese, addicted and
> medicated adult cohort in US history.
> —Brené Brown, PhD, LMSW, TED Talk

Overweight, Unfit, and Tense

We claim to not have time to prepare healthy meals or move our bodies. In some cases, it truly seems impossible to fit a habit of healthy cooking and movement into our overbooked schedules. Our society is set up to keep us overweight and stressed, not by intention, but by design. We simply do not yet have a habit of movement established in our culture nor do workplaces encourage movement during the workday enough; we do not commit to healthy eating at home nor do organizations focus enough on food choices at work; we do not take seriously the health of the mind and how a stressed state of mind manifests as dis-*ease* in the body. We also do not take seriously the health consequences related to holding tension in our bodies and how that manifests as stress in the mind. If organizations begin to accept that the necessary corollary of performance is the physical and mental health of the entire workplace, the leaders would establish effective and measurable holistic well-being plans for improving their own health as well as the health of their teams as part of their planning process each year. There are countless possibilities for incorporating well-being into an organizations culture depending up on the available space, resources, and general health of the team. We have become complacent of our size and some girth is accepted as normal. It doesn't help that we've created a system that allows fast, unhealthy processed snacks to cost less than a head of broccoli. As leaders, we serve as examples, and too many of us are among the cohort of the overweight and unfit, the stressed and medicated, and the disengaged and disconnected.

The first dimension is nourished by food. What we choose to eat creates our physical body from a cellular level. It forms our plasma, blood, muscles, bones, bone marrow, nerves, and fluids; it forms and nourishes the building blocks of our body and creates the physical form we see as we age. What we eat matters. We all know we need to make healthy food choices and to move our bodies to maintain health through out lives. Our doctors have been telling us this for years.

> Our diet is the most important component to our physical health and represents 70–80 percent of what we need to do each day to keep the physical body healthy.

We should be eating the highest quality food available. Our busy lives can easily distract us from taking care of ourselves. We are so busy that we seldom cook. We unconsciously overeat lifeless, processed food, and this makes us lethargic, so we drink caffeine or energy beverages to wake us up. We eat at our desks, in our cars, or while walking, and we snack on the run. We eat unconsciously, on autopilot. Much of the time, we are totally unaware of the taste and texture of the food we eat, the quantity of food we are eating, and the way the food makes us feel and behave during and after eating. Because we are lucky enough to have an abundance of food in our culture, we take it for granted. We eat without consideration for the nutrients contained in our food. Did that lunch nourish you and make you more productive and energetic? Or did it make you feel heavy, hurt your gut, and make you want to take a nap? Listen to the intelligence of your body, and use the information as a guide to make choices in your day.

Do you take a walk after a meal? Do you chew your food sufficiently so that it is easier for your body to digest? Do you notice how you feel after you eat? Is it time for a shift? You can make a profound difference. You have the power to make different choices. Serve as an example. Do it for yourself, and do it now. Give yourself permission to take good care of yourself.

Conscious Eating

Speed eating is a surefire way to eat too much in a manner that inhibits proper digestion of food. Furthermore, when we don't chew food well, we skip over the bulk of our taste buds in the back of the tongue and consequently miss the opportunity to really taste what we are eating.[48] Food should be savored and appreciated, if for no other reason than to feel grateful for having food when so many other people in the world are starving. The next time you sit to eat, try to eat consciously. This does not mean obsessing over your food or your body, but rather loving exactly how you are today and knowing that you can make choices that will make you feel better.

Ten Steps to Conscious Eating[49]

1. Apportion a smaller amount than you typically would.
2. Sit down for your meal in a place without the disruption of technology. Unplug completely.
3. Look at your food closely. Notice its texture and color.
4. Think or say a few words appreciating and being grateful for your abundance.
5. Bring your partially-filled utensil to your mouth, smell your food, and feel its temperature before placing the food on your tongue.
6. Put your empty utensil down on the table as you chew.
7. Notice the texture and flavor of the food as you move it around all areas of your pallet and tongue.
8. Chew the food slowly until the food is fully mashed up, and then swallow.
9. Take a full breath, smile, and begin again.
10. Eat until your stomach is three-quarters full, and then tell yourself that you've had enough. Begin to identify *enough* with that feeling of fullness.

Balanced Eating

Ultimately, we want to make choices and habits that help us move toward a more balanced or sattvic way of life. A sattvic diet is also called a yogic diet. It focuses on pure, clean, fresh, and seasonal foods that keep your body light and your mind calm. In a sattvic diet, we attempt to avoid foods that will cause destruction or imbalance to the body or the mind.

The traditional textual understanding of the first social principle of non-harming considers the ultimate yogic practice to involve eating only foods where no living creature is harmed. While this is the ideal according to yoga, it remains a vast disparity from the current dietary trials of a nation largely seeking to lose weight by following certain meat and protein centric diets. Further, given family preferences and time constraints, I too have not yet found my way to adopting a vegetarian diet. So, the guidelines below are shared with a view toward eating in a conscious, balanced manner each day, including what to eat and what to avoid and does not exclude high quality, humanely treated animal products. These recommendations are for the most part commonly known and are aimed at choosing foods that do not harm the cells (the building blocks of the body), deplete our energy, or unsettle the mind. We eat this way in an attempt to improve our health and well-being and to mitigate to onset of diabetes, heart conditions, cancers, chronic stress and fatigue, and mental illnesses like anxiety and depression.

Lifestyle Guidelines Related to Eating

1. Practice conscious eating at mealtimes.
2. Notice how different foods make you feel after you've eaten them and into the next day.
3. Eat all of your meals including breakfast.
4. Allow yourself to feel hungry, maybe even stomach-growling hungry. If you are not hungry at mealtimes, consider reducing the quantity you ate at the prior meal.
5. Don't eat after 8 p.m. or, even better, within four hours of sleeping or allowing a twelve-hour fast between meals.
6. Use smaller plates, cups, and bowls and invite the *portion control board* to each meal.
7. Keep meals simple.
8. Plan your weekly meals in advance.
9. Take shortcuts. (Tip: Buy pre-chopped vegetables, leverage salad bars, and purchase whole prepared foods at trusted grocery stores or hire personal cooks/prep-cooks.)
10. Poop daily.

General Dietary Guidelines

1. Eat the highest quality food you can find and afford. To be the most vigilant, eat as much local, organic, and non-GMO (genetically modified) food as you can find and afford.
2. Eat a rainbow of colors every day.
3. Eat whole real food. (Tip: Unbleached, ancient whole grains and legumes are whole foods that are nutritious and give us energy. Eat them especially for breakfast and lunch. Know what portion of carbohydrates you need in your day for energy that you will burn off before bed, and don't load them up with sodium. Balance carbs at meals with protein to help regulate blood sugar levels. Look for high-protein, low-processed cereal, granola, and muesli.)
4. If you eat processed foods, eat only those with short, recognizable ingredient lists. Over time, minimize or eliminate processed foods from your diet. Many processed foods are received in the body as sugar and contain chemicals that do not support the body's function.
5. Focus on decreasing sodium intake.
6. Eliminate trans fats from your diet completely.
7. Apportion your dinner plate so it is 50 percent non-starchy vegetables, 20 percent carbohydrates (starchy vegetables, grains, fruits), 20 percent protein, and 10 percent healthy fats. (Tip: Non-starchy vegetables include: broccoli, green beans, leafy greens, carrots, asparagus, cauliflower, beets, pea pods, cucumber, mushrooms, onions, red/green/yellow peppers, zucchini, and cabbage.)
8. If you're trying to lose weight, reduce the carbohydrates and consider salads, stir-fry, and green smoothies with protein powder for dinner and/or lunch.
9. If you are doing a lot of muscle building activities, boost your protein to carb ratio to support the healing of torn muscle fibers.

10. Bring awareness into your food choices. Consider the environmental footprint in the food choices you make and your responsibility to future generations. Consider buying more from farmers' markets and the local food sections found in conscientious grocery stores. Consider joining a food co-op to share in the fresh bounty during the growing season.

Foods to Eat and Those to Avoid

Recommended food intake is a complicated and ever-changing science. You are unique. Use common sense and make small changes paying close attention to how you feel along the way.

Specific Food Guidelines

1. Triple the non-starchy vegetables in every recipe you cook.
2. Make vegetables the star of the show.
3. Snack on nuts, nut butters, hummus, avocados, whole fruit, and/or drink plant-based protein drinks without sugar and fresh-pressed juice. Pre and post workout nutrition, when one engages in vigorous exercise, is important and may necessitate these off mealtime snacks, otherwise skip the snacks.
4. Pasta and breads are carbohydrates and processed foods. Buy freshly made pasta and bread prepared from organic, whole grain (heirloom if you can find it) that has not been genetically modified. Eat them in moderation. They should expire quickly because they do not contain preservatives. (Tip: Reduce your carbohydrate intake especially on days that you do not exercise vigorously. Carbohydrates turn to sugar and then fat when not used for energy.)
5. Minimize or eliminate added sugar. Sugar is a carbohydrate that too often leads to weight gain. (Tip: Honey, maple syrup, and agave sweetener are sugars, too. In limited quantity, choose these natural sugars in lieu of other processed and artificial sweeteners.)
6. Increase plant-based sources of protein such as lentils and other legumes.
7. Eat fermented foods daily for gut health: pickles, raw milk cheeses, miso, tempeh, sauerkraut, kimchi, yogurt, kefir, or kombucha. Adding one to two tablespoons of apple cider vinegar containing 'the mother' to your water one to three times a day likewise supports the gut.
8. Eat *only* lean, grass-fed meat and free-range pasture-fed poultry, eggs, and dairy products (raw milk and cheese are good choices), and low-mercury fish (typically non-farm raised or purchased from sustainable farms that are making a business out of raising the healthiest quality fish). Limit red meat consumption to once a week and eliminate processed meat.
9. Watch the Omega-6's: David Servan-Schreiber, MD, PhD discusses protein intake in detail in his eye-opening, international bestseller *Anticancer: A New Way of Life*. If you are going to eat cows and chickens in particular (including eggs and dairy), you want the animals that you eat to be eating healthy food for them—grass—and not Omega-6-laden, in Servan-Schreiber's words, "junk food for cows and chickens." [50] Why? If you eat grain-fed, Omega-6-laden meat, eggs, and dairy products, the Omega-6 excess in your body will overly stimulate

the production of fat cells, promote rigidity of cells, and promote inflammation. An imbalanced inflammatory response is the root of many diseases, including cancers—and we are trying to decrease rates of obesity and diabetes, which runs counter to an increased production of fat cells. In addition to Omega 6's also decrease consumption of other inflammatory foods including: sugar, processed white flour, trans-fats, alcohol, and gluten. Boost anti-inflammatory foods and herbs including: leafy greens, blueberries, shiitake mushrooms, fermented foods, Matcha tea, ginger, rosemary, cinnamon, oregano, sage, thyme, cloves to name a few.

10. Know your protein requirement. Protein requirements are also related to the muscular intensity, frequency, and duration of exercise that we do each day. If you are not doing muscularly intensive exercise, you may need less than you think. The more strength training and high-intensity-interval training that you do, the more protein you require for repairing muscle tissue. Although some protein is recommended at each meal to regulate our blood sugar levels, our understanding of portion sizes and protein needs tend to be incorrect.

Nutrition – Keeping it Real

Food is not for the tongue; it is for the mind.
—A.G. Mohan, BelovedYoga lecture 2013

The "Diet" Dilemma

As leaders, we are tenacious and want to perform, so we are looking to do anything that increases our energy. We often choose to eat by following diets that include marketing messages promising weight loss and increased energy. The field of nutritional science has evolved meaningfully in recent years alongside advancements in other sciences like molecular biology, biochemistry, and genetics. Nutritional science concerns itself with physiological and metabolic responses to diet. Even so, there is still no settled science as to the absolute best way to eat. As our knowledge of food continues to develop, so will the flurry of new "diets."

Behind the various diets are various companies trying to profit off diet products and services. Like any business, these companies leverage savvy marketing techniques to lure you into buying their products and services. Many of the diets promising the same results conflict with one another entirely, making it difficult to determine which diet to choose. Here are some statements from various diet plans:

Eat like a caveman. Eat according to your blood type. Eat according to your personality type. Eat to maintain an alkaline condition in your body.

Eat small meals every three hours. Eat three times a day and don't snack.

Don't eat dairy. Don't eat fruit with anything else. Eat food raw. Eat food fully cooked. Don't eat gluten. Don't eat grains. Don't eat meat.

Eating animal products is toxic. Red meat causes cardiovascular disease. Eating grass-fed red meat is okay. Eating carbs makes you fat. Eating dairy makes you fat.

Juice daily. Cleanse quarterly. Don't cleanse; our colon doesn't need help.

Vitamins and supplements are necessary; our diets do not provide us adequate nutrition. Vitamins and supplements are a waste of money; we get all we need from food.

Stop the Madness!

Eat to Feel Mentally and Physically Strong

Focus on what is important, building a sustainable foundation for well-being in life. There is a direct link to what we eat and how we feel. Eat to feel mentally and physically strong, which means eating in a way that does not harm the body or unsettle the mind. Know that what you need to eat to feel good may be different from what someone else needs.

> The objective of eating is to feel good and energized in our days and not to satisfy desires and cravings.

Many of the statements above are supported by good science and may be true based upon the individuals who were studied and the intention behind the research. But you are a unique person. Your needs are unique to you and will change over time. The totality of issues of genetics, age, weight, body composition, digestion, disease, allergy, activity level, mental health, quality of sleep, sensitivity to seasons, stress, responsibilities, and other habits of life are factors in how we uniquely should eat (and exercise) to maintain balance in body and mind and optimal well-being.

Eat to Feed the Brain

Concerning yourself with a diet undervalues the point of eating in the first place. Many of us eat to maintain a number of points on a checklist, fill out a quadrant, or maintain a scorecard. The objective of eating is to feel good and energized, not to satisfy desires and cravings or to make us look like a touched-up image in a magazine. You may need the checklist to help you lose weight if you are overweight, but understand that you eat to feel good. You eat to feed the cells of your brain and the cells of your body. If you focus on how you feel and eat as a way to truly feel good over the long-term, you will end up healthier, happier, and more

> Call to action!
> Eat less and move more.
> Eat slowly and savor your food.

emotionally balanced. If you eat most of the time to satisfy desires and cravings, eating according to your wants and not your needs, this will more often lead to a path of illness and suffering, simply because we unfortunately tend to naturally crave unhealthy things like sugar and fried food and food made from flour. As you replace fried, sugary, processed, or sodium-laden foods with healthy foods, those cravings will diminish.

Eat to Fuel Your Cells

Orient yourself toward eating to consume nutrition that fuels the cells of your physical (food) dimension to maintain well-being. Consider eating for nutrition and weight management (or weight loss) during the week and for taste on the weekends. Use the 80/20 rule during the week: allow for a 20 percent slip in your diet so you can treat yourself to ice cream or pizza or dark chocolate. We all love to eat foods that aren't loaded with nutrition. We are human, and denying ourselves completely would be unkind. Treat yourself in moderation.

The first step toward developing a new relationship with food is simply to create an awareness of what we are eating and how we feel during and after we eat.

You Are What You Eat

1. What nutrients do I uniquely need? Am I getting enough nutrients from my daily food and drink consumption?
2. Am I easily eliminating waste (pooping) each day?
3. Do my food and beverage choices energize me or make me feel sluggish?
4. Do my food and beverage choices make me feel more calm or angry?
5. Do I ever feel hungry (stomach growling)? Or are my portions too large? Do I make intentional choices around when to eat or because it is that time of day or because of stress?
6. Does the frequency and content of what I eat and drink actually help me keep my rate of metabolism up, or am I overeating?
7. Am I at a healthy weight? If not, am I eating slightly smaller portions and lighter food to get to an optimal weight?

Take your time with changes to your daily food intake. You will not adhere to all the guidelines overnight. Try not to become fixated or obsessed with every single meal. If you begin to take a mental note of the foods you have eaten earlier in the day, you can choose foods to satisfy your remaining carbohydrate, protein, and vegetable needs. Most people will find they need to add a lot more vegetables into their diet and to become more aware of their protein and carbohydrate intake.

Portion Control Board

Studies have demonstrated a connection between the purchase of very large sizes of food products found at warehouse and "super" stores and the effect of such bulk-buying on obesity. Evidence is increasingly clear that when we buy very large portions of products, we eat more, contributing to a rise in BMI and obesity. It is human behavior to take a more generous portion from a huge bag of potato chips than one would from a small bag. So, a word to the healthy: buy organic fruits, vegetables, and healthy proteins in bulk, but it is better to leave the bagged, boxed, and frozen processed food items behind.

Being aware of this behavior pattern is helpful to understanding the importance of portion sizes. The more that is on our plate, the greater the likelihood we will consume more calories. Our portion sizes—along with our waistlines—have grown considerably in the last few decades. Interestingly, so have the sizes of the plates, bowls, cups, and mugs we now have in our kitchens. Seeing these giant plates and bowls invites us to fill them, thus distorting our idea of portion sizes. Consider eating dinner on a salad plate. We have forgotten what is a normal and appropriate portion of food. Managing portion sizes is not about obsessing over a number on a scale or living in fear of gaining weight. It is merely so that we can maintain a healthy and reasonable weight that makes us feel good. Healthy and reasonable is not analogous to skinny and obsessive.

> It is not helpful to your health and well-being to become fixated or obsessed with every single meal. Make honest estimates.

Why Are We Overweight?

Unfortunately, much of the time we don't know that we're eating non-nutritious food. We actually think we are eating healthy food and making good choices. As leaders, our time is precious, and so we are on the lookout for food that is both healthy and fast. But labels, marketing messages, and portion sizes are deceptive and incomplete. We trust them because we want to trust them. We trust them because we are often too tired and too busy to cook. If something is labeled as *heart healthy, fat free,* or *no added sugar,* we assume it's good, and we think that we know what that means and we eat it.

These labels and others like *natural, gluten-free,* and *whole grain,* are used to help us discern for ourselves what foods to choose. It is possible that the manufacturer has done a decent job at creating a product with a short list of recognizable ingredients, no additives or preservatives, and minimal sugar and sodium. However, such a product still is *processed food,* tinkered with in some way so that it can exist on our grocery store shelves for a long time. In reality, if it doesn't have a logical expiration date, it is probably not natural. Do you ever see *natural* stamped on an apple? Some apples may be treated topically with pesticides (therefore not organic) and others may be grown from seeds that have been engineered (genetically modified) so that the fruit can magically serve as its own insect repellent. Either way, apples are plucked off trees and (absent washing and sometimes waxing) delivered to a store for us to buy and eat. Whole foods do not have ingredient lists: an apple is an apple, lentils are lentils, chicken is chicken, chick-peas are chick-peas, spinach is spinach, carrots are carrots, quinoa is quinoa, barley is barley, dates are dates, cashews are cashews, chia seeds are chia seeds, parsley is parsley, cilantro is cilantro, turmeric is turmeric, and cinnamon is cinnamon. Many herbs, spices, and roots offer flavor to foods and are *potent* sources of nutrition. And any prepared food that you want to buy at a market should contain an ingredient list of similar whole foods and nothing else.

If we relabeled food on shelves of common grocery store chains according to what they really are, most of the processed goods are so highly refined that they could be called *disease-causing agents*. While growing up in the 1970s in Pittsburgh, the center for poison control encouraged families to place a now-famous green and scowling Mr. Yuk™ sticker on all toxic household products to deter small children from ingesting them. Most items today on traditional grocery store shelves should be stamped with a likewise deterring Mr. Yuk™ and labeled with a tobacco type of warning that reads, "This item causes obesity, diabetes, and heart disease." Sarcasm aside, consider asking yourself as you glance at long lists of unrecognizable ingredients on highly processed foods, *is this "food product" a disease-causing agent?* Make wise choices with eyes that are wide open.

Sugar Exposed

Sugar is the world's biggest crop by astounding numbers. Many studies have tested the effects of sugar, and scientists continue to debate the specific effects from different kinds of sugar (fructose versus glucose, for example). The aggregate body of research suggests a linkage between sugar consumption and various negative consequences, including high blood pressure, insulin resistance, high levels of triglycerides, fat in the liver, fat in the muscles, belly

> Make healthy eating a non-negotiable in your life.

fat, weight gain, and inflammation—all of which contribute to the epidemics of obesity, Type 2 diabetes, and cancer.

Added Sugar

The sugars that are contributing to disease in this country and driving the obesity and Type 2 diabetes epidemics out of control include the added sugar found in processed food. The American Heart Association recommends the added sugar intake by women and men to be no more than, roughly, six and nine teaspoons a day, respectively, yet the average American consumes *twenty-one* teaspoons of added sugar a day. Added sugar is not the natural sugar found in whole fruits and grains. Most processed foods (even organic) have some kind of hidden sugar added, including crackers, canned/jarred soup, cereal, bread, pasta, fruited yogurt, tomato sauce, soup broth, beverages and, of course, cookies, cakes, candies, and other treats. Read the labels carefully.

Anything that sweetens can be considered added sugar, ranging from processed cane sugar to honey. However honey is natural and has health benefits when consumed in moderation and uncooked. Agave sweetener is also natural and is said to spike insulin levels the least. It is widely known that high-fructose corn syrup (HFCS) is horrible on the liver and our metabolism and leads to a host of diseases.[51] We simply should *never* consume HFCS, and yet it continues to be included in all kinds of processed foods. An abundance of HFCS-sweetened disease-causing processed "food products" are shamelessly marketed to our children. Read the labels carefully on any products targeted toward your kids.

Sugar is Addictive

Sugar is highly addictive. In some research circles, sugar has even been called an opiate, considered as addictive as cocaine. The body gets a boost of energy and then crashes, so you want more sugar to feel better. The more of this type of food you eat, the more you crave, and the more you *will* eat, contributing to weight gain. Cravings are minimized when we consume foods that do not spike our glucose (blood sugar) levels.

Carbohydrates Become Sugar Then Fat

It is true that any complex carbohydrates such as brown rice, quinoa, bulgur, steel-cut oats, sweet potatoes, lentils, and beans are, when overeaten, broken down into sugars, which (if not burned off) will store themselves in the body as fat. To be clear, unprocessed, whole grains and legumes themselves are not to blame for our fat problem unless we are eating too much of them. Whole grains in their unprocessed state are good for us, particularly when balanced with protein at a meal. Complex carbohydrates provide us with the fuel necessary for energy. We must simply eat them in appropriate proportion to our individual activity level and body type so we burn them up each day.

Whole Fruit

Whole fruit is also very good for many of us, just not in a processed state. The sugars found in whole fruit are natural and easily used in our bodies. We must only maintain a sense of portion control and balance when we eat them. Fruit is a simple sugar and digests very quickly—in around twenty minutes—and as such makes for a good snack alongside some protein. Diabetic research would suggest minimizing fruit intake in general and always eating some protein along with the fruit, or any carbohydrate (sugar) for that matter, to slow the pace of digestion and help regulate blood sugar levels—fruit with nuts or nut-butter for example.

Chemicals and Preservatives

Most processed foods also contain chemicals or preservatives and coloring agents. Debate continues as to whether they are harmful to the body. The radically healthy avoid them by closely inspecting food labels. Most chemicals and preservatives do nothing to support the health of our body. That's not their purpose and for that reason alone it makes sense to try to avoid eating them. Why let them build up in your body and wonder if they are causing harm? Processed foods are often sweetened with sugar and typically contain chemicals and preservatives and coloring agents. Preservatives make good business sense for grocery stores because they keep products stable on shelves for a long time. You can do your best to avoid chemicals and preservatives by purchasing whole foods and reading labels carefully. If you follow the eating recommendations outlined above, you will avoid a lot of chemicals, preservatives, and added sugars. Further, you will be eating in a healthful way that helps to ward off the onset of diabetes and dozens of inflammatory and autoimmune conditions.

Make an Action Plan for Eating Healthy Food

Based on research, it seems safe to assume that we as a society are eating in a matter directly contributing to our health problems. Our movement toward processed, fast foods and away from home-cooked meals and whole foods has contributed to our changes in diet. Busy lives and busy leaders find it difficult to get a healthy meal on the table at night. This is normal. But high quality and sustainable leadership depends upon feeding your body and mind healthy food. You are disciplined and strong. Figure out a way to take control of your food intake, make a plan, and execute.

Ten Critical Success Factors to Getting Healthy
Food onto Your Dinner Plate Each Night

1. Make healthy eating a non-negotiable in your life
2. Plan in advance (Tip: Involve the family in choosing the weekly meals; over time figure out the five to ten go-to weekday meals that work for your family each season.)
3. Shop in advance (Tip: Hire someone to shop, have groceries delivered, or sign up to have them bagged by the grocery store in advance for pickup at the store.)
4. Prep in advance (Tips: Have kids help chop, pay to have someone chop, or buy pre-chopped.)
5. Choose simple meals (Tip: Implement a five-ingredients-or-less rule on weekday meals.)
6. Delegate, delegate, delegate (Tip: don't push the full burden of meal planning on one person. Instead, delegate certain days to certain family members—even your kids. Teach your kids how to prepare healthy food early on.)
7. Take shortcuts (Tip: buy pre-chopped, whole-foods-based and labeled meals that are prepared daily at grocery stores. Leverage the hot and cold food bars at healthy grocery stores. Order take-out from restaurants that offer meals that are consistent with your healthy eating rules.)
8. Get help! Consider one of the many healthy meal delivery services. Consider using a meal assembly kitchen service where you assemble and pack pre-prepped, nutritious, whole-foods-based meals, or even buy them preassembled, and store them in the freezer for quick cooking when you need them. Or even better, hire someone to come and cook your dinners a couple of times a week.
9. Savor your newfound energy and savor your food.
10. Share your successes (and your chefs) with others, make it a matter of discussion, and inspire others to do the same.

Eat the Rainbow—Vegetables 101

The reason we struggle so much with healthy eating is that we are not accustomed to having the vegetables be the star of the show. The idea of organizing our meal around vegetables is foreign to us. I told my son when he was four that we must eat a rainbow of colors every day, and that he had no colors on his plate. He said, "I have brown,

> We hire people to watch our kids, to clean our homes, and to tend our lawns. Why not hire someone to help you get healthy meals on the dinner table and pack a healthy lunch for you while they are at it?

Mommy." I smiled and responded that brown doesn't offer enough nutrients to give us lots of energy, prevent us from getting sick, and improve our vision. Of course, there are a few whole-food based *brown food* exceptions such as shiitake mushrooms, but most of the browns in our diet are processed carbohydrates like bread, crackers, and pretzels.

Too many of us eat like a picky child. Strive to eat a rainbow of whole, unprocessed foods every day. Eat a diet with a lot of green and orange and add in some red, purple, yellow, and blue. The whole-grain brown, tan, and white foods are best in the morning for bulk and energy. Other than that, just eat a little as a side dish. The list below offers some super easy ways to make veggies the star of the show. Add a protein (lentils, beans, fish, chicken, grass-fed beef, tofu, quinoa) and/or a whole grain (bulgur, farrow, rice, sweet potatoes, or a pasta made from a protein) to any of the vegetable preparations below and you have a meal.

Tips for Getting Veggies on Your Plate

1. Don't overthink the vegetables, and keep preparation simple.
2. Buy pre-washed baby greens, and put them on your plate at every meal. Serve them underneath whatever you are cooking or serve them lightly dressed on the side.
3. Cook spinach with garlic, onion, and light oil over low heat to serve at any meal. Never burn your oils as its said to make them produce potentially carcinogenic compounds, choose oils for cooking that have a high smoke point like ghee, macademia oil, avocado oil, coconut oil, or organic canola oil. If you want to cook with olive oil, do so over very low heat.
4. Have simple salads of greens, tomatoes, and cucumbers particularly in the spring and summer using the freshest vegetables available. Top lightly with high quality oils, vinegars, or juices. Mix in any variety of sprouts as a change. Always choose organic, pure, mechanically-extracted, fresh oils that are not highly processed, refined, or temperature-treated.[52] Simple dressings include extra virgin olive oil and balsamic vinegar, or try avocado oil with champagne vinegar, pomegranate vinegar, or lemon juice. Add walnuts, sliced almonds, or pistachios if you need more protein. Add a little feta, goat cheese, fresh mozzarella, or shaved Parmesan for additional flavor.
5. Steam vegetables in a basket or simply get a microwavable bag of vegetables meant for steaming to have as a second vegetable at any meal. Broccoli, green beans, and baby carrots are great steamed.
6. Have packs of frozen peas and frozen chopped spinach on hand and add a few handfuls to every sauce-based dish you make particularly in the fall and winter, including soups, tomato sauce, pesto sauce, and Indian food.
7. Sautee fresh garlic and pine nuts in oil until they begin to brown, add broccoli until cooked but not too soft.
8. Buy pre-chopped stir-fry vegetables and cook them with a generous amount of ginger and sea salt. Douse with Braggs Liquid Aminos (tastes like soy sauce).
9. Bake Brussels sprouts, asparagus, grapes, fennel and/or onions in the oven season with a little sea salt. Include pistachios for a little crunch. Douse with balsamic vinegar.
10. Buy zucchini spaghetti and sauté with chopped walnuts. Toss with pesto and top with shaved Parmesan cheese.

11. Halve a squash or zucchini, a sprinkle of cumin, and shaved Parmesan cheese, and bake.

12. Sautee a lot of sliced red, orange, and yellow peppers with onion and a protein in a pack of fajita simmer sauce by Frontera to make fajitas. Always include fresh chopped avocado in your fajitas or tacos. Try using a pack of prepared lentils as the protein.

13. Eat raw carrots, sliced red peppers, and cucumbers on their own or with hummus as an appetizer while cooking.

14. Put chopped, fresh, organic, perfectly ripened avocado on top of nearly everything. The oil in this fruit is satiating.

Perfect Poop

Let us now transition the topic from the eating of food to the digestion of food. When one has a child, one begins the daily conversation about poop that continues for years. Did baby poop yet? What color was it—yellow, green, or light brown? Was it mustard-like, runny, chunky, or solid? Did it smell normal (yeah, right)? How many times did baby go today? Did baby struggle or not? It was green; did she eat peas yesterday? Black, it must have been the blueberries. It was runny. It must have been the prunes. It was solid and he seemed to struggle, perhaps his cereal is a bit too thick for him. *What is our goal?* Perfect poop for baby, right? Perfect poop.

This conversation between mothers, fathers, and childcare support people continues on a daily basis for years. Why? Because, initially, the pediatrician requires parents to report these details, understanding that they are indicators of the health of your baby. As your baby gets older, you still continue to discuss your kid's feces. Why? Because you know that your kid should defecate at least once a day and you want to make sure they've wiped properly.

Adult Bowels

You should empty your bowels each day, too. And your waste product is also a measure of *your health*. Why would that change? I wonder if we are the only place in the world where we accept stagnant waste sitting in our bodies for more than a day as normal. Walking around filled with crap all day is not helpful to your well-being. Excreting nice, solid, brown logs every day is a good measure of your health. Explosive or runny evacuations are a sign of imbalance. The gut is of huge importance to well-being. Dr. Michael Gershon, an expert in the field of neurogastroenterology, has spent his career studying the brain-gut connection. He coined the term *second brain* in 1996 in reference to the gut and its importance to the human condition.[53] Perfect poops are a sign that your bodily systems are functioning properly, you are managing your levels of stress, and that you are eating in a way that supports your health.

Bowel Disease

Twenty percent of the American population now has IBS or another similar bowel condition, the majority of cases being diagnosed in people age thirty to sixty-four. [54] It's not a disease that strikes us when we are old. Functional bowel disease is extremely costly, given its diagnosis first requires ruling out other, more serious conditions.

If you have a problem, take the function of your bowels into your own hands before your problem turns into a bowel disease. Eat healthy food daily. And consider the medications you are taking. SSRI medications are commonly used to relieve anxiety and depression, but also seem to cause the bowel, in Gershon's words, "to writhe, then churn, and finally to freeze up," which, in lay terms, means nausea and constipation.[55] With lifestyle changes, you may not need drugs anymore.

Stimulation

If you are already eating well and moving each day, you probably defecate every day, too. As we age, things may slow down. If you still aren't enjoying daily evacuations, perhaps you need a little stimulation down there to jump-start the system in the morning. Drinking eight ounces of water bedside upon rising helps, as does adding some fresh acidic juice, like half a lemon or lime, to the water. You can also do this prior to eating. A small shot (one to two ounces) of pure aloe vera juice upon waking does wonders. Drink a mix of Bragg's Raw Apple Cider Vinegar, water, and agave a couple times a day. Add some probiotic-rich, high-protein Greek yogurt to your diet. Make it plain, no-sugar; you can add a little date syrup, smashed fruit, 100 percent maple syrup or honey (if you aren't diabetic) at home.

Are you eating too much sugar that feeds the bad bacteria in your gut? Consider balancing your intestinal flora with a probiotic supplement, or by drinking some kombucha tea each day or eating another fermented product like kimchi that has the function of increasing the good bacteria in your gut. Are you eating enough fiber from vegetables to push out the waste from the day prior? Consider drinking herbal digestive aids or tonics (teas). Ginger tea is very helpful. Or learn about herbal digestive supplements like Triphala. As you begin to take note of what's happening down there, you'll notice the impact of a salad the day prior versus, for example, French fries and a burger.

Diagnostic Testing and Supplementation

In order to know what specifically to eat to support your health, it is very helpful to first know what you need. If you tell your physician that you just don't feel yourself or you frequently feel really tired, the current protocol at most offices is to test a few specific elements of your blood. It's an ad hoc, trial and error approach to tease out what might be wrong. It may also involve multiple random guesses at what to test, until something is found to appear out of range. Often the one to three tests still come back with a result that you are within normal levels, and then you go home still tired, lacking energy. This was my story. Or this energy-draining, nutritional imbalance is often misdiagnosed as depression and treated with drugs. It's an unsatisfying, unproductive, and unhelpful approach. Nor is it the least bit holistic.

There is a solution. Ask your doctor about getting a comprehensive nutrition panel that offers a complete picture of your blood. You may need to see a physician from an integrative and/or functional practice that encourages and authorizes such comprehensive testing. The samples are sent to a number of diagnostic facilities. For example, Genova Diagnostics offers a test called NutrEval FMV® that measures core nutrients and shares the findings in a color-coded, graphical report explaining your ranges and, importantly, your nutritional deficiencies. The report maps your deficiencies to potential consequences of long-term deficiencies, to foods that contain the needed nutrients, and to a recommended minimum daily supplement necessary for you to get that nutrient back into a recommended range. This comprehensive test now gives your physician a comprehensive view into your blood health at a cellular level and offers a roadmap to tracking and supporting your well-being, starting with your blood. Some high-end gyms like Lifetime Fitness now offer similar types of tests. But do it with your primary care doctor or nurse practitioner instead, because it becomes part of your health maintenance program. It is a point-in-time test so you may want to have the complete panel done every few years and your outliers retested periodically to make sure you are on track. Your doctor, nurse, or even a staff nutritionist will recommend dietary changes and supplements to take that support your body's function. This is a relatively simple way to start feeling your best today. What you eat and what you supplement are fundamental to your showing up healthy, happy, energized, and engaged. It is the foundation on which the rest of your holistic well-being resides.

As a side note, there are many other tests that use samples of saliva or blood to look at genetics and other blood components that can help you understand your body further, including factors like your propensity for storing fat in different parts of your body and your levels of stress measured by the presence of certain hormones. Some of these diagnostic tests will then include practical recommendations, including the type and intensity of exercise you should do, the foods you should eat, and the supplements you should take to maintain a healthy body composition and/or reduce your levels of stress hormones. Get that perky you back by feeding your cells the nutrition and type of movement they need.

Movement

Movement Practices—aka Exercise

It's important that we move our bodies in ways that support our well-being through balance. We oftentimes find ourselves working in highly competitive situations. If you know you are a naturally competitive A-type that can tend toward imbalance like me, then finding a non-competitive form of exercise that centers the mind–body in a supportive and positive environment would be helpful to you. Exercise choices that can also be mind–body practices involve anything where you have the opportunity to focus on your breath and the beating of your heart in settings that do not send your mind reeling in a negative direction. Although yoga movement training is an obvious choice as it targets the mind-body in a very intentional and sophisticated way, swimming, cycling, and running can be done in a conscious way that yields mind–body benefits for people too. As yoga has become more mainstream, more and more top fitness instructors and classes are incorporating a mind–body element into their classes, mostly near the end where they have their students relax, release, and center. Alternatively, if you know that you often find a reason not to move your body you need to be pushed. It is essential for you to find an exercise partner(s) and to choose challenging classes led by motivating teachers.

Exercise causes us to sweat and increases our levels of many hormones that boost our metabolism, help us burn fat, and support a positive mood. Sweating is a necessary way to excrete built-up toxins like lead, mercury, arsenic, and cadmium that are present in the environment and in some of our food. Sweating supports our immunity, our health, and our skin. Some choose to sweat in a sauna or a steam room and others choose to sweat through movement.

We all know that we should move our bodies every day. Make conscious choices that balance the body *and* mind. I know that yoga movement practice is an essential part of my mental and physical well-being, so I choose to practice several times a week. I practice for my family because I've found I need the yoga movement practice, together with a daily meditation practice, to help me keep my mind and emotions in check in the frenzy of a very full life. I choose a variety of challenging, powerful, advanced, and sometimes very sweaty classes. As already mentioned, I have found my yoga practice releases the tensions in my body that lead to low back pain. I also leverage the expertise of personal trainers, who continue to challenge me in high intensity exercise two to three days a week to target and strengthen muscles differently, to balance the sides of my body in other ways, to build endurance and stamina, and to boost metabolism. With a mid-forties metabolism and following two births, high-intensity interval training has helped me burn fat on my body, gain muscle (hence increasing metabolism), and consequently supports weight loss. It also makes me stronger so I don't injure myself in the challenging yoga classes that I enjoy so much. I learned long ago the importance of mixing up the routine and moving the body in different ways. What assortment of movement do you need in your life that supports a healthy weight, vitality, emotional control, discernment, clear-thinking, and equipoise?

I've been around the fitness community for some time now having taught aerobics and weight training at a women's gym in my teens and becoming a regular at many gyms in the decades subsequent. I have a great deal of respect for all fitness instructors and the alternatives for keeping in shape. A good trainer is worth every penny as is a good yoga teacher. Since this is a yoga inspired book, we'll focus next on the benefits of yoga as a movement modality so that you will begin to incorporate it into your weekly routine.

Benefits of Yoga Movement Practice (asana)

Yoga *asana* practice (poses done on a mat), in the context of modern yoga, is a mind–body physical practice involving conscious movement with breath awareness and is the third of Patanjali's Eight Limbs of Yoga. Yogis understand that what we do to the body affects the mind and what we do to the mind affects the body. They are one. This makes us an integrated unit, the *mind–body* or sometimes called the *bodymind*. A regular yoga asana practice helps us remain strong, mobile, and erect as we age by countering the negative consequences of sitting, by releasing tension from the body, reducing pain, and creating balance. Asana practice can even be done in your chair at the desk. With open and unstuck bodyminds, we have an increased capacity to manage stressors in our minds, reduce distraction, control our emotions, connect with our teams, and increase our efficiency and productivity. Further, the modality involves paying attention to the present moment, a skill that allows us to learn about ourselves, support our well-being off the mat, and engage in life with a more positive outlook.

Strength

Yoga asana practice, like any weight-bearing exercise, strengthens bone and muscle. Keeping muscles strong is critical to maintaining our metabolism and allows us to age and exist comfortably. When we move slowly and consciously in an asana class, we require our muscles to remain toned throughout the transition from pose to pose. The term used for lengthening a muscle while maintaining some tone is called *eccentric stretching*. While many forms of exercise strengthen predominantly through contraction of muscles, a yoga movement practice strengthens while lengthening the body. That's why, when you see yogis doing amazing arm balances, holding their own weight while defying gravity, they are strong but do not generally have huge muscles. Many yoga poses require the practitioner to use all of their muscles the same time as an integrated unit to establish a strong foundation that allows them to be still and to breathe while holding the pose. Disengaged and weak muscles instead have a practitioner wobbling in the pose until they build strength overtime. Yoga is a whole body, balanced, strength-training regimen.

Tension Release

The continuous lengthening of the body during a yoga asana practice releases tension within the myofascial system, which is the highly complex, web-like system of soft connective tissue that offers our body form. Our myofascial system holds our bones, muscles, organs, nerves, and blood vessels—among other structures—in the right place so we can stand erect in our human form. Without this system, we'd be a pile of bones, fluids, and tissue. Since the vast majority of our nerve endings are found in the myofascial system, it is oftentimes referred to as the *emotional body*, where we tend to hold stress. Hence, it can be thought of as our *feeling* center. Yoga can cause a practitioner to release stored emotion too. During particularly deep stretches in a yoga class unexpected emotion can surface like pent-up anger or sadness. In this way a yoga class offers a safe environment for working out and releasing unnecessary and unhelpful emotion, including emotion associated with stress. When we release both physical and emotional tensions we relax our bodies and minds and have a more positive outlook.

Mobility

Our daily habits impact our myofascial system. If we do not move our body and our joints regularly, they will start to get gunked-up and we'll feel stiff, leading to physical and mental tension. Over time, a regular yoga asana practice will lengthen bound-up tissues, allowing for fuller range of motion and enhancing mobility as well as mitigating aches and pains. The practice enhances flexibility and mobility by freeing tension bound up around the joints. When this happens, we also relax and feel better, so it has a mental and emotional impact. Another way to think about the myofascial system is as a huge interstate with lots of roads crossing all over the place and tons of traffic. When traffic flows, the energy is consistent. When traffic gets backed up and even comes to a stop, the aggregate energy stops and sits in that spot. When we allow the energy in our bodies to sit in a spot, it gets stuck there.

Our myofascial system has a slimy surface, so when it's healthy, all the other structures can move about freely within this web. When we build tensions in our bodies through our daily habits, the slimy surface of our fascial plane becomes sticky and glue-like in places. This stickiness makes us inflexible and inhibits mobility. When it becomes really sticky, it is referred to as an adhesion. These adhesions form according to the positions we put our body in when we sit all day and constrict movement and through other habits like muscle-building exercise when not complemented sufficiently by lengthening. When we release these sticky, glue-like adhesions, fluids move more freely through the body's web, and we move more freely in our lives.

Alignment

The poses done throughout a yoga asana practice also improve mobility through proper alignment of the body and balanced use of its tissues. Without movement, these tissues can get locked in a short position and result in poor posture, leading to future injury. Visualize the Hunchback of Notre Dame. You've seen such people—forward head, internal rotation of the shoulders, and curvature of the spine that can be caused by long-term sitting, reading, or typing. Importantly rounded shoulders, tight necks, and mobility limitations are also the unfortunate consequences of years of poorly aligned pushups and an imbalanced training regimen heavily focused on large muscle groups. Let's examine just this one alignment issue common among desk sitters. Gravity exacerbates this poor posture, weighing heavily on our necks and backs and causing pain. This hunching also causes the psoas muscles in our core to shorten, which can lead to a deeper curve in our lumbar spine that can cause compression and pain in the low back, shorter strides when walking, and tight muscles at the bottom of our feet. You can see how poor posture can have a domino effect on our bodymind.

Yoga is a bare foot exercise where we stretch and release tension even in our feet. Our energy body becomes more vibrant when points of stuck tension are released and we walk through our day upright with ease and comfort. Opening the front of the body— especially the psoas muscles—allows us to stand more erect and breathe more easily, which also gives us energy. We stand taller as yoga focuses on the correct alignment and movement of the spine and the lengthening of the musculature of the body. Our spine moves in seven directions, and many yoga classes are sequenced to fully move the spine in all seven: flexion (forward bending), extension (backward bending), rotation (twists right and left), lateral bends (sideways bends right and left), and axial extension, which happens when we *get taller* by lengthening the spine on its axis and creating space (and releasing pressure) between our spinal discs. Because I now practice standing erect, I measure a three-quarter inch taller (per the doctor's measure) than I did in my twenties!

Yoga poses seek to keep the spine correctly aligned and maintain the health of the intervertebral disks or the cushions/cartilage between each of the vertebrae. These cushions suffer imbalance from years of sitting, which results in backaches and later trauma like arthritis. Yoga improves posture, mobility, and locomotion, which we depend on every day of our lives.

The Mind–Body

What makes yoga asana practice different from conventional forms of exercise is that it is a guided mind–body practice. We are guided to become more conscious and pay attention to a wide variety of things of which we typically do not pay attention. Ultimately, we learn a great deal about ourselves through that attentiveness, through that conscious awareness. And what we learn is incredibly useful to living a life of health, happiness, and engagement. The mind piece is the most important aspect of a yoga practice and is what the majority of this book involves.

Conscious breathing is the connection between the body and the mind. Through the breath, we move from a state of body awareness to a state of mind awareness. The breath links the two. Breathing is detailed in the next chapter and involves bringing awareness to each inhale and each exhale. In many yoga classes we seek to *fully* breathe every inhale and exhale through the entire practice. This breath consciousness can be highly relaxing to the nervous system. Breath consciousness takes the practitioner to a different state of awareness, a calm and meditative place. To maintain a focus on the breath through the entire class requires full concentration and also serves to strengthen our cardiovascular system and enhance our lung capacity. In particular, maintaining a long, smooth, consistent breath pattern for the duration of a strong practice is very challenging. Consequently, one way to consider an advanced yoga practice is how well the practitioner can maintain an even breath through the class.

Focusing on the present moment over and over again while moving from pose to pose teaches us to concentrate, focus, and move out of distraction. It is simply not possible to smoothly move through the sequence without paying attention. Talented yoga teachers understand how to cue in ways that support the basic principles of the practice. The practitioners begin to pay attention to their bodies and over time learn not to push or force their bodies beyond their ability, which keeps them safe and in control. Teachers elegantly guide students to become aware of their thoughts and habits as they move from pose to pose. The cues help the practitioner to identify with habits of mind that are helpful and those that are not. In time, the practitioner begins to see clearly that in each moment they have a *choice* to do what they habitually do or to make another choice. These are empowering moments where students begin to appreciate that when they slow down a little and pay attention, they have within them this level of control that they hadn't benefited from before. The process fortifies from the inside out, builds courage, and strengthens resolve. This newfound awareness is refreshing and yields positive moments of self-realization that support positivity, health, and happiness.

Yoga Safety and Selecting a Class

Like any other form of physical exercise, a yoga asana class involves movements that when taken too far or when done with poor alignment can cause injury to the body. We can get hurt in life generally when we follow poor teachers and leaders. We can also get hurt when we lack humility and allow the ego to push us far beyond our current training and ability. In yoga asana class, the lengthening of the muscles may feel intense at time, but we should never feel pain. Nor should we ever feel that our joints are compromised. Correct alignment and use of the muscles maintains safety around the joints.

If your muscles aren't strong or flexible enough for certain poses, modify your pose and use props in every class, or take a gentler class. If you have an injury, let the teacher know and s/he may have modifications to recommend as time permits, but never move into pain. If your injury causes a lot of pain, you should probably be in rehabilitation or doing private therapeutic yoga lessons. It's not the role of a teacher in a group class to rehabilitate an injury, so it is important that you know how to modify your own practice so the teacher can teach to the group.

Heated Yoga

There are strong opinions in the yoga community for and against heat. Provided you have adequately hydrated before class and continue to hydrate subsequent, heated yoga may be appropriate, but heat is not necessary for a yoga practice. I like participating in a heated practice at least once a week especially when it is cold outside or when I know I need a detoxifying sweat or a deep tension release. A heated room will help warm up the body a bit more quickly and support muscle lengthening and may challenge your heart more than an unheated class, but extreme heat can allow you to bend much more than your body is ready for and lead to injury. There are different levels of heat. Classes in heat over one-hundred degrees are very taxing on the mind–body and will send many people into a fight or flight response when we should instead be relaxing. Extreme heat can also take practitioners away from being focused on safe movement of the body, because they are focused instead on the extreme temperature, the sweat pouring down their faces, and not slipping on the wet puddles they've created. So if you like heat, incorporate a non-distracting level of heat into your yoga practice and drink a lot of water.

Repetitive Stress Injury

Mix your class assortment up. Fitness professionals have long held that it is never good for your body to do the same things repetitively, day after day. Overuse of the joints can lead to repetitive stress injuries. This includes any form of strenuous movement, including an intense yoga asana class. Likewise, it is not advisable for most of us to take daily yoga classes that do the exact same set of poses every single day, particularly if it is the only form of exercise that we do.

Yoga Styles, Brands, and Specialities

The newest yoga celebrities create their own styles of yoga that have stemmed from modern lineages. Some yoga styles are more alignment-based, some are flowing, and others are oriented toward strength and challenge. Some are restorative, and still more are therapeutically inclined. Experience them all! Some do a lot of push-ups, while others avoid them. There are a wide variety of special classes targeted to just men, athletes, runners, pregnant women, teens, kids, and babies. The broader base of teachers today infuse a blend of styles and traditions and will differ meaningfully in the poses they teach, cues they use, the degree to which they focus on alignment, breathing, meditation, and philosophy. Practice with a variety of teachers until you find a few that resonate with you and offer a mix of movement that supports your weekly routine. After twenty years of practice, I still thoroughly enjoy participating in classes led by a variety of talented teachers who continue to inform my practice and my teaching.

Class Confusion

The abundance of styles creates confusion in the market, which may make it difficult to choose a class or a studio. Based upon a studio owners experience and beliefs, he or she may dictate alignment or sequencing rules that teachers are to follow to ensure student safety and mitigate business risk. Some studios may have rules around what teachers are permitted to teach in their classes while others may allow the teachers the freedom to teach to their personal style. You may ask a studio owner if they have established such standards. This table below may help you choose the type of class that may be suitable for you to balance your mind–body. Keep in mind that this table is subjective and will always be incomplete, as new brands of yoga emerge every year. Yoga studios should be able to direct you to a class suitable to your level and personal goals. At times a studio may even have to direct you to another yoga location for classes more suitable to you.

How to Select a Yoga Class

I am neither fit nor flexible. I do not regularly do any form of exercise.	Gentle, Beginners, Introductory Classes, Private Lessons. Ask the studio for guidance.
I am somewhat fit and somewhat flexible. I walk and exercise a little each week.	Beginners, Introductory Classes, Private lessons, Hatha Flow, Level 1 Vinyasa/Flow, Yin Yoga, Kundalini.

I am fit but maybe not flexible. I exercise fairly regularly a few times a week and practice a little yoga.	Hatha Flow, Vinyasa/Flow All Levels, Intermediate Vinyasa/Flow, Level 2 Vinyasa/ Flow, Prana Flow, Power Yoga, Dharma Yoga, Jivamukti Yoga, Anusara, Kundalini.
I am very fit. I exercise most days of the week and practice yoga regularly. I was/am an athlete.	When you want to advance your physical yoga practice beyond the options in the Fit category above, you may want to try Level 2/3 classes, Advanced Vinyasa, Advanced Anusara/ Iyengar, Ashtanga, or specialized series, workshops, and private lessons that focus on advancing your practice.
I am one of the following: a gymnast, a body-weight athlete, an advanced yoga practitioner, or a yoga teacher looking for a different physical challenge.	If you are very strong and interested in inversions and arm balances, you may like Rocket or Fly Yoga. For offerings that are completely different and remind me of Cirque du Soleil, there are aerial yoga and Acroyoga. Note: unless the teacher includes breath, meditation, and internal awareness practices, they will not really allow you to experience the mind-body benefits of yoga; they will merely let you have a little fun and enhance the bodyweight conditioning aspects of your physical asana practice.
I simply need to relax!	Yoga classes should be relaxing but everyone finds relaxation a little differently. Consider these options: Slow Flow Vinyasa, Restorative yoga, Yoga Nidra, Yin Yoga, Meditation, or private lessons. Ask the studio for guidance.

Being Your Best – Sleep First, Think Later

Quality Sleep

One way to deplete health and well-being is to short-change our sleep. The National Sleep Foundation reports that the average adult needs seven to nine hours of sleep, and many of us get less than six.[56] Sleep is fundamental to our health, well-being, and ability to lead. When we are not well slept, we will not make the best choices. The qualities of nature can be considered with regard to our sleep choices as well. Although sleep is meant to be a time of inactivity and rest, we can choose to sleep in the mode of goodness by going to bed early, with an empty stomach, in a clean bed, in a dark and uncluttered room, with clean air circulating, and rising with the sun.

Sleep Deprivation

Researchers at Berkeley found that sleep deprivation enhanced the connections in the part of the brain associated with depression and anxiety, while a good night's rest helped with mood and coping mechanisms.[57] Lack of sleep slows the activity in the prefrontal cortex, the higher-functioning part of our brain involved in complex thinking and judgment. When this happens we rely on the lower-functioning parts of the brain that deal with survival instincts. In other words, when we are sleep deprived, we see more of life as a threat. Our amygdala, the emotional center of our brain, reacts swiftly and without the help of the *voice of reason*, the prefrontal cortex.[58] Absent the help of this voice of reason, we tend toward *overreaction*. We lack emotional control when we do not have enough sleep. Our prefrontal cortex also helps control our behavior and affects our judgment and decision making abilities. When impaired, we also make poor choices in the food we choose to eat, linking insufficient sleep to obesity.[59] Those who slept less than six hours a night were found to be 30 percent more likely to be obese than those who slept seven to nine hours a night.[60] Further, poor sleep has been clinically associated with most mental disorders.

The effects of lack of sleep are numerous. We may think we function fine with less sleep, but an impaired prefrontal cortex not only impairs our ability to concentrate, pay attention, problem solve, and learn but also impairs our judgment and decision making abilities.[61] Lack of sleep inhibits memory and we become more forgetful. Chronic sleep disturbance can lead to physical problems including heart disease, hypertension, and diabetes.[62] Finally, when we do not get enough sleep, our immune system is affected and we are less able to fight off illness and disease. Quality sleep is essential to good leadership.

Pineal Gland

It is helpful to understand our bodies a bit better in order to really appreciate how one falls asleep and stays asleep. One notable participant in our pattern of sleep is the pineal gland. This small, cone-shaped gland resides behind the forehead, toward the center of our brain. It is part of our endocrine system, responding to and communicating information about light in our environment, thereby helping to maintain our biological rhythms and, of importance here, the circadian rhythm.[63] The pineal gland is, in a sense, activated by conditions of lightness and darkness. Historically called *the third eye*, the pineal gland resembles the human eye. A primary role of this gland is to synthesize and secrete the hormone melatonin, which helps our body maintain its circadian rhythm, including our sleep-wake cycle. Melatonin also chemically induces drowsiness and decreases body temperature. Our melatonin levels decrease as we age, which contributes further to aging.[64]

Due to its powerful ability to neutralize free radicals, melatonin is being investigated as having a role in fighting disease.[65] Consistency in sleep schedule is important, as melatonin production begins to rise about two hours before a consistent bedtime to prepare us for sleep. It peaks around 3 to 4:00 a.m. and, for the most part, ceases with sunrise.[66] Taking a melatonin supplement orally has been an effective way to fake your body to sleep while traveling in different time zones, when your circadian rhythm would otherwise be out of whack. Sleeping without light is an important way to help your body stay asleep.

Sleep Routine

The bottom line is that sleep is essential to our ability to do our best work. A healthy night's sleep begins with establishing a routine for sleep and tweaking it until it works for you.

Ten Tips for a Deep Sleep

1. Try to get as much sunlight during the day as possible.
2. Don't drink caffeine after 2 p.m., or the equivalent of six to eight hours before bed.
3. Finish eating two to four hours before bed so your body can focus on growth and repair instead of digestion allowing you to have as close to a twelve hour fast as possible.
4. Dim the lights after dinner to allow your pineal gland to start telling the body to wind down. Make choices that help you wind down, not wind up, such as listening to softer music and watching nonviolent television shows.
5. Turn all LED alarm clocks away from you so they shed no light toward your face. Stating the obvious, do not have your phone buzzing in your room or anywhere that you can hear it during the night. Close your blinds and allow it to be as dark as possible.
6. Make sure the room while sleeping is a cool, 65 degrees or lower[67], comfortable temperature. Wear loose, breathable, cool, natural clothing to bed. Bedding should also be breathable and natural.
7. The environment in your room should be calm and not distracting. Get rid of clutter. Use a sound machine as necessary to mask sounds from inside or outside the home. If traveling, consider wearing earplugs. The sounds at hotels are unpredictable and foreign to you and may disrupt sleep.

8. Skip the nightcap or have it early in the evening. It takes one hour to digest one ounce of alcohol. When you have a drink before bed, your body spends hours metabolizing the alcohol. This makes your sleep lighter and more fitful and you feel less rested in the morning. You will sleep better if alcohol has had enough time to clear your bloodstream before bed.

9. Allow the hour before bed to be non-stimulating. Watching television, using the computer, notebook, or a smartphone during this time can be stimulating. Pick two: read an inspiring book, take a bath (use Epsom salts), give yourself an oil massage, do yoga stretches, meditate, have sex, drink chamomile tea.

10. Maintain a consistent sleep–wake cycle each night as best you can. Go to bed at a time that allows you to sleep seven to nine hours a night. Consider taking melatonin capsules to manage time zones while traveling and get a good night's sleep on the road.

Personal Pride

Personal Principle 1: Cleanliness – Purity (*sauca*)

The first of the niyamas or personal principles is *sauca*, which means cleanliness or purity in body and mind, including our thoughts and words. To live in observance of sauca involves our external and internal mind–body, kept clean through a healthy diet, a clean living environment, and a pure mind. A clean living environment is just what it sounds like: keeping our home and workplace clean and tidy, which will support a tranquil mind. A pure and clean mind involves choosing clean content to read and programs to watch. A pure mind is a balanced and tranquil mind.

A pure, balanced mind is supported by a humble kind of pride. A humble pride honors both the body and mind as gifts to be cherished evidenced by our daily choices. With humble pride we also honor the possessions we are fortunate to have by keeping them clean and tidy. Yoga philosophy sees possessions as impermanent and temporary things that we are never really entitled to but if we happen to have them, we are to care for them. Humble pride is not to be confused with the kind of pride directed entirely on outward appearances where our false ego takes over. Ego is discussed in the chapter covering the knowledge dimension.

Begin to recognize how you feel when you choose overly stimulating or violent mental content when you are already stimulated or stressed. There is an understanding in Ayurveda, the traditional system of medicine in India,

Like attracts like, opposites heal.

that "like attracts like; opposites heal." We are attracted to what we like, but we may *need* the opposite. If we consider our lives to be too full and stress-filled, overly stimulating television or music will not allow us to elevate our mood and nourish a serene mind. Inundating our minds with violent or highly chaotic content will not help us relieve stress in our days. Choosing instead to read inspirational materials, listen to pacifying music, or watch inspiring TED talks will typically help us move toward a balanced state.

Making a habit of thinking and saying words that are light and clean is a way to cultivate a balanced mind. Manipulative, critical, and controlling thoughts and behaviors are not light. Passing judgment is not light. They are, rather, a way of imposing your will instead of accepting the present moment as a pure, raw, and essential part of your life experience. We are meant to acknowledge and experience our lives in a full and honest manner.

Questions for Leaders: Personal Pride

1. Is your diet light, clean, and balancing?
2. Do your exercise choices promote mental balance, strength, and heart health?
3. Do you drink sufficient and purified water? Do you enjoy fresh air daily?
4. Does your leisure time support harmony and balance in your life or disharmony, imbalance, and stress?
5. Does your choice in television shows, movies, and music create calm and happiness or distress and imbalance? What about your choice in friends?
6. Do you have a good sleep ritual in place?
7. Are your spaces organized and clean? Is your desk free of clutter?
8. Do you dress comfortably?
9. Is the organizational culture light? How about your leadership style? What about the personalities on your team?
10. How can you add more lightness, balance, and harmony to your life?

Create a Foundation for Healthy Habits

The future depends on what we do in the present.
—Mahatma Gandhi

Habits develop when we do things over and over until we no longer have to think about doing them. At every new moment, we have the opportunity to make choices, to develop habits that keep us connected to ourselves, or to develop habits that keep us separated from ourselves. As we repeat the same choices, they become an increasingly meaningful part of our lives, impacting our attitude and personality. This imprint on our psyche is called a *samskara*.

Seldom do we take time to consider why we developed certain habits to begin with. Drinking coffee in the morning, for many of us, is a habit that started as a way to awaken our minds and prepare for our day. We oftentimes don't question or give much thought about whether to drink the cup of coffee. We drink it out of habit. Our habits shape our personality, so we become that person who drinks coffee in the morning. We and our coffee habit become enmeshed; the habit becomes part of our self-identification. We self-identify with many things in our personal and professional lives, which shape our identity and dictate our habits of life. Some of our chosen identifications may be helpful—others, not so much. Examine your habits. What habits have you had for a very long time for which you have no truly rational explanation for continuing to do them?

Concluding Statement

One tiny step can cause a monumental shift. Reflect upon your current state of affairs. Choose one small habit in the physical dimension that could use improving and commit to improving it. After a period of time it becomes part of your life. Then choose another habit, then another, then another until, over time, you find that you have simplified your life; you eat healthy food daily, you move your body regularly, and you sleep soundly. Focus on seeing personal growth on an annual basis. Working on your holistic well-being is a lifelong endeavor. You will look back reflecting upon how you have improved the health of your body, released a lot of tension, and increased your energy level, leading to a more positive outlook. At work, others will be drawn to your renewed vitality and positivity, serving your ability to lead. Through your example, you will also share your positive habits with others, inspiring them to tend to their holistic well-being.

Chapter 5
Yogi Secret #3: Energy

Old Maxim
Working until I drop is appropriate.

New Maxim
Working in consideration of my energy level is appropriate.

Resolve: I use only the energy necessary for the task at hand.

Yogi Secret #3 allows me to develop or maintain personal qualities inherent in inspiring leaders including: vitality ~ emotion awareness and control ~ calm demeanor and controlled temperament ~ creativity and personal expression ~ clear and focused communications ~ confidence and self-esteem ~ strength and courage ~ authenticity and vulnerability

Bathe deeply in that ocean of sound
Vibrating within you, now as always,
Resonating softly,
Permeating the space of the heart.
—*The Radiance Sutras,* Lorin Roche

The second layer is the energy dimension called the *pranamaya kosha.* This is the layer of our physiology involving our life force or vital energy, called *prana.* It represents our energetic quality of being. As atomic beings, this is the same energy that is in exchange with the world around us and is considered in terms of its quality or vibrancy. It is the extant vibration throughout the body that is stimulated by sound, breath, and movement. Movement, breath, and chanting in a yoga practice directs the flow of prana through thousands of energy channels, called *nadis.* There are countless energy systems around the world, each having their own energetic "map" of the body. Prana is called *chi* by the Chinese and *Ki* by the Japanese.[68] The energy channels are sometimes called meridians or pathways, with central points or energy vortices, ranging commonly from six to more than ten in number, which typically run up the axis of the body. In many systems, including yoga, these central energy points are called *chakras*.[69] The pathways and points create maps of the body, used as the basis for healing modalities such as acupuncture, shiatsu, cupping, reflexology, qigong, and yoga movement practice—all of which attempt to remove blockages to the flow of energy to heal and ultimately restore vitality. One cannot see energy channels or *prana*, yet they are both a vital element to maintain the life of an organism.[70] Energy modalities are broadly and effectively used in ways to include boosting vitality during intense chemotherapy treatments, alleviating migraine headaches, tempering hot flashes, managing pain, balancing imbalances in the body, and improving mood.

Prāṇamaya Kosha
(Energy)

Our Layer of Vitality

Riding the Wave[71]

Paying attention to energy in life can be thought about like surfing and riding a wave in the ocean. When balanced right on the sweet spot of the crest of the wave, we have an amazing ride (so I've been told). But it doesn't happen that often. Patience is essential. Most of the time is spent sitting on the board and waiting for a wave to appear. Sitting and waiting may seem mundane and boring. From that perspective, we lose interest in the waiting part and disengage from what's right there in front of us, instead looking out in anticipation of the next wave. Anxious to ride every single wave, we may ride too far ahead of the wave, tire, and miss it completely. Focused exclusively on *the wave*, our life becomes a series of exhausting attempts to go after the next and better wave, getting frustrated when we miss the wave, becoming increasingly detached from the serenity and majesty of the waiting part, and living only for the future.

When we always ride ahead, we are merely skimming the surface of our lives, living in a disconnected manner, checking off boxes on a never-ending to-do list. The everyday grind is that time spent sitting and waiting. Riding ahead, we completely miss out on the wisdom of the moment. Instead, when we are present to each moment along the way, we are open to the greater wisdom that life offers. Importantly, riding too far *behind*, we never come close to catching the next wave. Riding too far behind blocks us off from the possibility of really experiencing something magical and exhilarating. Experienced surfers find pleasure in both the ride itself and in all the waiting—noticing and enjoying the water, the sun, the shore, and the birds. They know the art of catching a wave is in waiting for *the* wave and timing it right. Can you envision the parallel in your daily life? Can you identify examples of too much effort or too little effort in your life?

The Razor's Edge

Similarly, in a yoga class, I often speak of finding the *razor's edge*, that edge between effort and ease, and then softening there. This is the path of balance that exists uniquely for each of us between too much and too little, avoiding either extreme. That is where we find the wisdom of the practice. In a yoga classroom, it is common for students to move more quickly than the pace of the class, riding ahead of the energy of the class. They are trying to get things done. They are worrying about what's next. They are living in the future and avoiding the present experience. Arriving with the breath and feeling every inch of movement are ways to ride the energetic wave of the classroom. On the mat, the razor's edge is the place where you can arrive in a pose and keep your body still while breathing fully. Here, we can safely and skillfully find and test our limits, our edge. A commonly-cited Sutra involving yoga asana is number II.46 in *The Yoga Sutras*, which reads *sthira-sukham asanam* and means "a steady ease-filled posture." By finding the ability to soften while existing in a physically challenging pose, we can find calm on the mat and then in life.

Ride your edge. As first time snowboarders learn, it takes some doing to tease out your edge and stay balanced. As I know first hand, when a person believes she will be able to snowboard easily since she can downhill ski and impatiently and aggressively tries to learn, a lot of time is spent painfully slamming the body against a snowy mountain over and over and over again. It is a skill in and of itself to become acutely aware of our edge, to live fully and patiently there without falling over into a state of stress and anxiety. We seek to ride the energy of the edge, releasing into and allowing it to take us on its ride. At work, we want to work hard and excel but not so hard where we burn out, make careless decisions, or become a poor example of a leader. At home, we can fight with our kids, pushing them, hurrying them, and controlling them. Or we can choose to be carried by their energy, which seems to be unlimited in my household.

The Energetic Web

We are energetic beings comprised of atoms that make up molecules that make up cells that make our blood and our tissues. We are in constant motion, a multitude of protons, neutrons, and electrons that interact with all energy around us as well as with the radiating, pulsating, electric field within each of us. One way to feel our energetic dimension is by feeling the effects of movement and vibration. When we exert energy by exercising, breathing rapidly, or singing loudly, our body remains energized for a while after we stop. We still feel movement inside. It is easy to feel this for yourself. Take five minutes and simply dance around in your living room or belt out a tune with all your heart. Then stop and feel the sensation running through your body.

As leaders in an office setting, we are desk sitters. Half of us don't even leave our desks for lunch. Our bodies aren't designed to be so sedentary; they have evolved to move and stand. In this holistic model, our energy dimension is, of course, tied to all other dimensions. When our bodies are tight and bound up and stiff, our energy stagnates. We may even feel discomfort, and it becomes more difficult to focus on our other needs.

Begin to consider the impacts of sitting, not just on the physical well-being but also on your mental and emotional health. Small shifts in your work habits can result in big shifts in your energy level.

Ten Tips to Increase Energy at Work

1. Park farther from the office. Take the train.
2. Take the stairs at work. Run up them.
3. Have a stretch break every two hours, using your chair, desk, walls, and door jams as props to deepen stretches.
4. Find a place to stand and work for part of your day.
5. Find a place to sit on the floor to work.
6. Walk during conference calls.
7. Have walking meetings.
8. Walk to lunch and/or take group walks outside after lunch.
9. Call a good friend.

10. Listen to uplifting music. Sing.
11. Look at pictures or videos of people or animals who are special to you.
12. Plan something really special for yourself.
13. Eat slowly a square of dark chocolate (over 70 percent cocoa).
14. Smell an uplifting essential oil.
15. Listen to an inspiring TED Talk and/or spend time with people who inspire you.

Yoga Energetics – The Subtle

We tend to be very disconnected from our energy dimension. We tend to focus on the health of our physical bodies and to notice the state of our minds. And we are often on a quest for increased energy, yet we seldom talk about how we can affect the health of our energetic layer. When we increase our energy, our desire and passion in life, *ojas* in Sanskrit, also increases.

We have all felt the effects of someone else's energy. This can happen when we encounter someone who is contented and joyful, which impacts us in a positive manner, or when someone is stressed and unhappy, and we find ourselves growing more stressed as well. We cannot stop this from happening. For example, when we see someone at a conference for the first time, it is all too often that we know, we feel, whether we are comfortable approaching that person or not. We can sense it through the energy, the vibe they give off. Their vibe connecting with our vibe—it often jives or it doesn't. We *all* feel this energetic exchange, all the time; sometimes we notice and sometimes we don't.

This is the energetic dimension and we have a measure of control over it. We want to keep the energy in our system flowing and healthy. Becoming aware of your subtle energies can help you work effectively and with confidence and self-esteem, knowing when to assert yourself and when to hold back. It can help you assess your own vibe and how it affects others.

Maintain the Mojo

A constant and powerful yet subtle feeling of *joy* is a useful and powerful inner experience that is very positive, strong, grounded, in control, and content. It is a place from which magnetism and charisma are borne. Magnetism and charisma come energetically from the inside and radiate out from a natural place when one feels joyful. Magnetism and charisma appear in ways to include our expression, our gestures, our word choices, our tone, our emotions, our mood, and our attitude. We then powerfully impact the emotions, mood, and attitude of everyone around us. These two powerful leadership attributes are not forced, are not boastful, and nor are they an in-your-face kind of energy. When rooted in subtle joy, we can change our entire team's energy for the better. This is what I call *mojo*. Mojo by definition means magic spell or hex, but is used colloquially in reference to operating at a highly functioning state. And it's infectious. Inspiring leaders that wield great followership are vibrant—positive, strong, and happy; in other words, they *exude* mojo. Inspiring leaders are also authentic and courageous, able to be fearlessly real. But our mojo needs maintenance. When we are depleted, we lose our mojo, and sometimes it is difficult to get it back. By doing things to boost our energy dimension, we support our mojo, our strength, courage, and charisma, and we find ourselves able to take risks and put ourselves in new situations where we feel vulnerable but are less fearful.

Begin to notice the energy exchanged between people and how your energy is reflected toward others. Begin to notice how others can impact your emotions, mood, and attitude. Notice how others are drawn to you when you feel in that place of subtle joy, full of mojo. When you have to interact with a lot of people in a business context, assess your energy and the vibe you want to give off *in advance*. Our energies shift all the time. When we become more intimate with energy we can use it helpful ways. The more we learn about energy, the more we can choose ways to influence our energy in the joyful direction and boost our mojo, thus enhancing our interpersonal skills and team engagement.

Movements of Energy: The Winds

There are five subtle aspects of energy, called the *vayus* or winds that refer to movements of energy in yoga. When we take students through a yoga class, we sequence poses that will affect these subtle energies. The upward flowing energy called *udana vayu* that is seated in our throat and skull is particularly worthy of discussion for leaders and office workers. When this energy flow is strong, it presents as enthusiasm and willpower, self-esteem and self-expression—but an imbalance can result in anxiety, repressed emotions, and difficulty expressing oneself. It is important to balance this upward flowing energy with grounding energy called *apana vayu*. As leaders with fast-paced lives, we often spend all our time in our heads, the place where the upward-flowing energy rises. Too much energy spent thinking and processing depletes the other forms of energy that allow us to feel and digest our experiences. Yet a full assimilation and proper digestion of life experiences is what allows us to feel grounded, safe, stable, and balanced. Strength and courage stem from a safe and grounded place that allows us to be authentic, honest, and real.

Too much headspace energy stirs up our nervous system, too, which can lead to feelings of stress, anxiety, instability, and anger. Our speech becomes less articulate as we have too much going on in our heads. To find balance, we need to slow down, to find ways to relax and to experience some quiet. Take a holistic perspective and make conscious choices in what you eat, drink, watch, do, and listen to. If you have a full and hectic life already become really comfortable in your body by giving it warm, nourishing, non-agitating food and beverages and spend time moving in ways that are grounding, not stimulating. For example, burpees, handstands, loud heavy metal music, movie thrillers, and spicy food are stimulating choices, especially to a person who is stressed, anxious, or high-strung. Make energetic choices that keep you in control of your conscious mind and senses and out of overdrive. Also consider whether the energetic choices you make for your kids are benefiting their well-being or not. We all need down time that is non-stimulating and we all need a little solitude.

In a yoga asana class, to relax people we focus on balancing the upward flowing energy with the opposing energetic flow found in grounding poses, where more of our body makes contact with the mat, and by using stabilizing cues that may involve our feet and hands pressing into the mat. Many yoga practices are calming to the nervous system, even if they are challenging. The use of the breath, the lengthening of the body to release tensions, and conscious cuing and pose selection all serve to calm our nerves.

Managing the Energy of Communications

Establish Guideliness to Control Your Schedule

One of the best ways to feel grounded in a busy workday is to regain control of your schedule. Effective leaders take control of their workday, establish boundaries with their team, and block off segments of time each day to do their own work. Without established precedents it is easy to be sidetracked with the team's efforts, which can derail your plans for the day. Establish communication guidelines with your team, recognizing that the guidelines pertaining to interactions with you will likely be different from the guidelines the team should honor amongst themselves. If you aren't in control of your schedule, make suggestions to your boss on ways to manage communications that will support the entire team and reduce stress. Or simply cocreate guidelines with your peers that will help all of you. Guidelines concerning the format and expected response time for communications are helpful and will allow everyone to manage priorities in their day. For example, consider setting a twenty-four-hour rule, letting the team know you will respond to e-mails from them within twenty-four hours, and that they should contact you only if you do not happen to respond. Include your expected response time in your signature line. If your team has come to expect instantaneous responses from you, it is likely you are too entrenched in the day-to-day. In this case, allow your team to operate more autonomously. Work on trusting them.

Cocreate a Communication Plan

Communications have a moving energetic quality to them that can become hectic and chaotic. Rein them in with enforced guidelines and rules. I have never met a person who does not feel slammed with a variety of communications—e-mails, meetings, voicemails, texts—every day at work. Cocreate a communication plan with your team with the goal of making everyone's work days a little easier to manage and improving the quality of the interactions. The guidelines established should simplify the process and allow the team to work together more effectively, resulting in a flow of communications that feels less burdensome, more manageable, and more useful. Review and reinforce the communication plan with the team regularly at meetings to make sure it is working. Consider creating a plan using the ideas below.

Communication Plan Guidelines

E-mail:
- Limit email to brief updates or very simple questions only.
- Keep the length of e-mails to one paragraph or a few bullets.
- Limit the back and forth, since we know that the effectiveness of the communication degrades as the number of e-mail exchanges on a topic increases. After one or two e-mail exchanges, establish a rule to pick up the phone or add the topic to a small workgroup meeting agenda.
- Ideally, you trust your team and are not included on every e-mail exchange.

Meetings:
- Minimize meeting duration.
- Not all meetings require your attendance. Prioritize them.
- Honor time limits.
- Weekly team update meetings: thirty-minute to one-hour meetings that serve as brief reporting on progress and general updates.
- Small workgroup meetings: one-hour meetings. Working meetings intended to progress an initiative. You may not have to be involved in all of the small workgroup meetings.
- Individual team meetings: thirty minutes maximum. Weekly meetings with direct reports to answer questions and concerns in a private forum. Seek to connect with, engage, and empower each team member.
- Ad hoc meeting requests: when team members want to address individual concerns. Minimize random drop-ins. Try to require the team member to make an appointment on your calendar, including a brief summary of the topic to be discussed.

Managing the Energy of Meetings

Great leaders know people extraordinarily well. They know and can anticipate how people think, behave, and feel. They can get people to do what they want, while allowing them to feel good and be heard. They are able to open people up and inspire them to act. To do this, they first must understand that in themselves. They know how to assess their own energy and rev themselves up or calm themselves down. They know what in life will make them feel good or not so good, and they manage their choices and emotions accordingly. They find their own balance that invites harmony and well-being into their lives, and they lead from a happy, optimistic, and positive place. By managing the energy of meetings you can build and maintain not only your vitality but also your confidence and self-esteem, which stem from a positive energetic space.

Learn to Use Energy to Your Advantage

Pay attention to what is really happening as you engage in dialog with others in your life. Begin to enjoy watching energetics play out in a meeting. Notice how you can manifest what you want when you allow the mind some space and ride the present. Work on noticing and intelligently using the energy in the room. Consider the suggestions below.

Eight Tips for Keeping Your Own Energy Up in a Meeting

1. Know your base of support in advance.
2. Have your base of support sit closest to you to hold an anchor of positive, supportive energy near you.
3. Connect through eye contact with your base of support in particular and to others who appear to be agreeing with what you are saying (clue: nodding their heads).
4. Give a bit less attention to those who look like they are not supportive.
5. Pause from time to time, allowing those who are not sure if they agree to think.
6. Create some energy. Move around. Nod your head as you speak. Use your arms. Or even stand up or walk around from time to time.
7. Try to bring people on board through eye contact, using names, and nodding as they speak. When you nod you are acknowledging them as they speak and they feel *heard*, even if you end up having a different opinion.
8. Find subtle ways to connect with each person in the room. This makes everyone feel welcomed and included, and it invites them to share. This positive energy will reflect right back to you building your own stores of energy.

An Engaging Energetic Environment

Create and maintain an energetic environment that feels positive, open, vibrant, and supportive. Creativity emerges out of this kind of environment as does motivation and inspiration. Constructive dissent and constructive feedback happens in open, positive, and supportive environments thus bettering organizational outcomes. Consider the suggestions below.

Energy Tips for Group Meetings[72]

1. In advance of the meeting, send a clear meeting agenda and stick to the timing. Let the team know what they will be asked to respond to in the meeting and why. Be specific, so you can call on each person by name.

2. Before the meeting, visualize how you want it to go. See the people around the table and convince yourself that everyone in the room is supposed to be there, that they are there for a reason, and connect to that belief. Be so firmly established in that belief and intention that you create an energetic glue, a magnetism, with every participant before the meeting even begins.

3. Just before the meeting, emotionally connect to your important role as a leader to help, serve, and guide. Get very clear on your personal responsibility to your team.

4. At the meeting, connect with every person in the room before and/or during the meeting. You can connect through eye contact, by personally addressing them, or by honoring their words as they speak. In conference calls, welcome each participant by name as they enter the call and, as time permits, ask a few participants how they are. Connecting with all participants collects the energy of the space and creates a boundary of safety and trust.

5. At the beginning of the meeting, take several breaths to quiet the energy. Your breaths may unconsciously encourage others to do the same. Then restate the agenda and timing and explain what kind of discussion you are intending. Set an energetic expectation, a tone for the meeting. For example, if you are looking for a lot of creativity and discussion and you want to build energy, *tell* them you are looking for active dialogue. You may even be inspired to use a story, a quote, or a poem to set the stage. Once the meeting starts, don't give them a way out. Keep the dialogue rolling along until what you wanted out of the group has manifested.

6. Start the meeting in a positive way, extending accolades and appreciation, even if their work is actually not good and you want them to shift gears.

7. During the meeting, keep the pace of discussion moving. Don't let any one person drone on and/or deplete the energy through negativity. If one team member is taking too long on his or her point, it is likely something that should be discussed and reconciled in another format and/or amongst a smaller group. In this case interrupt, and indicate that the issue is unresolved and how you would like it to be addressed offline, and then move on.

8. If there is an issue on the agenda to be addressed, get it into the open quickly. If there is a festering issue with regard to you and you are aware of it, ask one of your trusted participants to introduce the issue in the meeting. Thank them for bringing up the concern, offer an explanation, and suggest ways to resolve and then move beyond the issue. Proactively invite others to weigh in. Acknowledge that everyone should feel safe addressing concerns in your meetings. This establishes a template for how to handle sensitive subjects in the future.

9. During the meeting, if you are feeling sensitive to the energy in the room, perhaps you feel you are losing control of the meeting, connect again to your own breath. Establish a subtle connection with your base of support, and remind yourself of your intention to be a good leader and your belief that everyone belongs there. Be your own cheerleader. Feeling a bit stronger yet calmer, assert yourself and regain control.

10. During the meeting, if body language, facial expressions, and tones of voice tell you that the meeting is spiraling in an unproductive direction, quiet the space. Ask everyone to close his or her eyes, be silent, and breathe for five minutes. Then continue. Some people may balk at first, but even their nervous systems should calm after a few minutes, even if they merely sit in the presence of everyone else quietly breathing. We feed off the strong or calm energy of others.

Caring for Energy on Phone Calls

It is more challenging to move toward a goal on a conference call, where you do not have the advantage of body language and the participants can tune out. To keep people engaged and focused, keep calls well organized and actively managed. Participants will have to be called upon more proactively than might be the case in a meeting. Consider the following suggestions.

Energy Tips Specific to Conference Calls

1. Cocreate a baseline of rules and expectations around conference calls with the rest of your team. Expect, at a minimum, punctuality, participation, and preparation. Work hard to create a safe environment where the team can be honest, not only about the work tasks at hand but also with regard to interpersonal effectiveness and team cohesion.

2. Without the benefit of seeing a person's face, it is even more challenging to know how he or she is feeling, so it is best to encourage concise, relevant, and helpful discourse and attempt to assess energetics through a person's tone of voice.

3. At the onset of the call, remind the participants of the meeting agenda, timing, and any requisite conference call guidelines of your choosing. Let them know that you will facilitate the conversation and that all participants will have a brief opportunity to comment as appropriate.

4. On a conference call, there is often an uneasy silence at the onset. Consider communicating with a trusted participant or two in advance. Assign them a question to ask of you to get the dialogue started and a question to ask of another team member. Once the dialog begins, others naturally feel more comfortable sharing.

5. Encourage respectful discourse where everyone is honored and heard. If the exchange moves outside of the boundary of respect, address it immediately.
6. Control the dialogue and keep the pace moving, which is particularly important on a conference call. Facilitate by calling on specific people as appropriate.
7. If there are relatively few participants, call upon each team member, so they all have an opportunity to offer their comments without feeling as though they must interrupt to be heard. This is particularly important on a conference call.

Managing Uncomfortable Energetic Experiences

There are techniques you can use in a meeting to help manage an individual who makes you feel tense or uncomfortable. The list of tips below can help you reclaim control and may even result in an energetic shift in the other person that will set the stage for a better relationship. Consider the suggestions below.

Energy Tips to Reduce Tension in a One-On-One Meeting

1. Before the meeting, center yourself with your breath while maintaining an attitude of equanimity.
2. Wear a natural, soft smile but not an unauthentic grin. Maintain a calm appearance on your face, in your eyes, and with your posture.
3. Laugh. Tell a joke. Tell a self-deprecating story (be a little vulnerable).
4. Ask them how they are or something about their personal lives.
5. Stretch a little and roll your shoulders and neck as you take some breaths.
6. Take a huge inhale and a slow, audible exhale. You can begin this way and/ or do this a few times throughout the meeting without saying anything, while appearing to be thinking or reviewing some notes. Similar to the contagiousness of a yawn, at some point the other person will feel the urge to take a breath. This is one way to attempt to calm another person down, to help him or her relax a bit and ease tensions.
7. Allow the other person several minutes to vent his or her issues. Sit and listen, but say nothing. Simply be silent, breathe, and nod while maintaining a pleasant and calm expression. After the person is done speaking, do your best to allow a few moments of silence where you are breathing, nodding, and thinking before speaking; he or she will probably say something else in that space. At that very point, through your silence, it becomes clear to you especially that you are in control. The person should be a bit calmer having just released a bunch of strong energy.
8. Maintain a calm tone of voice that is not too loud yet is assertive. Make eye contact. Speak intentionally, very slowly, with almost-stretched out speech. Nod slowly as you talk. Repeat a summary of what you understand to be the issue or concern. Ask if your understandings are accurate.
9. Express initial agreement and advocacy toward *something* they said, or flatter them in some way. Talk about the entire scope of the work and the people and efforts involved. Be transparent and clear. Then, while nodding, go in with your decision.

10. If they are ever out of control, establish a boundary by getting up and leaving the room, even if it's your office. As you calmly stand up, state assertively that they will need to schedule another appointment to discuss further when they have a clear head. Do something to clear your mind like taking a short walk, centering your mind, or breathing deeply to shake off the negative energy, so you can get back to work relatively unaffected.

Every meeting is a teacher. Get curious about what you have been taught. Spend a few quiet moments after your meetings contemplating the energy exchange.

Breath Regulation

Once upon a time, our vital senses engaged in a superiority contest. It was to be determined that the most important sense was the sense whose departure most worsened the bodily condition. Speech departed first. When Speech returned, the other senses said, "the body got along mute but was otherwise fine." Sight departed next. When Sight returned, the other senses said, "the body got along blind but was otherwise fine." Hearing followed suit. When Hearing returned, the senses said, "the body got along deaf but was otherwise fine." Thinking departed next. When Thinking returned, the the other senses agreed, "the body behaved like a child but was otherwise fine." Then the Breath began to leave. All other senses were drawn along with the Breath, tethered and tensing like a racehorse waiting behind the gate, and at once they exclaimed "*Stop*. Please don't leave! It is *you* who are the superior sense."

—Chandogya Upanishad, XIII

The Breath

I once did a series of private lessons with a yoga studio owner to help me understand some of the concepts I was learning in my first yoga teacher training. He immediately honed in on my breath, indicating that I needed to learn to breathe. Then he proceeded to try to educate me on the faculty of the breath. Apparently after nearly forty years on this planet, I didn't know how to breathe!

Breathing is a fact of life, yet the majority of us do not give much thought to our breath. We inhale and we exhale. It happens pretty much automatically, right? What more does one need to know? Well, there is *much* more to know. What I now understand is that what I really could not do was relax, and relaxing goes hand in hand with certain ways of breathing.

An important aspect of a yoga movement practice is the use of the breath as a means to direct the flow of prana affecting the body-to-mind balance and corresponding emotions. Using the breath, we impact not only the flow of energy throughout our bodies, but also our emotions. Although we are often not conscious of it, we use our breath regularly to get stirred up and upset. We can also use our breath to calm us down. There are hundreds of different breathing exercises that have been around for thousands of years. Many breathing practices have been rigorously researched and the merits of these practices are well documented. Through breath work, we can regulate our levels of stress and moderate feelings of anxiety. Proper breathing influences our physical body including our nervous system, which directly affects the state of our minds.[73]

The Breath and Emotions

Our ability to breathe is fundamental to living. We typically hear about breathing only when one has a problem doing it, such as those with asthma or emphysema. Such folks with limited capacity to breathe understand quite acutely the importance of the breath. The rest of us sit all day at the office in our chairs and breathe in and out without even thinking about it.

The way we breathe yields certain results at work, results that are different from those we would achieve if we were breathing a different way. The way we inhale and exhale has a direct impact on our thoughts, our responses, and, ultimately, on the decisions we make. It has a direct impact on our well-being. Our breath is a tool that we have with us all the time, and we can use it to improve our work outcomes and our lives.

Fostering a fullness of breath and understanding the basics of breath regulation is a powerful—and free—tool that is extraordinarily valuable in keeping us balanced and calm. We want to breathe in a way that optimizes the functioning of our respiratory system. That, in turn, improves our circulatory system and maintains healthy digestive and elimination systems.[74] Since our systems work together in a holistic manner, health presents itself as the vibrant life force within us. We want to have a relationship with our breath so we can assess our state of being and make choices that support our ability to be discerning leaders with emotional control and equipoise.

Leaders have been taught how to create a sense of urgency around tasks to improve productivity. We lead and work in fast-paced environments. In such climates, it is easy to have our emotions controlling our behavior and unconsciously say or do things abruptly, without much thought or consideration. The breath can help us pause, notice, reflect, consider—and then formulate a more thoughtful response. Controlling emotions is not an easy task for many of us who operate at lightning speed and tend to have swift reactions. It is possible and desirable to make quick decisions while in control of our emotions and from a calm, collected state. Learning to anticipate times when our emotions may tend toward being impulsive will give us a better likelihood of managing these emotions. People with emotional control rebound more easily when faced with obstacles and challenges.[75] From a biochemical perspective, Candice Pert discusses the peptide-respiratory link in *Molecules of Emotion,* where she explains that the rate and depth of our breath directly impacts the quantity and kind of peptides released from our brain stem, including peptides that make us feel better—endorphins.[76] Some examples of emotion and the corresponding breathing tendencies are as follows:[77]

- **Anger:** short and thin inhales, charged exhales; tension in the body
- **Fear/anxiety:** uneven and shallow inhales and exhales at odd intervals; a tightness in the belly
- **Depression:** shallow, lifeless inhales and long apathetic exhales; lethargy in the body
- **Impatience:** short, irregular inhales and exhales; tension at the heart space
- **Vibrancy/Happiness:** deep inhales and exhales; pleasurable feeling in the body

It is in times of stillness, when we are breathing and calm, that we are able to get out of the way of our minds and tap into our creativity, where new ideas and original thinking comes to us. Become a student of your habits of breathing, the breath patterns of others, and parallel emotions.

The Breath and the Nervous System

Now you see that the breath is the connector between the body and the mind. You also see how it offers clues into our current state of being. We can begin to become aware of our habits of breathing and use them to identify the state of our nervous system. Through breath regulation, we can move from a state of fight or flight to a state where our demeanor is calm. The breath can reign in the nervous system and, consequently, the mind. We accomplish this shift by slowing down the breath, taking full long inhales, and matching them with slow, even, and very long exhales.

> The Mind is the Master of the Body, but the
> Breath is the Master of the Mind.
>
> —B.K.S. Iyengar

When we practice breath regulation techniques, we can move ourselves into our parasympathetic nervous system, our resting state. Our bodies are meant to spend most of the time in this state of repair and growth. Through regular practice, we begin to breathe more efficiently, intentionally controlling our pace of breathing while increasing our breath capacity. We breathe more fully and improve our state of being in the process. Elite athletes practice breathing techniques to optimize performance in their sport.[78] Actors are trained in using the breath as a tool to help them alter their bodies and minds to mirror the emotional state and personality of the character they are trying to portray. As leaders, we too can benefit from assessing and regulating our nervous system through breath regulation to improve our well-being and performance.

To be clear, if we are in a really stressful situation and feel very anxious or angry, we can't simply breathe our way out of it into a completely calm state. I wish that were possible, but realistically, when the fireworks display has started inside, you often may have to take more active measures until the finale has ended. In this case, funneling that emotional energy into something—such as a difficult project, a challenging workout, or even singing loudly—may be a useful way to both leverage its power and diffuse it. If you are really worked up, you may have to simply go outside and scream alone in your car to let the strong energy pass through you. Perhaps you can express in writing your strong feelings in a journal. But doing absolutely *nothing* is damaging to your health. Holding on to strong emotion again and again and again is analogous to creating mental injuries that are left untreated, become infected, fester, spread, and eventually cover our mind with an armor-like scab fixing those emotions in place. Holding onto to strong emotion and suppressing it is like saving it for later only to come back stronger leaving damage in its wake. Who wants to save vast stores of anger and anxiety for later?

That said, since we now know that we shouldn't be breathing as though we are in a really stressful situation all the time, the fireworks are less likely to go off in the first place. Good leaders are self-aware, proactive, and can control their emotions, which is facilitated through the breath work discussed in this chapter.

The Mechanics of Breathing

Before we go into the breath practices it is helpful to visualize how breathing happens in the body so you can feel the breath better in your own body. The mechanism of the breath involves the diaphragm, which is a large "dome shaped muscle"[79] connected to some of the ribs and spine. It shades the lower abdominal cavity, including the stomach, intestines, sex organs, and bladder. Above the diaphragm are the lungs. The diaphragm descends on inhale, creating space for lungs to fill with breath. When we inhale fully and the diaphragm lowers, we compact the space for the organs of digestion: the stomach, intestines, and bladder. And when we release or relax the belly at the same time, we create more space for those organs and can take more air in. In the words of my yoga therapeutics teacher, Doug Keller, breathing a relaxing and grounding full diaphragmatic breath, "brings the breath in deep while massaging the heart and toning and nourishing your internal organs,"[80] contributing to their optimal functioning.[81] When we exhale, the diaphragm rises, helping to push air out of lungs and creating more space for the organs of digestion. We use the muscles in the abdominal region, our core muscles, to help push all the air out of our lungs. Drawing the belly in at the end of each exhale not only helps with this but also serves as a core strengthener.

Mechanism of the Breath: The Diaphragm

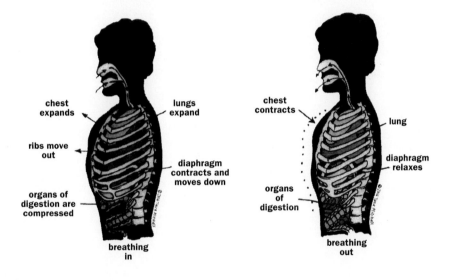

As the lungs fill with air, they extend forward, backward, right, left, up, and down, roughly sixteen to eighteen times per minute—bringing in fresh oxygen and expelling carbon dioxide. Few of us leverage the full capacity of the lungs when we breathe. Most of us are either collarbone breathers who largely use the top of lungs, ribcage breathers who largely use the mid-lungs, or belly breathers who largely use the bottom part of the lungs.[82] This is important to recognize, because not only can we begin to discern someone's emotional state based upon how they breathe, but we also contribute to our own emotional state based upon how *we* breathe. If we are anxious and continue to breathe high and shallow, that breathing will continue to contribute to our anxiety. Poor breathing over time also negatively affects pulmonary function, contributing to heart disease.[83]

Constrictions of the breath can be eased through the simple breathing exercises. If you have lived as a shallow breather for much of your life, you would typically have tightened intercostal muscles. These muscles reside between the ribs and allow the ribcage to open and close around the lungs. If these muscles are really tight, it may be difficult to breathe fully at first. With practice, they will loosen. If you wear clothes that are too restrictive, such as belts, bra straps, waistbands, and neckties, you are likely inhibiting your breath. If your body is generally tight and inflexible, the back muscles in particular, it may also be difficult to breathe fully into the back body. Practices like yoga that open the front and back of the body, allowing for full breathing, enhance vitality by facilitating the use of the full lung capacity. During breath regulation it is helpful to visualize a teacup. The tea first goes to the bottom of the cup and fills to the top then pours out of the top emptying last from the bottom. As we fill our lungs with each inhale, from the very bottom to the very top, imagine the ribs relaxing away from the lungs to make space. As we exhale from top to bottom imagine the ribs contracting some and the belly drawing in at the end.

Stages of Breathing

There are four stages of breathing: the inhale (*puraka*), the pause at the top of the inhale (*antara kumbhaka*), the exhale (*rechaka*), and the pause at the bottom of the exhale (*bahya kumbhaka*).[84] The inhale pause is referred to as *retention*, the exhale pause as *suspension*. Adding all stages together—the length of our inhale, the length of the retention, the length of the exhale, the length of the suspension—is called our total breath capacity.

We each have a unique breath capacity. Some people may not suspend their breath at all, some may not retain it, some have a longer inhale, and some have a longer exhale. It is unique to the individual. For most of us, our total breath capacity can increase with practice. It is important to have a relationship with your breath and become aware of your natural breath capacity and tendencies. How you address your breath throughout the day will directly affect your physical, mental, and emotional well-being.[85] Donna Farhi calls this *tuning* the breath in *The Breathing Book*. Check in with your breath throughout the day until it becomes a habit. Using your breath to center yourself will allow you to operate from a clear and calm place. This is the only place from which we should be making decisions.

Breath Regulation and the Mind–Body

In yoga, breathing exercises are used to help control and regulate our life force energy or prana. The science of controlled, conscious breathing is called *pranayama,* the fourth of the eight limbs of yoga. There are many types of breathing practices, each for specific purposes. There are breathing exercises for stress management and calming, for energy creation and vitality, and for clearing or balancing the mind. Breathing techniques have benefits in addition to emotional control, nervous system control and respiratory health. The organ massage offered to the kidneys while breathing fully helps to maintain kidney health. The pumping action in some of the more energizing forms of breathing exercises also helps stimulate digestion. There are even breath practices for specific health conditions, such as asthma, allergies, back pain, headaches, and depression.

For the purposes of stress management and focusing the mind, a simple practice of slowing and lengthening the breath, working toward an exhale that is longer than the inhale, will begin to calm the nervous system. We start to relax just by breathing differently, even if life around us is exactly the same. Lengthening our exhale sends a message to our mind–body that everything is okay,[86] moving us from our sympathetic nervous system (fight or flight) to our parasympathetic nervous system (rest and relax). This shift initiates with a big inhale, followed by a long exhale and an intentional relaxing of the body for a few minutes. This method of conscious relaxation will help slow the heart rate and reduce blood pressure.

Traditionally, a regular yoga breathing practice is encouraged in the morning before the start of the day, in a seated position with eyes closed, for eighty cycles of breath. For most of us, that means eight to ten minutes.[87] You can also practice simple breathing exercises on the train, in a car, or at your desk to establish a pattern that can set you up for optimal breathing during the day. For the exercises offered that involve counting each breath, you can certainly watch the seconds on a clock or count in your head, but it is helpful to use a metronome in the beginning so you can close your eyes and move out of distraction. The seconds of the clock or the tempo of the metronome allow you to consistently measure a baseline number of counts of your inhale, your exhale, and the pauses in between. Many free metronome apps are available for download. Choose a tempo that feels right to you—not too fast and not too slow.

Breath Awareness Practices

Below are several breathing practices. Consult with a physician prior to attempting any breath regulation practice, particularly if you have a heart condition, lung issues, chronic anxiety, or are pregnant or asthmatic. Breathing exercises are taught at yoga studios all over the world and an abundance of how-to videos can be found on YouTube.

Shape Change

This is a feeling-based practice that allows you to become aware of how the breath changes the shape of the body. The practice involves ten cycles of breath. All inhales and exhales are through the nose.

Feeling Your Breath in Your Body

1. Sit comfortably with a long erect spine.
2. Close and relax your eyes, and keep them closed and still through the practice.
3. As you inhale through your nose, place your hand on your belly, and notice it go out with the inhale. Then exhale, and notice how the belly returns to its original location.
4. As you inhale, place your hand on the front of the ribcage near the heart, and notice how it moves forward. Then exhale and notice how it moves back toward the body.
5. As you inhale, place your hand on your collarbone, and notice how your chest rises and the collar bone spreads. Then exhale and notice how the chest falls.
6. As you inhale, place your hands on either side of your ribcage, and notice how your ribcage expands to the right and to the left.
7. As you inhale, place your hand on your mid-back, and notice how your back body moves or does not move with the breath. If the back body is tight, it will not expand.
8. Now, as you inhale, take note of the length of the inhale as compared to the length of the exhale.
9. On the next five cycles of breath, think about how to describe your breath right now. Is it warm or cool, thick or thin, choppy or regular, short or long, high or low, comfortable or distracted? Are there any pauses? Does it feel constricted in any places?

Against the Grain (Viloma) Breath

The objective of this practice is to learn to give attention to the breath flowing into the body and the full capacity of the lungs. It serves to activate the ribcage and expand the breath as you focus on one piece of the breath at a time. You will also learn to give attention to both the inhale and exhale and to discover the pauses that happen at the top of the inhale and bottom of the exhale. This practice is best experienced while lying down and can be practiced pausing during the inhale or pausing during the exhale.[88] All inhales and exhales are through the nose.

Creates Awareness of the Full Lung; Expands the Breath; Calms and Relaxes the Nervous System

1. Begin by lying down, palms facing up. Relax your body.
2. Close and relax your eyes and keep them closed and still through the practice.
3. For two counts, inhale through your nose, taking one third of your breath into the belly so your belly inflates. Then pause for two counts.
4. For two counts, inhale the next third into the ribcage so your ribcage inflates. Pause for two counts.
5. For two counts, inhale the final third into the collarbone area so you can feel it expand. Pause for two or more counts.
6. Now, slowly release all the breath in an even, slow, thin, quiet manner. Draw the belly in at the end pressing all the air out. Then pause and begin again.
7. Repeat five to ten times.
8. Relax and feel.

Breath Baseline Practice

Once you have some familiarity with the breath awareness practices above, you can examine more closely your natural pattern of breathing, including your total breath capacity, the length of your inhale, the length of your exhale, and the pauses that you make at the top and bottom of the breath. All inhales and exhales are through the nose.

Finding Your Baseline Breath Capacity

1. Start your metronome.
2. Sit comfortably with a long erect spine.
3. Close and relax your eyes and keep them closed and still through the practice.
4. Begin to breathe naturally through your nose. Try not to change or force the breath. If you don't naturally pause between breaths then don't pause in this practice.
5. As you breathe, count your breath, counting separately the inhale, the retention (pause) at the top of the inhale, the exhale, and the suspension (pause) at the bottom of the exhale (IRES). You will have four numbers in the end.
6. Do twelve cycles of breath, counting each cycle. By the end of twelve rounds, you will have a good sense of your average count.
7. Write the average down. Examples of IRES could be 4:2:3:0 or 5:1:4:2 or 5:2:6:2.
8. Your total breath capacity is the addition of the four numbers. The length of inhale is the first two numbers added together. The length of exhale is the last two numbers added together. For instance, in the three examples above, the total breath capacity, the total inhale and the total exhale are 9/6/3, 12/6/6, and 15/7/8, respectively. The result will be unique to the individual and his or her current emotional state. There isn't a right or wrong set of numbers.

Breathing Techniques to Calm the Nervous System

Now that you know your natural way of breathing, your breath capacity, you can slightly modify it. The key word is *slightly*, as this, too, is a process. As above, do not force or push the breath or put a lot of effort into breathing. Simply *breathe*. If you try too hard to inhale and exhale, you may become lightheaded and dizzy and the practice becomes counterproductive. This next step is just a way of breathing a little more consciously and using the lungs a little more fully.

Lengthen Your Exhale

When the objective is to calm the nervous system, as mentioned previously, we want our exhales to be longer than our inhales. This technique is another way to get to understand how you breathe and to see if you can use your breath to keep your emotions in check and find calm in your day. And, certainly, when you are already doing something to relax, you can use your breath to help you find an even deeper relaxation.

**To Calm and Relax the Nervous System: Cultivates a
Calm Demeanor and Controlled Temperament**

1. Always breathe through your nose.
2. The objective is to inhale fully and make your exhale longer than your inhale.
3. Sit comfortably with a long erect spine.
4. Close and relax your eyes and keep them closed and still through the practice.
5. Relax your ribs and inhale fully and *slowly* while taking note of the count.
6. Exhale fully and *slowly*, pulling the belly in and up to aid in pressing all of the air out with the goal of extending the exhale longer than the inhale.
7. For our examples of IRES, above (4:2:3:0, 5:1:4:2 and 5:2:6:2), example 1 has an inhale of 4+2= 6 and an exhale of 3+0=3. This person might be a little anxious or excited. Example 2 has an inhale of 5+1=6 and an equal exhale of 4+2=6. This person may be feeling ordinary, neither anxious nor particularly relaxed. Example 3 has an inhale of 5+2=6 and an exhale of 6+2=8. This person might be feeling rather calm already.
8. To extend the exhale, simply try to expand the exhale itself *and* the suspension. Keep the inhale the same. For example, the anxious person above might at first try to balance his or her breath with a 4:2:4:2. Then, overtime he or she may try to lengthen the exhale, moving toward, for example, 4:2:6:2.
9. Do ten rounds.
10. Relax and feel.
11. Practice extending your exhale, noticing how you feel throughout your day.

Bees Breath (Bhramari)

This practice is a little strange and requires you to be a bit uninhibited. It is easy to feel the energetic shift it creates and it feels good. This practice can help you clear your head, refocus, or transition between activities. And it is a bit like a reset button for when you are anxious, stressed, irritable, or angry. Since it also vibrates the vocal cords, Bees Breath practice can be helpful before giving a presentation or attending a meeting where you have some important speaking to do. The hand placement is necessary to close off the senses so you can feel the vibration in your body and mind.

The instruction below includes a simplified hand placement; if you watch a video of this practice you may see the practitioner with all fingers in use on the face. The Sanskrit name of this breathing practice means *humming bee,* because of the sound you make during the practice.

Calms and Relaxes Body and Mind; Reduces Tension and Calms Strong Emotion; Clears the Throat; Cultivates Clarity and Personal Expression

1. Sit comfortably with a long erect spine.
2. Close and relax your eyes, and keep them closed and still through the practice.
3. Close your lips, and keep them closed throughout the practice.
4. Press your index fingers firmly on the flaps of your ears to close off sound completely.
5. With closed lips, touch the tip of your tongue at the place where the back of your front teeth meets your palette.
6. Inhale fully through your nose.
7. Maintaining that position, slowly exhale while making the humming sound of a bee as loudly and as high pitched as you possibly can. This is an internal sound because your lips are closed.
8. Focus your attention on the middle of your forehead and the vibration that is taking place there with the intention of increasing that vibration by making the bee sound louder.
9. Do five rounds. If comfortable, you can build to fifteen.
10. Relax and feel.

Breathing Technique for Centering the Mind

Alternate Nostril Breath (Nadi Shodhana)

This practice can be done by most people all the time and is useful for calming and centering. It involves creating an even flow of breath (life force, prana) through your energy channels (nadis). The name itself means clearing the channels.

Calming and Centering; Cultivates Balance

1. Sit comfortably with a long erect spine.
2. Close and relax your eyes and keep them closed and still through the practice.
3. With your right palm directed toward your face, place your right thumb near your right nostril, your index and middle finger on your forehead, and your ring finger near your left nostril.
4. Press the right nostril closed with your thumb.
5. Inhale fully through your left nostril while keeping the right nostril closed off.
6. Close the left nostril with the ring finger, open the right nostril, and exhale fully through the right nostril. Then inhale fully through the same, right, nostril.
7. Close the right nostril, open the left nostril, and exhale fully through the left nostril. This is one round.
8. Begin again by inhaling through the left nostril.
9. Then close the left, open the right and so on, concluding each round with an exhale through the left nostril.
10. Do ten rounds.
11. Relax and feel.

Breathing Techniques That Are Energizing

Breathing practices are not just for calming; they can also be practiced to create energy and rev up your body prior to a big meeting or presentation. Energizing breath practices strengthen the cardiovascular system as your heart is forced to pump harder, as it would during exercise. It's important to note that cardiovascular exercise that forces us to breathe fully but not *too* heavily is good for the lungs and will also expand our breath capacity. Do not do these practices while pregnant and consult with your doctor before practicing if you have heart or respiratory problems.

Bellows (Bhastrika) Breath

This vigorous breathing practice is a great mid-afternoon pick-me-up that improves circulation, clears the mind, strengthens and tones the abdominal muscles, and massages the organs of digestion.[89] Aside from giving energy and power, this is also said to help raise metabolic function, which aids in weight loss. This breath is called Bellows Breath because it is like stoking an internal fire with powerful, even inhales and exhales.

**Energizes; Stokes the Fire; Cultivates Confidence
and Self-Esteem; Activates Power**

1. Sit comfortably with a long erect spine.
2. Close and relax your eyes and keep them closed and still through the practice.
3. Inhale fully to begin.
4. Exhale sharply, quickly (about one second long), and forcefully through the nose. Power this by drawing the belly strongly in and up.
5. Inhale sharply, quickly (about one second long), and forcefully through the nose, releasing the belly out.
6. Repeat for ten cycles of breath the sharp inhale followed by a sharp exhale both powered by the belly.
7. At the end of ten cycles, fully inhale a regular breath and retain the breath for up to five counts.
8. If comfortable, start again and continue with this breathing technique for up to five rounds of ten cycles. Cease the practice, or do fewer cycles of breath if you get dizzy.
9. Conclude with a huge inhale and a slow, deep exhale.
10. Relax and feel.

Skull-Shining (Kapalbhati) Breath

This practice has an energizing effect on the body and a clearing effect on the mind. It is also helpful during the spring and fall, when there is a tendency toward allergies and sinus congestion.

Energizes; Clears Mental Stress and Sluggishness; Improves Concentration

1. Sit comfortably with a long erect spine.
2. Close and relax your eyes, and keep them closed and still through the practice.
3. Inhale fully to begin.
4. Exhale sharply, quickly, and forcefully through the nose. Power this by drawing the belly strongly in and up.
5. Take a *passive* yet full inhale through the nose. Allow the inhale to take as long as it takes; this is different from the short, sharp inhale used in Bellows Breath in that it is not at all forced.
6. Repeat.
7. Do a few rounds to start, increasing the number of cycles when you are comfortable. Over time, you can increase to five or more minutes. Cease the practice or do fewer cycles of breath if you get dizzy.
8. Relax and feel.

Summary: The Breath

Therapeutically-trained yoga teachers can help you learn about your unique habits of breathing and teach breathing techniques. Develop a relationship with your breath and the state of your nervous system and focus on extending your exhale whenever you can. This habit alone will help you manage stress by improving your capacity for handling what comes with more grace and control.

Philosophy: Manifesting Vitality

Social Principle 3: Non-Stealing—Generosity (asteya)

The principle of non-stealing (*asteya*) is one of the five social principles (yamas). Asteya has to do not only with material theft, but also with intangibles like time, energy, pleasantries, happiness, trust, economics, and comforts. At the office it includes the obvious, like not taking office supplies for non-office use and not abusing expense accounts, which is essentially stealing from someone. Taking credit for the work of others is a theft worsened by not giving credit to appropriate parties at all. More broadly, asteya extends to environmental stewardship in the sense of not taking the health of the planet from future generations and can be practiced through measures such as energy conservation and recycling at the office. Having a completely clear picture of all of the direct and indirect consequences of your work and making efforts to mitigate harm is a great way to practice this principle.

The Energy Vampire

From the perspective of a leader, an important nuance of this principle involves the idea of not stealing the *energy* of others, of not being an energy vampire. Some energy vampires have persistent personal problems and a variety of unappealing qualities including hostility, despondency, or misery. They also like to complain and gossip. In excess, these qualities and traits are emotionally tiresome for others, waste a lot of time, and suck energy. As a leader, setting boundaries and limiting time with such people will help you to manage your own energy and honor your team.

Don't be a Spirit Sapper

The best way you can support your team is to build them up. Don't steal the team's spirit. Add to it. We have often heard the saying *raining on someone's parade* or *stealing someone's thunder*. Avoid this. Take care not to be cavalier about an issue that is of importance to a team member. Avoid saying or doing things that would embarrass or humiliate members of your team. Too many people in leadership roles are simply not incentivized to care about their impact on the well-being of employees, so it does not factor into their behavior. People in leadership roles can easily steal the life and vitality of their team. We have all known unenlightened managers who simply believe employees should be happy to get a paycheck and that's all they are owed by the company.

Give Broad Appreciation

It can be easy to take advantage of efforts or to take efforts for granted. People work hard and, if you marry their effort with positive reinforcement, they will feel full and complete, never lacking. Give accolades openly and frequently that are consistent with your principles. Be overly generous with compliments of work well done. Seek to discover where each and every member of the team contributes *well* so that the accolades are broadly shared. Elevate the spirit of the team through supportive measures. Give credit where credit is due. Be vocal. This applies equally to you. Allow others to elevate your spirit by accepting accolades and appreciating compliments. Avoid self-sabotaging behaviors and take care not to minimize or marginalize the work you've done. Don't steal from your own spirit. What you may not realize is that generosity is a form of giving and helping, which lights up the pleasure centers of our brain. Science has shown that helping others gives us pleasure and so through the practice of generosity and appreciation we reward ourselves.

Honor Your Commitments and Your People

It is easy to feel we are entitled, that we deserve things. Furthering on the avidya (ignorance, misconception of reality) discussion, at the office we work very hard to overcome challenges, and so does our team. It's typical for hardworking people to expect to be rewarded with promotions, money, projects, good clients, or preferred territories, for example. It's natural to feel this way. But expectations and entitlements are like a zero sum game, since there are a limited supply of the best clients and territories, few promotions, and finite pools of cash to split. Armed with expectations, someone *always* feels he or she loses. Expectations set the stage for guaranteed disappointment for someone. Knowing this, leaders can attempt to mitigate disappointment through clear and honest communication all through the year, a genuine focus on fairness and equity, regular feedback, a systematic focus on the growth of every employee, appropriate non-monetary benefits and perks, and huge expressions of gratitude all the time. This is how we can honor a commitment to our team. Further, a well team is a happier and more cooperative team and that itself will temper feelings of disappointment. Keep yourself on your high priority list as a way to mitigate your own feelings of entitlement and expectation. Honor your commitments to yourself, your commitments to your employees and customers, and your commitments to your family and friends.

Be Prudent with Time

Asteya also applies to time, something we never seem to have enough of. Lengthy meetings without agendas and poor preparation are simply stealing the time of the participants. Ways to honor asteya at work from the perspective of time include expecting attendees to be punctual for meetings and prepared and keeping meetings short and mandatory only for those directly involved. Importantly, do not serve as the bottleneck. As the leader you can be responsive to the needs of the team and as generous with your time as possible. Empower your team and help them prioritize. Delegate and hold people accountable to a crystal clear, agreed-upon set of deliverables. Honor time constraints. All of these practices help to maintain the principle of asteya at work.

Be Considerate of Others

Not stealing the time of others involves being considerate toward others. To be considerate, one must have enough space in life to pause and acknowledge in each moment what is considerate behavior or not considerate behavior. We often go through the motions without regard to the impact we are making, sleepwalking through life. It takes time and practice to begin to change unconscious habits into conscious actions, to act in a manner that is considerate and generous. It can help to begin to notice the people to whom we typically don't give much attention. These are the people whose faces we neither see nor remember, even though we may flash them our badge, order a drink from them, or simply walk right by them every single day.

A director of a touching YouTube video dressed several actors up as though they were homeless. The director had each actor sit on a sidewalk in a location where a member of the actor's *own family* would pass them to see if the family member would notice them. No one noticed. Not one family member paid attention to the homeless actor, even though they happened to be their wife, their cousin, their sister, or their uncle. Later, the family members were shown a video of them walking by the homeless person who was actually a member of their own family. When they saw the truth they were visibly affected: dumbfounded, ashamed, and openly disappointed with themselves. This is our wake-up call, too.

How many people do we walk by every day to whom we pay absolutely no attention? Begin to become aware of how a wide variety of people within and outside of the office serve to make our lives a little better. Look people in the eye. *Smile* and *seek to connect* at the most rudimentary level. Learn their names. This practice will allow you to learn to be more considerate of others and will go a long way in helping you connect better with your team.

Non-Stealing at Work

In a healthy work environment where the enterprise values and honors all relationships with employees and external parties, feelings of entitlement become less pronounced as people feel more content and whole. You can foster such an environment by being generous with your time, patient with your people, and forthcoming with feedback—both good and bad. In vibrant work environments, contributions are rewarded and appreciated. Leaders add to the good feelings of their teams by propping them up and taking care not to bring down the team by marginalizing or under-appreciating efforts.

Questions for Leaders: Non-Stealing and Generosity

1. Do you greet your staff pleasantly and express appreciation for their efforts, even in times when things are not going well for the business?
2. What measures do you take to build up each member of your team? How do you recognize and support your team? Do members of your team recognize, support, and build up one another?
3. Do you or your team take credit for actions of another employee or a competitor?
4. Do you or your team compare yourselves to others? Do you or your team suffer from feelings of lack and inadequacy? Do you or your team suffer from feelings of superiority and arrogance? Does the team have a healthy dose of self-esteem?
5. Do meetings begin punctually? Are people well-informed in advance about the purpose of meetings so that they may arrive prepared?
6. Do you delegate to your team clearly established and widely communicated goals and deliverables each week? Is the team clear on what they are expected to accomplish each week? Do you hold people accountable?
7. Do others honor your time as a leader? Do they schedule time to meet with you?
8. Are meetings long and drawn-out places for discussion of issues that more effectively could be resolved in small work groups? Are meetings full of wasteful talk from folks who like to hear their own voices?
9. Do people make eye contact during meetings? Are they listening and engaged? Do team members multitask during meetings, thus not fully listening and disrespecting the time of others in the meeting or on the conference call? Are participants calm and controlled? Are you calm and controlled?
10. When employees need time to discuss their work, do you afford them that time and help them manage their workflow?

Cultivating Courage and Strength

Obstacle to Growth: Fear (abhinivesa)

> There is nothing enlightened about shrinking so
> that other people won't feel insecure around you.
> We are all meant to shine, as children do.
>
> —Marianne Williamson

Living Fearless and Free

Rolf Gates suggests that the root of stress is actually fear. He suggests that this fear is based on our self-created beliefs and worldview, having to do typically with an unknown future situation that we are comparing to something in our past. *Fear*, in this sense, isn't reality, but rather a mental phenomenon that we invent in our minds. Living through fear has us living in three moments as we worry about:

1. what we want to preserve from the **past**
2. what in the **present** we are unsatisfied with and therefore feel we need to change
3. what will happen in the **future** as a consequence

It is far less energy intensive and much less stressful to live in one moment, the present one. When fearful we are more reactionary and less in control of our emotions. When we can let go of some of that fear, we are emboldened gaining courage and strength. With renewed internal power we carry ourselves with confidence, are appropriately assertive, and have a healthy amount of self-esteem. We are more immune to the stressors that can be consequences of uncertainty, ambiguity, and change as well. A healthy amount of self-esteem allows us to express ourselves truthfully, being honest about both our talents and our flaws, without the fear of self worth. This is a humble place where we are not afraid to highlight our limitations. With humility we acknowledge that we are imperfect and that's ok. It is only through struggle that we source strength and freedom from fear. When we can let go of some of our fear we have a greater desire to dig deep and create and share our new ideas with others.

When we attack our fears head on we become less afraid of taking risks. Mistakes and even failures are welcomed because we know that they mean we actually tried something new and we have the opportunity to learn from them. Entrepreneurs start businesses knowing the vast majority of companies fail but they take the risk and do it anyway. This requires faith and enough inner strength to trust yourself and to know that you can pick up the pieces if you fail. Overcoming fears and taking risks can come in many forms. Some of mine have included skiing black diamonds, handstands against the wall, moving to new cities with dreams in tow, traveling alone to many unfamiliar places on the other side of the world, but most of all publishing my words and ideas in this book. What fears have you overcome? Can you develop enough inner strength so you can cultivate the risk-taking side of yourself?

Fear of Loss

The *klesha,* (obstacle) of fear called *abhinivesa,* leads to negative stress, anger, and sadness. Abhinivesa in the classical context of yoga means fear of death. Philosophically speaking, when we are riddled with fear, we aren't growing. When we live a stagnant life, we are dying. Rooted deeply in our subconscious, this fear affects every choice we make. This can creep into the everyday and become the fear of losing the lives we are working hard to create. It can become the fear of losing our self-created identity. It can become the fear of having a life filled with work, people, and things we don't like and the fear of losing the things, people, and work that we do like. Abhinivesa can be thought of as clinging to the *house of cards* we worked hard to establish, wanting to preserve it at all costs—no matter how impermanent, instable, or weak its base of support. If we cling to our house of cards, we aren't trying new things. We aren't growing. I had a saying that I told myself while downhill skiing that went *if you don't fall (softly) once in awhile you aren't trying hard enough.* Try harder. Stretch your limits. Push your edge a bit and you might access a new threshold. Embrace the fall and get back up again.

Our Fear "Story"

Fear holds us back. My daughter at age two was very afraid of the sound of the surf and the wind, and so she never wanted to step in or near the ocean. One day, I pressed her feet onto the beach during our family vacation and walked a few steps away from her as she screamed in fear. I continued in the days to come noticing how each day it became easier for her; she overcame her fear in a few short days. I reflected on her fear and what I'd done. We ask (or force) our children to conquer their fears all the time. Yet I found myself feeling hypocritical because I didn't feel as though I was pushing my own boundaries on much at the time. In what ways was I forcing myself to conquer my fears? How was my fear of loss holding me back from discovering something new?

Holding onto fear stifles our enjoyment of life and stifles growth and innovation at work. Stress is fear. Anxiety is fear. Anger stems out of fear. Sadness can come from fear, too. Fear is negatively correlated to confidence and self-esteem. When fear increases, confidence decreases. Fear, stress, and anger are often based on deep-seated, self-created stories about the unknown future that involves negative outcomes, like losing a job, making a mistake, becoming destitute, losing the love of family or the acceptance of friends. Professionally, fear, stress, or anger can involve many things, such as the fear of losing a client, losing a deal, not getting a promotion, being seen as not knowing or doing enough, not getting a big bonus, or not getting the prized project to work on. Professional fears often circle back to those deeper personal fears. Deep-seated fears and anxieties are also found in undue concern for the future and meticulously planning for some unknown future in an attempt to prevent anything bad from happening. Fears can limit us and will direct and control our everyday experience if we let them, and it is hard to escape them. Do you have a *fear story* playing out in your life?

Control Freaks

Many leaders have a tendency to be control freaks. It's certainly been part of my constitution, which also stems from this obstacle of fear. How does a need for control impact our lives and our team? Solving for unknowns is one manner in which fear appears strongly in my life. I planned out my life just so, accomplished my milestones: undergraduate school, business school, good job, marriage, career success, world travel, and kids. I intentionally planned out all of these things. But the kid part put a halt on the control aspect of my life. Suddenly, I could not *plan* for whether they would make friends, whether they would learn to speak clearly, or be good at math, or integrate into school. These are unknowns that I wanted to solve for to mitigate any possible harm. I can't plan how much time they will need from me. Since they always change, I will never know that answer because there is no answer. It is an unknown that I try to solve for anyway.

Kids are free spirits, not meant to be tightly controlled. We can discipline along the way, but generally, the traits about them we try to control or change stem from our fears the most noteworthy being our desire for control. They dillydally to get out of the house, take forever to eat their food, refuse to sit still, freak out over toys, and throw food all over the floor. That's what little kids do. If we pay attention, we come to learn that they are great teachers. There are times when we procrastinate, don't like our food, are too stressed or excited to sit, get annoyed with bad drivers on the road, and throw insults at others. And there are times when we just need a hug. We can be like kids, too. To this day, I often find myself trying to solve for everything and control my life, to make sure everyone's needs are met well in advance of knowing what those needs might be. It's senseless and draining. I now try to make a conscious effort to consider the flip side of my fears and control a little less—the growth borne out of struggle, the strength revealed in uncertainty, the work ethic established when challenged, the humility and inner strength shaped out of loss, the opportunity in adversity. Also with regard to my kids, I spend more time acknowledging the socialization and learning associated with a variety of educators and caregivers and less time feeling guilty. A need for control of our lives is based on a variety of root fears including: fear of change, fear of creating turmoil, fear of disrupting the good things, fear of losing a semblance of order, fear of being wrong, fear of making a mistake, and fear of being worthy.

Working on courage and faith and letting go of fear is actually a much less tiresome way to live, honoring that we are strong and can pick up the pieces if things don't work out. Taking those risks is letting go of fear and boosts confidence and self-esteem. We can realize that showing up and doing our best at all times is the extent of what we can control. That's it. We can realize that sacrificing our well-being is counter to doing our best. Importantly, we can realize that allowing space for the unknown to happen is actually a *necessary* part of life. This includes space in our schedules and space in our minds. That space for the unknown affords an opportunity for growth and learning, surprise and wonder. Micromanaging and being hyper vigilant about every single task and e-mail and phone call and client need and personnel issue that confronts us in a day is our *self-created fear* playing out at the office. Making everything urgent and time sensitive and ultra important is also fear playing out at the office. We learn and growth through mistakes. Find the teaching moment in every happening, no matter how the cards may land. Find your strength and power in knowing you are a survivor and make good choices.

On Urgency and Vulnerability

Another way to consider the effects of fear is through an examination of urgency and vulnerability. There are certainly needs that we must address, but when we can figure out what drives our fears, we will realize that not everything is urgent. A good way to work toward becoming more *fearless and free* is to practice being vulnerable through self-expression. Work to let go of the urgency through vulnerability. It takes great courage and strength to be vulnerable, to challenge the status quo. It takes vulnerability and risk to catalyze something new. The more vulnerable we can learn to be, the more powerful and courageous we become. With a willingness to be vulnerable and some humility, we acknowledge our weaknesses, consequently releasing fear and building strength. We will find ways to address our fears and our limitations by communicating with others, seeking more information, asking questions, and working to understand our own feelings and how and why things affect us. We address fears by trying things even if they end up failing knowing we are resilient. Embracing failure as part of our process of learning and growth further fortifies our confidence and self-esteem. When we confront our fears, we emerge stronger, reclaim control over our lives, and we will feel more comfortable managing deadlines, people, and the vast number of requests that stuff our e-mail boxes. We will prioritize and feel content with our choices. We are able to be authentic leaders.

Frozen in Fear

When a constant fear of loss is coupled with a clinging to the contents of our lives, it immobilizes us. We become frozen in our worry and concern about losing things, instead of functioning productively and going with the flow. With such strongly embodied fears, we become inflexible and resistant to change. Our fear-driven, inflexible attitude comes out in how we manage our team. We cannot build trust when we succumb to our fears. Fear paralyzes and we find ourselves in a state of micromanagement, disconnection, and distrust. Our distrust of efforts and intentions results in a domino effect of unhelpful leadership qualities that disengage the team. We become intolerant and inflexible, we think less of our team and treat them poorly, and, consequently, they don't perform as well. We do not take risks or leaps of faith, and nor do we try to optimize goals. We can even become inoperable, where our minds spin and nothing gets done. Our confidence erodes when we hold back and do not try out of fear.

Faith

Instead, firmly believing and accepting that everything in our lives has a reason for happening, even if it doesn't appear that way, will cause us to embrace life more fully and not recoil from it. Some things are just not meant for us to understand. We can then function in the flow of life and roll with the punches, as the cliché goes. When we accept things as they come, however, we don't actually see them as punches, but rather as simply the ebbs and flow of life. Our outlook is more positive, we are willing to try new things, and we begin to embrace change, mistakes, and failures. Challenges seem less insurmountable. Obstacles and setbacks are now seen as opportunities. We walk around a bit lighter and feel less burdened in our bodies and minds. Sometimes the waves in the water are rough, but there is peace in knowing that they always calm down again and are but a small part of a vast and glorious sea.

Concluding Statement

Spending time working on your energy dimension will allow you to interpret situations more accurately, control them appropriately, and leverage energy to serve helpful purposes. Becoming aware of your own energy and having a relationship with your breath will help you to understand your emotions, to intelligently navigate the tasks in your days, and to work productively with all people with whom you must interact. Learning to use the breath as a tool to reign in your sympathetic nervous system, which otherwise causes us to feel stressed, allows you to live in a more balanced way. Acknowledging your fears, taking risks anyway, and embracing failure will help you build confidence. Reflecting on your attention to this layer, you will notice you have more productive meetings, clearer communications, a new awareness of your emotions, and a newfound control of them, an enhanced aptitude to read situations, and greater confidence and strength.

Chapter 6
Yogi Secret #4: Mind

Old Maxim
A chaotic and stressed mental state is normal.

New Maxim
An orderly and serene mental state is normal.

Resolve: I choose to marry effort and ease in my life. By reflecting upon my perspective and worldview, minimizing distraction, quieting my mind, and tuning into my reactions, I experience life with clarity and understanding.

Yogi Secret #4 allows me to develop or maintain personal qualities inherent in inspiring leaders including: equipoise ~ clear-thinking ~ open-minded and receptive ~ empathetic ~ self-aware ~ emotional control ~ realistic and pragmatic ~ objective and unbiased ~ positive outlook

People are disturbed not by a thing, but
by their perception of a thing.

—Epictetus

The third layer is the mind dimension called the *manomaya kosha*. The mind layer is our rapid-fire processing center, like the chip in our computer. *Manas,* meaning *mind,* is the aspect of mind that governs reaction and informs everyday thought and emotion, which are functions of perception, or how we see and react to the world around us. Our mind (manas) is also like a recorder that records all of the thoughts and memories we have ever had onto an infinite old-fashioned reel of film, that is then stored in our mental warehouse of mind-stuff, called *chitta*, the storehouse of memory. This warehouse of information is based upon what we were taught and what we have observed and experienced, influenced by our upbringing, education, society, and the world around us. Ultimately, what we uniquely draw from our memory bank governs our overall perception including our beliefs, worldview, perspectives, and attitude.

Manomaya Kosha (Mind)

Inner Awareness

In this chapter, we begin to take a deeper dive inside. We consider our brains and how they respond to stress, the way we live our lives, and what we can do to settle our minds. We will also seek to understand our worldview, our beliefs, and our perspectives—where they come from and how they relate to our present attitudes and behavior. Our principles are created in the mind dimension, as are our ideas about right and wrong. We will also pay attention to the *quality* of our interactions and how they serve our lives and the world around us. We will examine how all of this affects our lives, our well-being, and our ability to connect with others.

We need to look closely and really see ourselves, not in the sense of seeing with our eyes, but really seeing how we are unique from the inside, perhaps for the very first time. Most of our lives are spent understanding ourselves through the lens of how we *think* everyone else sees us or how we would *like* them to see us. Now we will peel a few layers of the onion and look deep inside into the truth of who we really are. We will allow that little archeologist[90] to bring out his little tools, taking great care in removing the dust and discovering what is there—what has always been there under the layers, behind the dust, hidden from view. This is how we become self-aware.

When we know ourselves very well from the inside, we can begin to cultivate leadership qualities like fairness, equipoise, and pragmatism.

Paying attention to physiological cues including the subtle sensations, emotions, and feelings, we examine how these inner events can let us know whether we are adhering to a way of life that supports our well-being or not. To support our efforts to be happy, healthy, and engaging fully with our team, we will learn how to seek guidance through our *inner* experience, through reflection and contemplation.

This *inner awareness*, also called *inner knowing*, is something many leaders, due to our full lives and meaningful list of responsibilities, ignore. And yet these sensations are there to guide us. For example, making decisions against our principles, our understanding of right and wrong, doesn't feel good. Yelling or even being stern toward others doesn't feel good. Hassling ourselves is self-defeating and also doesn't feel good. But we often operate at such a pace that we don't realize it *doesn't feel good*, or we notice it but just as quickly write it off as a necessary part of the job. Sometimes we simply accept at some level that we give ourselves a hard time. The bad feelings then get internalized, adding to stress and creating conditions for dis-*ease* in the body. Becoming aware of our feelings and sensations changes our inner monologue. We then can make helpful choices regarding our thoughts, actions, and words in consideration of what we're being told from the inner self. Not only are we more effective at the workplace but also we feel better.

Emotional Control

As we unpeel the layer of thoughts and feelings,[91] we importantly learn to control our moods and emotions using self-observation and self-awareness exercises and techniques. What we learn along the way and the choices we make shapes our character. With practice, we enhance our ability to *learn* things through our senses over time, *assess* what is going on, and *respond* accordingly. In our fast-paced world, we are constantly stimulated by a variety of inputs from our environment, including people, text messages, phone calls, e-mails, social media alerts, music playing, and our to-do lists. And our minds are constantly assessing these inputs and reacting to them based upon our current internal condition and what we've learned over time. This circular process of assessing and immediately reacting, assessing and reacting, assessing and reacting is what some call the spinning or racing mind. While the chatter in the mind is not specifically a bad thing, this chatter, when whirling and tumultuous, can serve to obscure us from seeing clearly the events and situations in our lives, and we find ourselves *reacting* and not *responding*. A response in this text involves conscious thought; a reaction does not.

A reaction stems from some, even minor, state of distress not to be confused with instinct. Instinct is borne out of special wisdom gained in a professional context from years of experience or maybe just something you are born with, like a mother knowing the needs of her child so intimately and immediately. Instinct is like a special gift we have. Our everyday thoughtless reactions would not be considered gifts. Connecting with our inner experience allows us some space to respond rather than react. As opposed to a reaction, which is governed by the fast and primitive emotional centers of the brain, responses are governed by the intelligence that manifests from the slower-functioning, most sophisticated parts of the brain.

Furthermore, when our mind is stirred up, racing, or jumping around like a monkey (aka the monkey mind), it is difficult to connect to ourselves or to others. This can often lead to what we call stress. When we are like this, our minds are *preoccupied*, degrading our ability to pay attention to the person speaking to us, even if we are looking him or her in the eye. Until we take a few breaths and snap out of the frenzy and into a mind that can pay attention, we may not even hear what was said and certainly will not be able to control our emotions. When we begin to understand our mind layer and observe our inner experience, we can anticipate our behavior and make choices that serve our well-being, consequently helping us become better leaders and better people.

Our Brain on Stress

Overreaction

Our prefrontal cortex is the part of the brain responsible for executive control. It is what should differentiate us from other species as intelligent and discerning humans. It helps us regulate behavior, control intense emotions, discern consequences of our actions, evaluate complex concepts, and practice sound judgment. Strong executive function also helps us with mature, clear, and lucid thinking. Fully formed by our mid-twenties, the prefrontal cortex tempers our *overreaction* to life. Importantly, when we are stressed, the function of our prefrontal cortex is weakened. When this happens, it is as if we slide back into the state of a teenager, with a lack of impulse control, less ability to control our temper, less mature judgment, and a diminished capacity for reason. Note that trauma and excessive stress experienced as babies and in our youth affect the development of the prefrontal cortex and consequently its function in the years to come.

Negativity

Our prefrontal cortex is the part of our brains most sensitive to stressors. Even relatively mild acute stress can inhibit cognitive abilities, while long-term stress can cause *physical changes* to the prefrontal cortex.[92] In *Buddha's Brain* (2009), neuropsychologist Rick Hanson, PhD, and neurologist Rick Mendius, MD, explain that we have a built in negativity bias, and if we are stressed too often, we begin to operate out of an even more negative place and view *everything* jaded by negativity.[93] Our memory of things while stressed is negatively biased and foggy; we have trouble knowing and articulating why, exactly, we are upset, because our memory is unclear.[94]

Loss of Emotional Control

We have less control over our emotions, and it becomes more difficult to regulate behavior, judge right from wrong, analyze a situation, focus, concentrate, or make decisions.[95] We begin to see and experience things in a more unpleasant light and become more distrustful of the efforts and intentions of those around us. If we suffer from a weak or damaged prefrontal cortex—as is the case when we live a life on simmer—we can become reckless and impulsive, irrational and anxious. A weak prefrontal cortex hinders our ability to make moral and ethical decisions as well.[96]

Impaired Judgment

Every time we perceive a threat, real or not, a part of our brain called the amygdala sends an unpleasant alert like an alarm bell, which kicks off our stress response system. When we continue to interpret and then experience moments of our lives as unpleasant threats or stress events—and subsequently allow our feelings to heighten—this becomes a habitual process with a negative domino effect on our well-being. Our amygdala gets used to sounding the *unpleasant threat* alarm and, like the boy who cried wolf, tends to sound it more easily. We worry more and see even more life events as stressful. We feel bad but can't point to a specific reason. Our brain (specifically, the hippocampus) tires out with overuse and makes it increasingly difficult for us to interpret things clearly and recall events as they occurred.[97] Our judgment is therefore impaired.

Anxiety and Depression

Directing our energy to the brain structures responsible for these alerts and reactions takes energy from our prefrontal cortex as well.[98] When we overuse our brain structures in this manner, we become predisposed to anxiety or depression.[99] Some people may say their nerves are shot, others may say they cannot stop their mind from racing, and some people just cannot get out of the rut of feeling sad. The bottom line is that we do not think nor act clearly when we are in any state of stress. To operate at our peak as a leader, we need to facilitate a strong connection between our prefrontal cortex and the rest of our brain by taking efforts to become calm, clear, and undistracted. As parents, cradle your babies, hug your kids, tell them how much you love them all the time and, importantly, *don't stress them out.* The more we learn about our own way of being, the more we will understand how we can support this connection. Make a chronically stressed state of being an unacceptable state of being in your life and make life choices that foster qualities essential to leadership.

Our *Way* of Being

> The mind makes a man its slave; again the same mind liberates him.
> —Swami Sivananda

The Baby Lab

In a 2012 *60 Minutes* episode called "Born Good? Babies Help Unlock the Origins of Morality," CBS correspondent Lesley Stahl interviewed a researcher at the Yale Baby Lab who was studying whether very young babies knew the difference between right and wrong. They used identical dog puppets, differentiated only by different colored shirts, and showed a skit where the puppets behaved in either a nice manner or an unkind manner. The puppets were then offered to the babies to see which one they liked. The vast majority of babies, at only six months of age, chose to hold—in essence *liked*—the nice puppet. The findings suggested that at the earliest of ages, we have subtle instincts toward right and wrong.

The next set of studies measured *preference*. Babies were first allowed to choose between two different treats. Then, two different cat puppets also chose between the same treats, and next the babies were asked to pick which cat puppet they wanted. In the majority of instances, the babies chose the cat puppet with the treat preference consistent with their own. The findings suggested that at the earliest of ages, we prefer those who are like us in some small way.

Next, the researchers measured *bias* by testing whether a baby would want the puppet who chose the opposite treat, the puppet who had a different preference from them, to be treated badly. This time, researchers used the two puppy puppets and the cat puppet that had chosen a different treat from the participating baby. In this skit, one of the two puppy puppets gave the cat a hard time, deliberately being unkind. Then the two puppy puppets were offered to the baby. *Eighty-seven* percent of the time, the babies chose the puppy puppet that gave the cat puppet a hard time. It seems that our earliest instincts from birth are to have a bias toward those who are similar to us and, even from six months old, we are supportive of unkind treatment toward those different from us. Whether an internal safety mechanism or an ethical flaw, it appears to be the way we are built. We seem to *label and divide* from the very earliest of ages.

Division and Separation

Knowing we have a natural tendency to create division between ourselves and other people is an important factor in our own evolution as adults. If we recognize this, we have the power to move beyond this tendency and intentionally begin to work to be more accepting of differences. Striving to unite, not divide and to *bring together*, not separate will allow you to move beyond those natural tendencies and become a more open-minded and objective leader. Not every employee will have the same skills we have or the same talents as another.

> Apply your focus on the perfection inherent in your uniqueness and consider the value that can offer to others.

Not every employee will see things as we do. Since our natural tendency will be to favor those who are like us and like-minded, we will be naturally distrustful and perhaps even fearful of differences. Knowing this, we need to work even harder to open our own awareness toward the preferences and views of others. We can begin to see people with a difference of opinion in a positive light by identifying, valuing, and leveraging their unique talents and opinions. Being very clear on our natural tendency to create separation between ourselves and others, to label and to divide, can also help us to be more accepting of our own self-designated imperfections. Begin to consider the *perfection* inherent in the uniqueness and distinctiveness of each member of your team, and consider the aggregate value that those special differences can offer to the organization. We are all imperfect and flawed. Also try to bring more of your attention to acknowledging all of the qualities that make us alike. Notice and contemplate the attributes that are identical across your team as a way to bring together and unite.

Finding Space

Reducing Distraction

To cultivate a healthy mind layer, we work to create space in our lives, simplify, decrease distraction, and tune into this subtle feeling-space in our bodies. The fifth of the eight limbs of yoga is *pratyahara*, or sense withdrawal. This is often used as a way to reduce distraction and concentrate for a meditation practice, which will be discussed further in the next chapter. At an even more basic level, a pratyahara practice can help us learn to control and limit the sensory input in our lives. A pratyahara practice allows us to consider the quality of the impressions we feed our minds and the amount of stimulation we need to maintain health. If we are depressed and sluggish, we need something different than if we are anxious and with a racing mind. The focus here is on reducing stress and anxiety and returning to a clear mind and a more conscious state of leadership. In consideration of all of the prior discussions concerning the layer of the mind, to exist in a mental state where you are not stressed, you are in control of your emotions, you are making choices in consideration of what you are feeling, and you are operating from an objective and united position—you need to be undistracted, clear, and rooted firmly in the present.

We are bombarded with a relentless amount of sensory inputs. We can learn to be present to our reactions and urges as a result of these inputs and proactively make non-agitating choices in our lives. This is not to say that we are trying to withdraw from all sensation in our lives; nor are we trying to flee from our emotions. We are merely becoming aware of where we are inviting unnecessary distraction into our lives and making sattvic (balanced) choices. These are the same choices that afford us the space to become self aware, clear in thought, and to cultivate equipoise in our lives. All of which also support happiness, health and connection with others, essential to a leaders ability to engage his or her team. This practice supports our ability to sleep soundly and improves our energy and vitality as well. A regular practice of pratyahara will help you decompress and tap into the quiet, calm, peaceful, silent spaces in your life. It is in the quiet that clarity bubbles up when we then can then choose an attitude that is mature and wise. Consider the following suggestions against the choices you might usually make:

Ways to Cultivate Pratyahara in Life

1. Decrease the number of inputs from devices.
2. Turn off chimes and alerts from gadgets.
3. Turn down the volume on the phone.
4. Turn down the volume of any music you listen to.
5. Turn off the radio in your car.
6. Wake up to a tranquil sounding alarm.
7. Listen to music that makes you feel calm.
8. Speak a little more softly and slowly than you normally do.
9. Watch television and movies that make you feel calm.
10. Watch, read, and listen to less news.
11. Read inspiring books more often.
12. Soften your gaze. Allow your eyes to relax.
13. Wear a slight smile all the time.
14. Consider light, simple, and natural food preparations.
15. Say no more often to the next task/duty/volunteer opportunity.

Cultivate Quiet, Calm, Peace, Silence

I was inspired by Sri Aurobindo's discussion in his book *The Integral Yoga*. Sri Aurobindo is an Indian nationalist, creator of Integral Yoga, and Nobel Peace Prize nominee.[100] He defines quiet, calm, peace, and silence in distinct ways,[101] not as a hierarchy or a path but rather as what I'll call *settling*. *Quiet* is describes as the condition of being in an environment without commotion or agitation. This can be an external environment, such as a quiet room, or, perhaps, a noisy room in which *you* are quiet, (not speaking). *Calm* has a subtle difference, described as a condition that has the characteristics of quiet but adds an internal stillness, a felt sense that is a bit stronger than quiet and less easily disrupted. Calm can be witnessed in our physiology. One can be quiet but not calm.

Peace is an embodied sense, a state of being or an environmental condition. It is more positive than calm, and very strong. Peace has both inward and outward qualities; we can be at peace within ourselves and also feel peaceful toward others. It is a sense of harmony and deep contentment with what is. One can have a busy chaotic life and still find peace, because it's an embodied sense. It is felt in our mind and body and spirit. A peaceful environment is described as a harmonious environment. We are unique. As such, we each have different capacities for chaos and for finding peace. Honor that about yourself and in others.

The last state is *silence*. In silence, one can also find peace. Silence has an unbinding tranquility about it. You can find silence in the very early morning or late evenings under the stars. You can find silence and peace while admiring natural environments such as the endless fog on a serene mountain lake at dawn. One can feel this deep, inner quietude in deeper states of meditation as well. Meditation will be discussed in the next chapter.

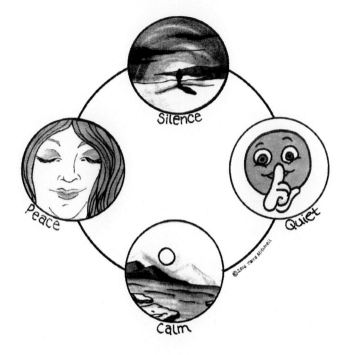

Allow yourself to sit in a quiet space every day for even a few minutes, in your car, home, or yard, where you can breathe, be still, and allow yourself to experience the feeling of being calm and centered. Life in full swing has our mind often in chaos. Pausing and breathing will overtime have enormous, positive impacts on your ability to manage your life in a healthier way, control your conscious mind including your emotions, and connect better with people on an everyday basis. Sometimes quietly sitting doesn't allow us to feel calm because we are too frazzled or stressed and we need an active approach to shift our state of mind. One way to accomplish this is by changing our internal vibration through music by chanting, singing, dancing, listening to music, drumming, or playing an instrument.

A calm inner space awakens us fully to the present moment. There could be a lot going on yet maintaining a calm inner space supports conscious leadership. Conscious leaders are present and aware and can engage in a happy and healthy way at work and in life. With control of the inner self, leaders connect and motivate others by making them feel safe and supported.

Consider how you might incorporate settling times more often in your life. There are many ways to allow for more quiet, calm, peace, and silence. Make time to be alone, doing very little. Keep in mind that even one or two minutes of quiet breathing will make a shift in how you feel.

Ten Suggestions to Find Quiet, Calm, Peace, or Silence

1. Turn off all sounds in your car.
2. Sit quietly in your car for five minutes and breathe before you go into work or into the house.
3. Close your office door. Turn off all sounds and focus on your breathing for a few minutes.
4. Use your office chair or a meditation cushion to sit and get quiet, calm, feel peaceful, and maybe even experience silence.
5. Consider reorganizing or redecorating your office so that it is harmonious. Remove clutter, create space, and keep it organized and clean. Place objects on the desk or hang pictures or quotes that feel peaceful to you.
6. Visualize a beautiful scene, the flame of a candle, or look at an object in your office that makes you feel happy yet calm to move out of the chaos of your mind and into a state of relaxation.
7. Diffuse or apply an essential oil topically that has a calming effect in your office and/or home.
8. Spend two minutes alone lying on your bed in quiet before dinner breathing and allowing your body and nervous system to relax.
9. Take a walk in nature recognizing the beauty of the earth.
10. Take a yoga asana class.
11. Take a meditation class.
12. Soak in a hot tub, and breathe with your eyes closed.
13. Get a massage.
14. Contemplate in a house of worship during off-hours when it is empty.
15. Listen to relaxing music.

Emotional Intelligence

In 1995, Daniel Goleman's best-selling book *Emotional Intelligence— Why it Can Matter More Than IQ*, popularized the term *emotional intelligence*. He proposed that that while IQ and technical skills are important, they alone do not make a good leader. He found good leaders have a high emotional quotient (EQ), and a mix of IQ and EQ should be considered as a competency framework for leaders. These modern findings dovetail nicely with some of the teachings of ancient yoga to be discussed here, as yoga focuses around a person's inner awareness and control serving ones ability to connect with, assess, and understand others.

Self-Awareness is a Function of Consciousness

Self-awareness is understanding what makes you *you,* including how you walk through your days, your everyday habits, the reasons behind the choices you make, and your emotional effect on others. Self-awareness is a skill that involves being so sensitized that you are aware of your feelings in real time.[102] Yoga, in both its ancient and modern context, is a path to consciousness that begins with awareness. This starts by first paying full attention to the present moment and becoming aware. Then through contemplation, philosophy, and meditation, aspirants become more aware of their thoughts, words, and actions and can begin to make conscious choices. In a yoga movement class, we ask the students to turn inward and pay specific attention to what they are doing with and feeling in their bodies and what is happening in their minds as they move through a sequence of poses. If a pose is challenging, for example, feelings typically emerge and self-talk happens. And this is exactly what happens during challenging times off the mat. Becoming aware of the present moment and making skillful choices is a keystone of the yoga practice.

With ongoing practice, we become more in-tune with basic human needs common to us all. As yoga is about getting to know yourself first— becoming conscious of your tendencies, habits, and idiosyncrasies—self-aware leaders can leverage yogic tools to train the mind, shift their choices, and adjust their actions in ways that serve the emotional quotient of their leadership. Leaders who are more conscious and aware are better able to connect with and engage their teams and can work skillfully and effectively with many different types of people in many different situations. The yogic practices in the Mind, Knowledge, and Bliss chapters allow us to understand our inner-selves better so that we can learn *how* to enhance our ability to serve as emotionally intelligent, effective, productive, and inspiring leaders.

Self-Awareness: Emotions and Senses

The etymology of the word *emotion* dates back to a French word from the 1500s meaning *to stir up.* This makes sense, as the physiology of emotion has a lot to do with nervous system arousal. In the office, we have moved away from sensation and toward suppression. We are taught to suppress feelings and emotions in the name of professionalism. Some lucky leaders with healthy emotional control also have a perspective that allows them to move through their days without becoming emotionally charged. They generally do not allow their nervous systems to be aroused by all that much. They are calm, open-minded, receptive, and able to see all sides of an issue. And they do not operate out of fear.

They are not the majority. Many if not most of us do get emotionally charged about things and suppress our emotion at the office, which damages our health overtime. Or we may control our emotions at the office, then react badly in line at the grocery store, in an e-mail or text to a friend, while sitting in traffic, or with our children or spouses. We call it a *bad mood*, but in reality it's pent-up emotion from feelings we haven't dealt with, a perspective the needs an adjustment, or too imbalanced a life overall. Perhaps our mood is a combination of the three.

Suppressing Emotion

Suppressing our ability to feel our own feelings and be sensitive to what is going on with the person right in front of us is like sleepwalking through life, and it is having deleterious effects on our health. To move toward sensation and away from suppression, we need to begin to know ourselves. When we have a tool like the breath to try deal with feelings as they begin to occur and when we are able to distinguish *perspective* from *truth,* soon to be discussed, things don't stir us up as much to begin with and our well-being improves. With a *beginner's mind*, prepare to introduce yourself to yourself, as though you have just met.

Mirror Exercise

Look at yourself in the mirror when you are alone. Stare directly into your own eyes, so you can see the color of your eyes and the size of your pupil, for five straight minutes, asking yourself who you are (silently or out loud), and see what answers come up. Then ask yourself if you are really that. Then, ask again. Keep asking and take note of the answers, of how they might change along the way.

Many of you will not be able to do this without having a massive sensory experience. You might feel elation, you might cry before the time is up, you might laugh hysterically, or you might do all of the above. Your respiratory rate will change. You will naturally inhale a little more deeply and higher in the chest. Why do you think this happens?

You've experienced a taste of your own spirit, your inner self, and that makes many of us nervous, leading to the physiological response. We typically hide.

Try not to hide.

When you practice observing yourself in your day, you will begin to know yourself so well that you can even anticipate times when you are likely to not be your best self. Ultimately, as a leader, you will foster an acute ability to manage the ebbs and flows with grace and ease and to help others do the same.

Whenever loved ones leave our house, my son gets sad. When he was quite young, he didn't understand how to process his feelings and typically refused to acknowledge their departure by ignoring their goodbyes and looking the other way. I came to realize that this is how he was expressing his grief. He was so sad that he used detachment as a way to quell this sadness and protect himself. As adults, we often do this, too. Even though we possess the communication skills to discuss and express our feelings, we often do not. When we feel anxious, offended, or hurt we could talk about it but too often do nothing. Instead, because it seems easier, we simply change our behavior. We internalize, suppress, ignore, and practice avoidance and detachment, which manifests as distress, unease, and disconnection. It becomes unconscious, a habit, until we no longer even recognize how we are feeling because these habitual actions take over.

Mindfulness and Consciousness

In 2014, *Time* magazine's cover boasted the title "The Mindful Revolution." Mindfulness is now a relatively mainstream catchphrase. This term comes from the Buddhist practice of paying attention to details in a non-judgmental way and is now widely used and studied by cognitive psychologists. In our busy lives some have come to see mindfulness as one more *to do* in an already full life. It happens to be, however, one of the best ways to move out of the feeling of being too busy to begin with.

In classical yoga, what is meant by one aspect of *consciousness* sounds very similar to mindfulness. Becoming conscious in our lives similarly refers to a commitment or intention to accessing a fully awake state of awareness that includes paying full attention to the present moment while practicing non-judgment (vairagya). Yoga is a comprehensive and substantive way of living consciously and when the science is applied allows for real change and transformation. As shared in this text, yoga, as the science of consciousness, also involves genuine efforts toward balance and is mutually reinforcing in its implementation both in the office and at home. This means it helps the leader and the enterprise at the same time.

> Social and emotional conditions can pack a wallop like physical ones, since psychological pain draws on many of the same neural networks as physical pain (Eisenberger and Lieberman 2004); this is why getting rejected can feel as bad as a root canal. Biology of Belief

Consciousness involves wakefulness, being awake or present, paying attention, and making principled choices. In a yoga movement class, we practice slowing the pace of our sequence and paying attention to the subtleties of movement. We fix our gaze, maintain balance, and move consciously, placing limbs, stacking bones, feeling muscle, and noticing thoughts. These on-the-mat seeds, with practice, begin to sprout and become part of our habits off the mat. We learn to become conscious or mindful of our unique habits of behavior to understand how our thoughts and feelings impact our behaviors. We start by becoming aware of our tendencies and our emotions and owning up to them. It is only by noticing and owning up that we can begin to change how we respond to the myriad of stimuli in our lives.

When we are heightened, some of us try to complete things at a frenetic pace, perhaps communicating in a terse or stern manner. By leading others when we are tense, we tax our bodies by engaging the overused fight side of our nervous system and we negatively influence the recipient of our charged emotion. Furthermore, authoritative leadership is an outdated style. Leading through influence has long since been proven the most effective style of leadership that allows a leader to engage his or her team. On the other hand, some of us, when overwhelmed, become frozen and do not know where to begin. We can spend quite some time staring at a list of to dos, with our minds spinning, waiting for an answer or path to present itself. Neither will optimize our ability to lead.

Emotional control is not an easy thing to accomplish for many of us, particularly if we are unsettled financially, emotionally, or otherwise. People who do not feel supported, seen, or listened to, will feel unsettled. When people feel repressed or marginalized they will feel unsettled too. Team environments that are neither supportive nor inclusive are unsettling. Everyone at work requires an advocate and a voice.

Take some time writing down when the emotions listed in the subsequent table show up in your life, both at home and at work. Reflect upon what you've written down, particularly the emotions that do not serve your well-being or your ability to lead. Then, consider using one emotion that you are trying to increase in your life—such as relaxation, confidence, or courage—as a single point of attention in your self-awareness practice, by attempting to fully feel and internalize that emotion. For example throughout your day you can say to yourself: *I am calm and relaxed.* Self-awareness involves a constant effort to live in the present moment and pay complete attention to what is happening there. Try using the same emotion in your meditation practice (discussed further in the Knowledge chapter) for a week or longer. Focus on the emotion by saying it repetitively to yourself in a moving meditation, while walking to work or enjoying a run. When you begin to realize that you can bring up an emotion through your own thoughts, you will discover you have an easier time keeping hold of emotions that support your happiness and effectiveness at work while letting the other ones go. It may seem a futile or silly exercise but the simple act of noticing, of becoming aware, is the first step in this process. Holistic choices are cumulative and each subtle impression has an impact.

> Emotions are like guests. They should be treated very
> nicely and gently, and sent away if they don't fit in.
> —Yogi Bhajan

Consider disallowing—for a full day, several days, or a week—an emotion that does not serve you. This is referred to as an *emotional fast* and is one way to practice letting unhelpful emotions go. It may help you negate an unhelpful emotion by focusing instead on one that is helpful. For example, make a short list of things you are really proud of, and keep it handy to focus on every time you feel anxious. Or, do something that relaxes you when irritation sets in, such as looking at a picture of your kids or your dog.

Emotion Awareness Exercise

Nine Principal Emotions/ Moods (*rasas*)[103]	When do they appear in your life? How often do they appear in your life?
Love (beauty, devotion, affection, compassion)	
Joy (cheerfulness, humor, optimism)	
Wonder (mystery, curiosity, surprise)	
Peace (relaxation, calmness, stillness, contentment)	
Courage (confidence, pride, fearlessness, inner strength, self-esteem)	

Anger (irritation, frustration, jealousy)	
Sadness (sympathy, despair, shame, guilt, neglect, humiliation, rejection, pity)	
Fear (anxiety, worry, distress, tension, apprehension, nervousness)	
Disgust (depression, self-pity)	

People like to be around leaders who are courageous, curious, and calm. Such leaders put people at ease, and they tend to not allow the daily grind to bring them down, using humor, often self-deprecating, to lighten the mood. We want to productively use, temper, or overcome the energy of fear, anger, and sadness and invite more courage, peace, joy, wonder, and love. There is an energetic quality to emotion, and it can serve to deplete us or fill us up. How we use it is our choice. The energy of anger that wants to explode out of us can be productively transmuted into something amazing. Learning to channel strong energy into a tough work assignment or mapping out a strategic plan on a white board may yield some very creative breakthroughs. If you simply use that energy to have an outburst, you waste energy that could have been used toward accomplishment. As already discussed, it is far better to scream in your car until a hint of a smile returns to you face, though, than to bottle that strong energy up and do nothing at all.

Emotional Control Technique: The S.E.V.A Method

If you want others to communicate with you but they are nervous and intimidated, you will never receive an honest report from them. They will instead avoid you and, if they must engage, will offer guarded answers and nervous statements. Or if your team thinks you are too distracted and anxious to listen to what they have to say, they won't bother telling you. It is challenging and can be intimidating to work with someone who tends to fly off the handle, cannot temper his or her emotions, or is visibly stressed. As a consequence, we miss out on having full information about day-to-day

A conscious leader starts from the vantage point that everyone before him or her has something of value to share.

operations. We also miss out on the opportunity to learn from the ideas and insights of the team, thus dampening the creative process and minimizing innovation. An environment where people feel intimidated is a hostile environment, a hostile workplace. The opposite is also true. As the leader, if you are nervous or anxious in a way that has you frozen in fear and indecision, this too, will not serve your leadership. People are more willing to be led by strong, confident, decisive, and discerning leaders. Leaders that are controlled in temperament and vibrant will have an easier time connecting with and engaging people, and consequently motivating and inspiring them.

If you are feeling heightened before you respond to your team, consider trying the next exercise.

The S.E.V.A Method
Sense, Exhale, Visualize and Question, Act

The S.E.V.A. Method is an in-the-moment emotional control technique that can help you foster healthier control of your reactions. *Seva* in Sanskrit means selfless service or something you are doing that helps others. Rooted in the highest common outcome, it would be an enormous and even transformative service to the world if we all made the S.E.V.A. method part of our everyday lives.

Sense. When we are about to react to something because of an abundance of emotion—we are *stirred up*. Like a tuning fork that quivers in reaction to sound, we too move in response to being stirred up. The first step is tuning in to our own sensations, and after we sense this, we move to E.

Exhale. As discussed in detail in the breath section, to calm down we need to focus on a long, smooth, even, and extended exhale. To do this, inhale a super-slow, giant-yet-comfortable breath through the nose, as big as possible without feeling light-headed. Then exhale an even longer, smoother, extended exhale through the nose. A few long, smooth, even and extended exhales invites our whole system to calm down. You may not be completely relaxed, but you may have given yourself a little space to stop from having an instant reaction, which is a part of managing your emotions. Then, move to V.

Visualize and Question. Now we have a moment to visualize what we can do right now that would yield the highest possible outcome in service to ourselves, to others, and to the enterprise. If you are certain that you clearly understand, the highest possible outcome may involve asserting yourself as calmly as possible and then suggesting a time to meet the next day to discuss in more detail, giving you time to calm your nervous system fully and reflect upon the issue at hand. Or if you are too stirred up, you may instead favor faking a smile, thanking the person for their perspective, and walking away to deal privately with your emotions. If you have fear, try to figure out why and ask yourself what is the worst thing that can happen. Build up your stores of confidence by having faith that your best is enough.

Working toward the highest good, though, almost *always* requires further questioning. Seldom are our heightened emotions a result of clear understanding, rather *mis*understanding. Asking clarifying questions may reframe the experience and change the tenure of the meeting. The reflective tool of simply asking yourself or another person "Why?" is a tool worth cultivating. Visualize the questions in your mind that might be unclear and the possible misunderstandings. After you visualize what you will do, then comes A.

Act. Once you have decided upon the best next steps, take the action envisioned. Highest common outcome decisions are those that, in the decades to come, we always feel good about. While you may choose to assert yourself or walk away to calm yourself, learning to always ask clarifying questions will support your ability to make highest common outcome decisions.

While this S.E.V.A method may seem basic, it takes practice. If we can give ourselves that extra space, we move from reacting from the emotionally-charged, fast-processing part of our brain to responding from the rational, slower-processing part. We just need that pause, that moment or two, and we can feel the shift. This practice helps to cultivate a mind that is more open and receptive. If we learn to employ this method, we can dramatically change the nature of a relationship or completely alter the outcome of a really tough situation.

Learn the S.E.V.A. method first for yourself. Notice when you begin to feel the sensations of unhelpful emotions like irritation or anger outside of the office too. Then take audible breaths focusing on a long exhale before you answer a question. Ask questions before you answer questions. Pause and reflect on the highest course and then respond. Begin to observe how it helps your leadership. Then, teach it to your team. Teach your team to take a breath before they answer in meetings. Begin to become rooted in a highest common outcome by committing to the understanding that we are both always wrong and always right, at least in some small way. Find the wisdom in the calm by slowing down and breathing deeply.

The S.E.V.A. Method

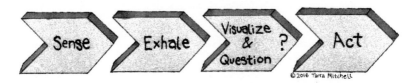

Practice with your family. Pay attention to the facial expressions that you share with your children and your spouse. Look in the mirror and make sure you know what kind of facial expressions you make and imagine how that might impact others in the office. Rolling eyes and grimaces appear immature, make a person look unintelligent, and can also be viewed as condescending. An intelligent, balanced retort with an appearance of equanimity is a more engaging response than eye rolling.

Self-Awareness: Perception and Knowing Oneself

> Ultimately, happiness comes down to choosing between the
> discomfort of becoming aware of your mental afflictions
> and the discomfort of being ruled by them.
> —Yongey Mingyur Rinpoche

Paying attention to how we perceive our lives is another way to get to know ourselves in a deeper way. Our perception of what we see, hear, touch, feel, smell, and taste helps us understand and process the world around us. Perception is a felt sense, shaped by our sensory input. Noticing how we receive our lives through our senses is yet another way to begin to understand ourselves better and make choices that serve our ability to lead. Through awareness comes acceptance.

Sound

We all have events, ideas, and experiences that cause us to perceive the world a certain way. It is interesting to contemplate and try to figure out how and why you, specifically, interact with the world around you the way you do. Growing up in a loud household affects how we feel about noise. As a response to this, we may as adults feel most comfortable in a chaotic, noisy household or, conversely, long to create a more relaxed environment. Some people born and raised in Manhattan can't sleep without the sounds of the city at night, whereas the same sounds may make rural people nervous. Consider the different internal affects of listening to heavy metal, hard rock, rap, blues, R&B, jazz, mantra, or classical music. Likewise, *savasana* or corpse pose, the closing pose in yoga when you merely lie down and relax in silence or to soft music, is unnerving to many new practitioners. The purpose is deep relaxation, quieting the physical body and the senses. It represents an ending only to be followed by a new beginning to take what one has just learned off the mat.

Smell

I once enjoyed a yoga workshop with best-selling author David Romanelli, who discussed the importance of savoring things several times a day, every day—in other words, peppering in little bits of happiness during each of our days. In a discussion about what he called *scent-oriented memories*, he shared that smelling Drakkar Noir cologne still makes him nostalgic and excited, as it may for many of us who grew up in the eighty's.[104] For me, I found the scent of the crown of my babies' heads deeply relaxing, whereas the smell of fermenting fish and putrid water on the banks of Tonle Sap Lake in Cambodia made me retch. Yet my husband stood by relatively unaffected by the smell but quite amused by *my* reaction.

Touch

Some people like a little personal space when speaking, while others get right up in front of your face to have a conversation. This is largely cultural, as are norms of touch. Some people adore massage and others refuse to be touched by a stranger. We have been taught to fear and restrain from touching in our society, although it is common for friends in other countries to hold hands while walking down the street. The intimacy of hugging a friend makes certain people very nervous, so they are stiff as a board when you hug them, yet others embrace and linger.

The point of these musings is merely to shed light on our differences and, accordingly, how we should expect that each member of our team will respond to our work tasks and work environment in very unique ways. With sensation comes truth.

Sensory Exercise

Take some time writing down the things, habits, or events that have shaped how you receive sensory input. Consider what will help you balance overly stimulating input. What causes you to feel tense? Is it meeting with a specific employee? Big presentations? Having too much on your to-do list? What causes you to feel calm? Is it spending time with a mentor? Taking a walk outside? Has listening to music or going to concerts as a teen affected how you receive loud sounds? How do you feel when the phone rings at work or when you hear the beep of text messages and incoming e-mail? Do flashing lights make you nervous? How do you feel when someone touches your arm when they speak with you? Do you like or dislike massage and, specifically, why? Are you repulsed by certain smells like strong fragrance? Do you feel a lot of internal turmoil when you walk past a homeless person? Use the table below as a start point. When we learn to become aware, to understand, to reflect and to sense we begin to accept, welcome, and see the truth—we become conscious.

Through consciousness we find liberation.

Sensory Exercise

	Past events that affect my sensory perception today	Is my sense heightened or diminished as a result? What am I sensitive to in my workday?	Ideas to promote calm and connection
Touch			
Smell			
Sound			
Taste			
Sight			

By observing ourselves, we can first begin to notice when we are feeling tense (heightened, negatively aroused, stressed). Then we can begin to identify when that tension stems from certain environmental stimulus, such as the persistent chiming of our gadgets or the sound of the voice (or the mere sight) of an angry boss. If the chime of our gadgets and the multitude of alerts cause us to tense up, we could choose to minimize them or turn them off. We may see our boss as the *angry boss* because he or she yells or simply because they look like someone else who ranted a lot in our lives. Identifying the things that cause us tension is the first step toward choosing to change our environment or our perspective.

Happiness and Perception

Next, we can remember the things that bring us joy. Happiness, joy, excitement, and enthusiasm are contagious, just like stress. If we remember what we really enjoy, we can begin to pepper little things that please us throughout our day so we can begin to fill our vessel with joy and share that contagion. Write down a top-ten list of your most memorable pleasurable sights, tastes, smells, feelings, and sounds. Get help from your partner or an old friend. Talk and laugh about it. You'll remember something about yourself: the things that make you feel good. Knowing yourself that much better just might translate into a better understanding of your team. As a leader, if *you* are happy and talk about the things you enjoy doing, you will learn more about what your team members like to do, allowing you to better connect, inspire, and motivate them.

Trauma and Perception

All of us have lived through various kinds of trauma that forever changed us and became part of us. Traumas vary on the spectrum from somewhat minor to very severe and what might be minor to one person could be more severe to another. All varieties of trauma affect our mind and our relationship to the world around us in some way.

In college, I opened my eyes at 5:25 one morning to find a masked, shirtless man hovering over my bed, stuffing a rag into my mouth. Luckily, I felt him first, had time to squirm and scream, and he ran. I initially experienced panic attacks and, for many years following, had tremendous anxiety and difficulty sleeping. I needed some light while sleeping, especially in hotels while traveling, for years after. It was difficult to fall asleep, jarred by every small click and sound. I now saw the world as a dangerous and threatening place. In other words, my *perception* had changed. My senses were now acute, and I often lived in a state of high alert. I became frightened if I found myself walking alone, particularly if it was dark. Every sound on the walk made the hair on my arms rise and my heart pound as I gazed around looking for any moving shadow. Even in daytime I sheltered myself, walking briskly and trying not to make eye contact with people. This was my new life. I lived this life for at least a decade until the gift of (mostly) forgetting set in. Not many people know about this event or how it affected me, certainly nobody with whom I've ever worked.

How many co-workers do you think have been attacked, mugged, shot at, or robbed? How many were in combat? How many have lost parents or siblings or friends? How many have had absentee parents? How many have gone through a divorce or are products of a divorce? How many have children with serious illnesses? Who was raised in a household of very limited means, perhaps homeless or nearly so? Who on your team grew up in physically or verbally abusive homes or communities or work environments? How many have suffered psychological abuse or another form of attack? How many grew up in households with alcoholism? How many have had major surgery or cancer? These are all different degrees and forms of trauma. Everyone has something—everybody. What about you? Every person you influence and every member of your team has *something*. And you will never know everything about your employees' lives; nor is it appropriate or necessary. Simply honor the fact that we all have traumas that we are dealing with, which influence our perception and perspective. Understand your own traumas and consider how they influence your perspective and perception. By being present to our traumas and becoming clear on their impacts on our worldview, we can learn how to skillfully work with our nuances in ways that are kind to ourselves and allow us to figure out exactly what we uniquely need to best function as a leader. Compassion and empathy develop out of work like this.

When we understand ourselves well, we also anticipate natural perceptions that do not serve us and can work to mitigate them by altering our perception or making different choices. Becoming skilled at anticipating how we will perceive the contents of our lives takes time, effort, and a great deal of self-awareness. Knowing in advance that a big presentation or an important meeting typically sends you into a panic will allow you to select from a variety of conventions such as diet, rest, exercise, breath work, visualization, music, and meditation to manage your perception well in advance of the panic. Knowing that spending time with certain people makes you feel low or angry will help you establish boundaries (such as time limits) in advance and also to come up with ways to redirect the conversation in a manner that may not impact you as much. When we begin to anticipate how we will perceive certain events, we can improve our ability to discern situations with clarity and understanding. We can also choose to move toward helpful situations and supportive people that allow us to feel safe and grow.

The Mind Made Me: Cultivating Clear Seeing and Vision

> If you suffer it is because of you, if you feel blissful it is because of you. Nobody else is responsible—only you and you alone. You are your hell and your heaven too.
>
> —Osho

Obstacle to Growth: Ignorance (avidya)

As previously introduced, the most important of the five *kleshas* or mental blocks that serve as obstacles to our growth is avidya (ignorance, misconception of reality). As earlier described, this has to do with our belief that our worldview is truth. The belief that things *are* as they are and not appreciating, rather, that they are the understandings we have come to in our minds based upon what we have uniquely learned and experienced. When we believe our understandings are truths, we are closed-minded, closed to other ways of seeing things, mentally blocked off from the broader picture. The concept is interpreted as lacking vision or knowledge, not seeing the truth of things clearly because we are bound by the impressions that fill our memory banks at this time. Our lifetime of impressions help us to shape our unique set of beliefs, which in turn shape our worldview. Our worldview fuels our perspectives on specific things, which shapes our attitude. Our attitude influences our actions and our actions lead to results. With a little space and intention we have the power to alter any member of this chain of events and change the result. Realizing our beliefs and worldview are neither truth nor fact, moves us into a position of clear seeing, inspiration, and vision—a more enlightened state where our minds are open. We are human and our tendency will always be to see our lives via our own mind-stuff, but we transcend this obstacle through humility and the intention to move beyond our own conditioning. Ignorance prevails when one is unable to see humanity and unable to embrace varied worldviews and a matrix of perspectives in an effort to find common ground. The subsequent sections will help you become more aware of and expand your perspective and worldview as a way to transcend this block.

Self-Awareness: Perspective

> There is no right. There is no wrong. There is *only* perspective.

Freedom Within Is Freedom Without

There's a yoga story in the book, *How Yoga Works*, about a young girl jailed for a misunderstanding. She was brutally beaten as the guards tried to get her to admit to something that wasn't true. But she was a wise yoga teacher, even in her youth, and she decided to change her perspective to see the inside of her cell as no different from the outside. She decided to treat her life as though she were free. She continued to practice and teach yoga to her jailers from her cell, in captivity, finding freedom in her decision. Among the many ways to interpret this is to say that freedom within is freedom without.

A Pen's Possibilities

Contemplate the meaning of an ink pen for a moment. What does that mean to you? When on a safari, I handed out little bags with a pen and notebook to orphans in Africa. To these children, a pen represented the opportunity to become something in life, because they knew they needed to learn to write, but writing implements were scarce. To a dog, a pen could be a playtoy. To a one-year-old, a pen could be something to chew on. To us, a pen is a common writing utensil. To aboriginal tribes, a pen could be fuel for a fire or a tool. To all of us, under the right circumstances, we could change our perspective of a pen and a pen could be a weapon.

Clearly, our perspective of the pen is self-created, based upon two things: (a) what we have been taught and exposed to up until that very moment in time when we encounter the pen, and (b) what we exactly need the pen to be at that very moment. This is true about our view of life as well: we create our view of our lives based on our perspective, which is shaped by a myriad of events in our lives, things such as upbringing, education, age, relative level of financial wealth, and material ownership. It's also based on what we think we need—what we are looking for or what we want to be true.

Generosity?

On the same safari, we also gave some of our old clothes and shoes to our guide, Emmanuel, who had a lot of mouths to feed. From our perspective, we had plenty, these were disposable, we wanted to help, and they needed some. From his perspective, it was a stunning act of generosity. Generosity? Emmanuel told us that his daughter, who fit into my old clothes, said it was like the *best* Christmas of her life!

The Choices We Make

Emmanuel's needs are at the basic level of food and clothing. At this level, we have fewer choices; our needs are simple and necessary—a couple of pieces of clothing, food, and shelter. But once we move beyond such basic needs, we enter a huge realm of *choice*. Good leaders understand this and take responsibility for all of their words and actions. Mentally strong leaders are not shackled by fear and feel empowered to change course and make different choices. Most everything in our lives is a want and a desire to satisfy a self-created need. This is where our worldview shapes our imagined life, the stories that our mind makes up and clips together. There are, of course, certain facts of life that are actual facts, but much of our lives and worldviews are not based on facts.

As kids, we are told what our worldview is supposed to be by our parents, and we try to match up to it through our choices—even though we don't always appreciate why. As adults, we gather insights from friends, colleagues, television, newspapers, magazines, and the Internet. We may choose to do no further investigation on certain things and believe exactly what someone told us. Or we may choose to learn more on our own and may consciously or unconsciously target sources of information to prove what we want to believe that satisfies our imagined life anyway. Or finally we may choose to triangulate across a wide variety of differing sources, including discussions with people having divergent views, leveraging our full capacity for reason, and then shape our worldview and beliefs with expanded insight. All of the information we receive helps us imagine how our lives *should* be and the choices we consequently make. We often even pressure ourselves to match our vision through the choices we make. In some way, we completely make up our ideas of what we should and must be doing in our days.

What we experience in the minutes and hours of each day is a function of the choices we make, including how we choose to see things, our perspective. When we begin to appreciate that the events and happenings in our lives are a function of the choices we make and how we choose to see things, we can begin to discern the message we are meant to receive from our experiences. Each happening is a moment to be savored, and every moment teaches us something about ourselves. We can then use those messages, those teaching moments, to guide our lives. Nobody benefits, however, when we learn nothing and allow our imaginations and its imagined life to run wild and interfere with our well-being.

Our Imagined Life

Our imagined life is a misconception that clouds our perception and can easily lead to always looking toward the future or clinging to our past, trying to meet that ever-changing vision of how our lives should be. Yoga is the continual process of letting go of the past and the future, so we can anchor ourselves fully in the present. It is very difficult to do. For example, dwelling on the fact that we could do a yoga pose last week but are unable to do it today is a misconception, a mistaken thought. A lot has happened in seven days that has affected our body and mind in the present moment. Apply that thinking to your biggest transitions in life and the consequent changes that you may or may have not found savory. Focusing on how we feel in that moment and working hard in our current experience, rather than missing what we used to be able to do or thinking toward what we might do tomorrow, represents our yoga in action. And such is life.

Poverty Mentality

I grew up in Pittsburgh, during a tough time with the demise of the steel industry, which once served as a very good livelihood for many. One of the times that my stepfather was laid off, his unemployment benefits included large blocks of cheese and powdered milk. My family seemed to be in a constant struggle for money. We wore hand-me-downs. We did not waste food. We did not have a room full of toys, as my kids do today. We did not go on grand vacations; we went camping. It was my job to make the milk, which was thin, chunky, looked gray, and tasted terrible. I, like many others in similar situations, grew up with a poverty mentality. Upon reflection, I see how this worldview has shaped the importance that I have always placed on my career and my desire to earn a lot of money. I am now aware that I am resource-rich, so there is no need to cling to this poverty mentality, yet it remains. Our worldview is often charged with emotion. It's not that easy to move beyond our conditioning, but awareness is an important first step.

Strong Women

Growing up in a household where my mother was the primary breadwinner helped to shape my worldview where I see women as strong, capable, and independent workers and earners. The idea of a stay-at-home mother is foreign to me, a huge departure from the realities of my childhood. My perspectives shape my experience in life through the choices I choose to make. When you understand the unique ways that you experience life, you will be able to make choices each day that help you stay balanced and open-minded and to not succumb to the self-created pressures you put upon yourself. Perhaps you will even open up to something new and become more meaningfully engaged in your work and your life.

Our Unique Perspective

Every single object, every event in our lives, everything we do, everything we think, everything we say—all of it is based upon an accumulation of our imprints that shapes our perspective. At work, our perspective determines precisely how we uniquely see everything. Contemplate the very many ways there are to see:

- every decision we make
- every deal we win or fail to win
- every task on our to-do list, every priority in our day
- every manager who manages us, every employee we manage
- every meeting we participate in and every one that we do not
- every coworker and every team we work with
- every department, every function, and its importance
- every e-mail, phone call, and text message
- every client we win or lose
- every quarterly return, every annual return
- every customer we service
- every competitor
- every operating plan, strategic plan, and planning meeting
- every product we make
- every service we offer
- every vendor that services us

Self-Awareness: Worldview

Worldview Exercise

Take some time completing the table below. Include all of the things that you know shaped your worldview and your beliefs. Consider some of the following questions as you move through the table: Do you feel you should live to work or work to live? Growing up, did you see your family working tirelessly? Did you see them also at play? How has this shaped your worldview? Were education and completing homework paramount in your household? Did your parents discuss politics at the dinner table? Did both of your parents work? Did you play team sports? Do you have siblings? Did you regularly attend a house of worship with your family? Were children to be seen and not heard, or were you running around freely? Did you go camping? Did you play in the woods? What has shaped your worldview and beliefs? After completing the table, consider how aspects of your worldview have served your leadership. Which aspects have made you more or less open, receptive, fair, objective, realistic, and pragmatic? Which aspects to you cling to so tightly that you lose emotional control and are not able to remain calm when certain subjects arise?

Worldview Exercise

	Worldview and Beliefs
Nature of Work	
Importance of Leisure Time	
Purpose of Education	
Importance of Family	
Role of Faith	
Role of Children	
Role of Spouse	
Role of Government	
Personal Responsibility	
Environmental Stewardship	
How Time Should be Used	

Importance of Community	
Volunteerism and Philanthropy	

Interference

If we feel someone or something interferes with our imagined worldview, we can become anxious, stressed, or depressed. If we cling too much to our imagined life, we become very impatient toward the interference and actually make it much more consequential. When we focus intensely on remedying the interference so that we can continue pursuing our imagined life, it can hinder our well-being. But when we choose to recognize that we create our worldview in our own minds, we can also choose to recognize that we have merely labeled things as interferences, and can instead see them as teachers in our path of life. This awareness helps you to more easily release into what comes and allow life to gently move through you. How might that feel?

Living in the Present

In our modern society, we have changed our wiring as adults, as teens, and as children, and we find ourselves in a rat race, running on a wheel with no sign of stopping. Operating at such a detached, frenetic pace makes us stressed, ill, and sad. Focused on chasing the future, on rushing and coveting, we become exhausted, impulsive, impatient, and self-interested.

Urgency is a perspective. When we treat everything as urgent and mandatory we have no space and our ability to lead becomes limited. Urgency necessitates that we lean on our current beliefs and perspective to get things done quickly rather than opening up to the unknown, to opportunity, to the creativity that leads to

Living the Dream

© 2016 Tarra Mitchell

innovation. If we search inside ourselves for the answers we seek, we might just find ourselves living more in the present rather than shackled and racing to an ever-changing imagined future. This involves honoring ourselves, being realistic about what is possible for us to accomplish in our days, while still maintaining our well-being. Take a fresh look at your list of things that you consider urgent or mandatory in your workday and in your life. Do you tend to chase the next big thing? Is fear driving your life?

Revisiting Anxiety

As defined by the Anxiety and Depression Association of America (ADAA), anxiety that does not go away and interferes with your life is called an *anxiety disorder* and is closely related to obsessive-compulsive disorder and post-traumatic-stress disorder. [105] According to the CDC, one in ten Americans aged twelve and over were taking anti-depressant medication between 2005 and 2008.[106] One in ten! This represents an increase of *over 400 percent* from the 1988–1994 period.[107] Many of the newest antidepressant medications are prescribed to treat anxiety disorders.[108] Anxiety disorders affect 18 percent of American adults.[109] The estimated cost of anxiety disorders in the United States in the 1990s was over $42 billion, representing one-third of the country's mental health bill at that time.[110]

Assuming we are beyond the level of acute poverty, our stress and anxiety becomes a function of the choices we make in our day influenced by our worldview and our perspective. We owe it to ourselves, to our teams, and to our families to become self-aware and consider whether our perspectives and worldview serve our well-being by affording us balance. Work toward accessing the balance of behavior that allows you to be healthy in body and controlled in mind so you can be a clear-thinking, open-minded, pragmatic and unbiased leader. Walking the path in the center, right between lots of effort and too much ease, is the balanced path where thinking is clear and judgment is sound. It is the path where we have learned to let go of results and accept what comes. When we no longer try so hard to keep up with the Joneses we will find connection, gratefulness, and happiness. Our team likes us more and our friendships deepen.

Never Give Up. Always Let Go.

Vairagya is one of two foundational tenets in yoga and refers to detachment from results. This idea of letting go was first mentioned in the discussion on tapas. It eases the edges and helps us welcome the flow of life. The other is *abhyasa*, or ongoing, uninterrupted and earnest practice. The two terms together ask us to work very hard but let go of—or be emotionally neutral toward—what happens. Vairagya is derived from the word *viraga,* meaning without or free from (*vi*) attachment or passion (*raga*). When we speak of vairagya to students in a yoga asana class, we reference letting go of the results of our actions, for example—how deeply you can go in a forward fold today—and instead live in the present and be okay with what comes. Yoga involves a disciplined effort to anchor yourself firmly in the present and not concern yourself with the past or future. The ongoing practice of letting go of attachments allows leaders to operate without the interference of strong emotions.

In our culture, this idea of not seeking a result or an outcome can be a foreign one. It seems to go against the idea of progress and productivity. The truth is, while it's important to work toward goals, we have no control over the actual result. We only have control over our effort and actions. There are a million different inputs that cause a result to happen. To think that we ourselves control all of that is an illusion, and when we link satisfaction or happiness to these results, we set ourselves up for stress and feelings of failure.

This letting go of results and outcomes is a challenge common among leaders who are often overachievers by nature. In 1998, during a rocky time for the stock market, I was working for a team of portfolio managers in Frankfurt when the Russian government devalued the ruble, rapidly sending the Eastern Europe emerging markets fund down the tubes. The team was lead by a very well known fund manager whose temperament aligned directly with the results of the market. He was friendly and fun one day and raging the next. His mood was tied directly to the results of the market, inextricably linked to something so very out of his control. His hot-temperedness was not good for his blood pressure or health, to be certain, nor did it support the engagement of his team, because, while we really liked him, we were afraid to talk to him on those days!

Letting go of results and relinquishing control is certainly one of my biggest personal challenges. Rolf Gates gave us this great way of thinking about this during his yoga teacher training: "Never give up. Always let go." Consider establishing that intention in your life, and see where it leads you.

Decided Positivity

Self Awareness: Outlook and Speech

We Find What We Look For

> There is nothing either good or bad, but thinking makes it so.
> —Shakespeare

Our perspective is colored by our current attitude or mood. Our attitude or mood tints our perspective in helpful or unhelpful ways. Our attitude sets our start point for the day, and we can choose to establish it as positive, negative, indifferent, joyful, curious, or opportunistic for example. Every time we choose a different attitude we see very different things as we move through our lives. And we consequently make different choices. In other words, we get what we look for. Good leaders maintain a positive attitude by reframing messages so they are rooted in optimism and seeing all sides in a balanced way.

Some years back I had the pleasure of seeing Jeanne Robertson, a six-feet-two, then seventy-year-old female comedian with a thick Southern drawl. She began touring professionally after discovering she was humourous during her year-long stint as Miss North America many years ago. Her gig is about finding the humor in everyday life, in those things that we would wish we could change but can't. Her message was that *you find what you are looking for.* Being six feet two since the age of thirteen was not always pleasant, and Jeanne ushers quite a bit of laughs sharing stories about how people tactlessly react to her stature. She finds the humor in the aging process, every single ache, pain, bandage, and wrap, and shares how spooking her husband in the middle of the night on one of his frequent potty trips adds some spice to the relationship. She has a wonderful gift of finding laughter in everyday life. *You find what you are looking for* is a simple yet powerful statement and such a wonderful way to elaborate upon influences to our perspective.

Word Choices

> We don't see things as they are; we see things as we are.
>
> —Anais Nin

We see and describe our lives and our work using a wide variety of labels such as interesting, good, busy, stressful, boring, or uneventful. Our words are choices, too. Unfortunately, too many of us use the words *busy* and *stressed.* Words used repetitively establish how you are choosing to see your life and you will intentionally or unconsciously attract more of what you seek, which validates your perspective. When stress and busy is the vision we are seeking, what we are on the lookout for, stress and busy are what we get. Those who look for laughter find it. When we look for grace and beauty, we find it, too. When we root our vision in joy, happiness, and love, we see it in abundance. We see it, because we are now *looking* for it.

You find what you are looking for.

It should now be clear that much of what we see as stressful in our everyday lives is based on our perspective. I am not refering here to physical stress like toiling in a coal mine, breathing soot, and trying to protect your ears from the sound of explosions. Clearly, these physical stressors will negatively impact health. I am also not speaking of the temporary stressors that happen if we find ourselves in a fender bender or contract a bad case of the flu. Although serious, those things happen, and then at some point they are over. The stress I am referring to is a reflection of how we choose to see ourselves and our lives in general, which can be due to the lack of balanced choice-making or due to simply our chosen perspective. Everyday life stress is, in this case, psychosomatic. Our stress has a lot to do with how we process and interpret the world around us. This kind of stress is negative and heavy. When we consistently seem to process and interpret our everyday normal lives as *stressful*, we attract more stress and often do nothing about it. Stressed people see every activity as burdensome, yet pack on more, never say no, and neither take time to decompress nor look for everyday joy. Overtime this leads to disorder or disease in the body and, important for leaders, affects the decisions we make and how we behave toward ourselves and others. We can decide how we choose to see the contents of our lives. We can choose to see a full (busy) life as an abundant life. And make choices to keep it abundant, which will necessitate time for self-care. We choose how we want to see our own story.

The Scrolling Reel

Every moment or event in our lives leaves impressions or imprints in our memory, called *samskaras* in yoga, of things we have seen, heard, felt, or thought. Our memories are like a really long film reel with clips and images scrolling along. Each time we take an action, think a thought, or feel an associated feeling, we create more imprints, which build and become stronger or more permanent as we age. When something happens to us, the imprints of our prior learnings pop into our minds, and we then create a series of labels, of adjectives, with which to associate this event. We arrange things into their boxes; this gives them meaning and lends sense to our world. It also makes us feel safe. When everything fits neatly into its box all is right in the world. But when it doesn't, we may feel fear and chaos and seek to preserve our view of what is right and sensible.

The Stories We Tell

Our perspective, our imagined view of how our life is today and must be in the future, is based on the stories we tell ourselves, stories we cling to as fact. As we've covered, this is *self-made*. We create the story of our lives based upon how we choose to see every single moment and all the various contents of our lives—the parts we see and importantly, *the parts we choose not to see.* Stated differently, our story is based on the parts we enhance and those we ignore. Then we invite the emotions that match the story. The story can be thought of as your biography, and in the words of bestselling author Caroline Myss, "Your biography becomes your biology." Our biography—along with all of its inherent molecules of emotion—becomes part of our physical bodies. It is very difficult for us to move beyond the level of the story; clinging to our perspective is human nature. In the end, however, it is through our perspective that we choose to see our current lives and our past in a way that causes us to be upset, angry, and stressed or calm, happy, and centered. There are pure facts or truths that are objective and absolute, and then there are the ways we *interpret* those facts and truths and deal with them. From getting cancer to losing a job to getting a divorce to having your house burn down, many people in similar situations will come through those challenges very differently. We own and control our conception of the various events in our lives.

I spent most of my life forcing and controlling things. Against all odds, I forced my way up a difficult-to-climb career ladder, even though such brute force of will did not feel good and didn't help me develop camaraderie along the way. As a woman, over time, I imagined that I had to do this because of my perception of a glass ceiling and a perceived token female problem. Whether legitimate or not, I perceived it to be true, and so I chose to work harder to ensure my advancement. Even more consequential, I also imagined that I had to do more to prove myself worthy because I lacked an Ivy League MBA amongst a sea of them in my field. Was my insecurity really because I was a woman or because I did not have an Ivy League MBA? Or were there other drivers of my hard-charging, bull-in-a-china-shop, take-no-prisoners behavior? My dad, who I love dearly, is the most authentic man that I know and has incredibly strong willpower. He dropped out of high school, joined the Marines, and became an alcoholic (now sober and proud of himself, as am I). Do any of these things have an impact on my beliefs about myself? Or perhaps the source was something else, such as growing up financially poor with memories of handouts and picket lines? Was it watching my extraordinary mother going to college while we were young only to then work tirelessly to offer my sister and me a chance at a *better* life? What does a better life look like anyway? Did I really deserve a good job in one of the most elite financial services sectors in the world? You can see how this train of thought is negative, limiting, expands insecurity, and is not rooted in inner strength. Whatever it was, my perspective dictated my behavior. It wasn't until I was able to step back and put in the inner work necessary to clearly see the story I was telling myself that I was able to consider other ways of looking at my life.

Limiting Beliefs

> Beyond our ideas of right-doing and wrong-doing, there is a field. I'll meet you there.
>
> —Rumi

Limiting beliefs prevent you from reaching deep within and becoming the inspiring, passionate, and innovative leader you were meant to be. Such thinking can also be a form of self-sabotage stemming from the manner in which we choose to color and create our story. My history, for example, can be interpreted with triumph and serve as a source of pride—or I can see it as a weakness and a source of shame. Either way, the interpretation is a figment of our imagination. If we allow our stories to taint our understanding of who we truly are and why things happen to us, we get it all wrong. We make choices and judgments based upon false realities and misconceptions, upon how we interpret our stories, and upon our imagination. The alternative is just allowing things to unfold naturally, while standing firmly in our inner strength, practicing gratitude, and going with the flow of life.

We choose how we see our story.

We decide whether a person, place, thing, decision, or event (henceforth *object* or *object of attention*) is good or bad based upon our perspective. We give the object detail, description, a label. We associate it with adjectives based upon our worldview, shaped by our perspective. Then we judge, opine, assess, criticize and size things up. We do that, and our set of descriptors will be different from the person's next to us.

The first step to becoming clear on the stories you tell yourself is becoming an observer of yourself in your life. Notice your habits and beliefs. If they are limiting you, begin to proactively intervene, regain control, and rise above the old, unhelpful story. We are strong when we believe in ourselves and take care of ourselves. Paint a new vision of strength and love, success and peace, connection and accomplishment.

The first step is awareness by observing and being a witness to yourself in your life.

Stories at Work

At work we choose to see things as good or bad, as opportunities or as threats, as successes or failures. We choose to see things as urgent or low priority. We choose to see things as effective or ineffective, as burdens or of critical importance. Work toward seeing the hidden potential in everyone and everything, learning to differentiate truth from perspective. From this place, former obstacles and challenges become opportunities. We begin to make more reasonable choices and move toward a stress-free way of living. We begin to create a perspective that focuses on the process and not the outcome. Knowing that you always do your best and you always seek to improve, you have an understanding that whatever the result may be, it represents but one ripple in the sea of life, a sea that has many ripples, many waves, and many torrents, each of which eventually settles back into the vast magnificence.

The Pause

Quieting the mind and sitting in stillness allows the cloud of misperception to vanish and clarity to emerge. This means seeing work situations and team members with a truly blank slate so that we can be objective, unbiased, and reasonable. To do so, we first must notice our habits of labeling things and recognize that these habits come from our perspective, which in turn comes from our pre-conditioning. Then we can begin to pause, reflect, and consider alternative ways of seeing things.

This pause is important and powerful. Rolf Gates once said "Music is the space between the notes." Inspiration, too, is found in the space, the pause. The pause connects a thought to the spoken word and to a decision or idea. That very pause has the power to alter the thought and what comes next. That pause invites the calm, objective, unbiased, humane, neutral place where choices can be ethically oriented and behavior upstanding. The pause can be a mere instant, but in that instant you allow the shift from reaction to reasoning in your brain.

> In the stillness of a posture we find the teacher, if we are the willing student open to learning.

By embodying the pause at work and moving from reaction to responses and then even to reasoning, solutions become more inclusive, ideas scalable, and creativity flourishes. Yoga philosophy considers that reasoning happens through a triad of direct perception, seeking knowledge, and guidance from discerning authorities. Reasoning is not instantaneous. The process of reasoning requires some time and effort. What we are describing is a mind that is open. With a mind that is open, life becomes a series of questions, such as "What if?" and "Why not?" Then genius and innovation can emerge.

Changing Your Perspective

Elevating Speech

Vendor is a word choice. *Partner* is also a word choice. Do you call third parties at work vendors or partners? Does your word choice reflect your behavior? Does it reflect how you treat them? Perhaps some you call vendors, others partners. Vendor has a certain connotation of inferiority that seems to require less respect, whereas partner implies you are all in this together. Do you use words that create unnecessary hierarchy and division? How might you change your vocabulary to bring together parties toward a united vision? How will this serve your ability to connect with and engage your team?

Angry Boss

Take the case of the so-called angry boss. When we always imagine a boss as angry, we label and see him or her as *the angry boss* before we even experience the person's actual temperament in that moment. Our bodies tense up and our tone of voice changes when we expect the angry boss rather than just *the boss*. A change in perspective will help us move from the image of the angry boss to simply the boss—and, eventually, maybe even to the boss with a lot of responsibility and multiple kids who is just doing his or her best. When we do this, we can perhaps feel empathetic and develop the courage to be more open with him or her. This is not easy work, but it will go a long way toward changing perspective in a way that will help you develop healthy relationships and meaningful connections. Try replacing negative words with more factual and compassionate words, like anxious or indecisive with unsupported and overworked, scattered with over stimulated, and apathetic with not challenged and underutilized. Consider the new words with the many other people who you interface with at work: employee, client, customer, or vendor. How might shifting your word use change your outlook toward a person and allow you to connect with and engage with him or her better?

Cultivating Empathy

In addition to being a key component to the pinnacle principle of kindness and non-harming already discussed, cultivating empathy is a skillful and positive way to adjust your perspective and circumvent unhelpful feelings, attitudes, and insensitivity toward the needs of other people. From an empathetic frame of reference, you are better able to connect with and engage others. This in-the-moment tactic involves seeing the person before you differently, in a more vulnerable light. Consider this tactic in conjunction with the self-awareness work to try to figure out what in you is causing you to be bothered by a person or to develop a negative attitude toward them to begin with.

If we put ourselves in the shoes of another, try to come to terms with the pressures he or she is under, and imagine all the possible challenges that person may have, then suddenly we can address him or her with a dose of empathy. We have also changed our perception, because now this person no longer causes us tension, irritation, or unease in some way. Instead, we merely see him or her as a human being who is struggling too, as we all do. Given our differences, it may be helpful to see your team as a group of people from different cultures. Cultural sensitivity, similar to empathy, has us practicing a host of things slightly differently from what we may naturally be used to. We become more forgiving, and it allows us to figure out how to communicate in a language the other person understands to get him or her to do the work that needs to be done. How can you operate with your team members a little differently so you may perceive them with intrigue and act with sensitivity? Like a game of cause and effect, testing various communication styles in intentional ways will allow you to figure out what will yield the outcome you want—team engagement. Can this experiment help you begin to perceive your team members with curiosity and wonder? Empathy is discussed with regularity in leadership circles, and cultivating empathy has been found to be a key way to competently work with others. How might cultivating empathy reduce your stress levels and enhance your ability to connect with others? How does it enhance your ability to motivate the team? What might happen to the bottom line if all leaders were to conduct themselves in this manner at work? What might happen to the top line?

From Perspective to Positivity

Words are not a small thing.
Words are the real power.
The whole universe is a magnetic field.
If we create positive words, we feel love.
If we create negative words, we feel hatred.
Communication is a gift to know, to understand,
and to realize.
Let your words be straight, simple, and said with a smile.

—Yogi Bhajan

Fact-Based Thinking and Fact-Based Speech

One way to move away from negative self-talk is to move toward fact-based speech. Now that you understand emotion in your life, you can remove the emotional influences from your speech and become adept at discerning fact from fiction. Fact-based speech is a way to practice stripping away the coloring, the opinion, the beliefs, and the emotions—whether they are yours or others'—and simply state the facts. This interim step is an important predecessor to moving toward less negative, more neutral, and even a more positive way of being. Once we can communicate effectively using just facts, then we can choose to overlay positive, helpful, optimistic words, if and when it is helpful to do so. Intentionally applying a positive tone and reorienting your words helps to establish a positive outlook and attitude. While this section is directed toward people who tend to go negative, if you are the type who sugarcoats everything just know that people may see right through the sugarcoating and disengage. The practice of fact-based speech may allow you to come across in a more authentic way to others and connect better with your team. There is a balance to everything.

Negative thinking, self-talk, and speech directed toward yourself or toward others is limiting and gives your mind a bunch of useless fodder on which to ruminate. This wastes your time and energy. Negative self-talk contributes to insecurity and stems from fear, stress, sadness, or anger. It takes away from your strength of character, your confidence, and your resolve. This is particularly true when it becomes persistent. Make a decision to take measures to remove all negative thinking from your vernacular and your thoughts. Visualize a red stop sign in your mind every time a negative word pops into your mind. Stop and revert to a neutral, clear frame of mind, orienting your thoughts back to pure facts.

The exercise below focuses initially on self-talk, the inner voice. The first list represents sentence introductions that are filled with doubt and uncertainty. The table below offers possible words to complete the sentences. Create the unhelpful sentences that you know you direct toward yourself or others. For the next week, pay attention to your thoughts and words. Each time you think something negative, critical, condescending, or judgmental, try to stop and reflect upon all the statements and words below that you find yourself saying in your mind or out loud. Through this practice, you will begin to discover whether negative self-talk is limiting your growth.

Statements

1. If only I were ...
2. I wish I was a better ...
3. If they had a better ...
4. Why can't they just be ...
5. Why aren't I able to simply ...
6. If they only had more ...
7. I wish I were more ...

Words

Leader	Healthier	Happy
Thin	Energetic	Intelligent
Athletic	Motivated	Attractive
Funny	Body	Fit
Confident	Nice	Listener
Empathetic	Parent	Sibling
Child	Academics	Training
Skills	Personality	Schooling
Time management	Concentration	Resolve
Sleep	Eating Habits	Friend
Time	Detailed	Technical
Job	Income	Projects
Boss	Co-workers	House
Patience	Successful	Wealthy
Powerful	Confident	Strong
...	...	...

You may be familiar with the field of positive psychology, which encourages positive speech as a way to help you see things in a more favorable light. Fact-based speech is a little different. Fact-based speech is neither negative nor positive. It does not look toward the future but is neutral and anchored in the present. It is simple and without drama. This kind of speech helps cultivate a neutral attitude of equanimity and allows you space to see the bigger picture. Over time, the peaks and valleys in life may not affect you so much. In his book *Meditation for your Life*, Bob Butera, PhD and founder of The YogaLife Institute, discusses a similar concept he calls *pure thinking* that influenced this section.[111]

Here are some examples from my own life. The fact-based speech below stems from things that I find challenging. My corresponding negative self-talk follows in parenthesis. It is easy to sense the emotion in the parentheticals.

Fact-Based Speech

- I try to cook healthy dinners for my family to keep our immune systems strong. (I loathe cooking dinner.)
- I try to go to bed early so I am well rested. (I try to go to bed early because I'm exhausted.)
- I am tired a lot because I am in my mid-forties and have very active young children. (If I did different exercises or ate different foods, maybe I'd have more energy. What's wrong with me?)
- I have childcare to help with my kids while I work, because I find intellectual work satisfying. When I am satisfied in this way I am more present and patient with my kids. (I feel guilty about leaving my kids in another's care so I can work.)
- Everyone has opinions, so I practice patience during election season. (I loathe the negative political bantering.)
- It has taken me a long time to write this book because I am scholarly and I want it to be thoughtful and useful, and that takes time. (Why can't I just finish this book already? Why is it taking so long?)
- Recognizing that I have too high expectations for myself, I practice patience and understanding when others are not responsive or thorough. (If only they'd get the work done in a reasonable amount of time and complete it fully.)
- I recognize that everyone is on their own journey, even if they make choices that end up hurting them. (Isn't it clear to them that they are making the wrong choices when they keep hurting themselves?)

To move beyond neutrality and cultivate some positivity you may choose to do this exercise a second time by changing the introductory statements to *I am* or *I have a great* and write down statements using the list of words that are true and reflective of your skills, competencies, and positive traits. Build self-esteem and determination by replacing the old unhelpful statements with the already true positive statements and say them to yourself often. Build a more positive attitude across the team by deciding to be positive yourself. Cultivate positivity and optimism in an authentic way by choosing to see the opportunity in adversity using intelligence. Find the factually positive angle, which is different from sugarcoating. This would be a way to move toward positive speech and building more positivity in your life. While negative self-talk is self-defeating and remembering what you are good at is necessary, inner strength is fortified when we learn to be content simply with what is.

In a YouTube video, BK Shivani calls the process of removing negativity from our vernacular a reboot for the brain. Our mind becomes fixated, stuck like a hung computer. She uses the interesting metaphor of pressing the

Ctr+Alt+Delete buttons in our brain to let go of the past burdens and restart fresh by looking for alternate ways of thinking. By considering the teachings in this book you are already beginning to do the inner work necessary to affect the outer experience. You are pressing the Ctr+Alt+Delete buttons and looking at life through fresh eyes.

In Pursuit of Equanimity

> Equanimity: evenness of mind, especially under stress.
> —Merriam-Webster dictionary

Mental Self-Sabotage

In the fascinating read, *The Biology of Belief,* stem cell biologist Bruce H. Lipton, PhD, offers his own discussion of the brain's built-in negativity bias, previously introduced. We play upsetting events from the past again and again in our minds, which strengthens the neural associations between an event and its painful feelings. This takes us out of the present moment and away from productive time spent. Allowing our minds, our simulator, to run wild and focus too much on all things negative builds negative strength, negative neural structure. It is like a cycle of violence. This includes how we see things. If we have to make a difficult decision at work and we consume ourselves with the *difficulty* of the task, it will become a bigger issue for us. By becoming aware of our mind-play and focusing energy in helpful directions, we can stop the cycle and build more positive neural structure.

> ...in relationships, it typically takes about five positive interactions
> to overcome the effects of a single negative one. (Gottman 1995)
> —The Biology of Belief

A lot of our negative self-play is a form of self-sabotage. We beat ourselves up about things we believe that we fail to accomplish or behaviors that we know to be not so upstanding. Practicing self-compassion is one way to acknowledge you are human and will inevitably make mistakes. Rather than giving additional weight and negative neural structure to the things that you are not doing well, invite warmth and compassion to yourself. Focus on betterment and improvement in the present time. This helps preserve self-worth and makes us more resilient as we seek to cultivate a more positive mindset focusing energy on our good qualities and attributes. A resilient leader possesses the inner strength to pick herself or himself back up after being knocked down and to press on with determination and drive. Supporting yourself in this manner opens your heart to others too, allowing you to be more accepting of their mistakes and idiosyncrasies. From that place, you can operate in a more reasonable and empathetic manner.

> The root of compassion is compassion for oneself.
> —Pema Chodron.

Hanson and Mendius use the concept of *darts* in our thinking.[112] The darts are our reactions. When a loved one or a person of importance in your life says something toward you that you find hurtful in some way, your reaction is like a series of darts. The first dart is a felt sense, maybe shock, sadness, or a felt ache in the heart or pit of the stomach. They explain that a deeper, more permanent dart like a scar forms, made of a wide variety of unhelpful feelings, like being unworthy, undeserving, or fears of being alone. These deeper darts have a tendency to mirror or stem out of scars (unhelpful belief patterns) generated earlier in your life, perhaps during childhood. We create and more likely *awaken* these scars all the time. As leaders, we owe it to ourselves to do our best to act in a manner that does not scar ourselves and focus on building up our teams and supporting them no matter what. Show support even when you are letting someone go. If you know in your mind–body—if all of your logic and all of your senses are telling you that it is in their best interest to find work elsewhere—then support them fully. By understanding how these darts play out in our own minds, we can choose to soften tough conversations, seek to balance dialogue with something positive, and importantly clearly communicate a view of a positive path forward that makes sense. If they are upset, invite questions and dialogue, and give them some time to absorb the information in the view of the new vision you've laid out.

Become aware of your reactions and your unconscious habits of communication that throw darts, and seek to cultivate new habits that better serve you and your team. We can choose to not get upset by a person displaying anger toward us and instead recognize that the words directed toward us are coming out of the emotions of the other person. We can choose to understand that the emotion has nothing to do with us. Beginning to understand that everyone carries their own set of mind-stuff is one way to begin to cultivate different habits. If someone says something that feels hurtful to you, ask clarifying questions and tell them that it felt hurtful. This simple process will do more to change their future habits and neutralize any impacts the words may have on us than internalizing and overthinking what was said ever will. Encourage people to discuss hot topics through active inquiry, honesty, and openness; the root of the issue is often not what it may seem but will come about through extended dialogue. Make people connect and talk issues through until you can see how to work through the issues, so they can re-engage fully in work. Festering emotional issues are problematic. A wound that festers too long leads to infection, pain, and discomfort that spreads throughout the body. Proactively work through emotionally-charged issues so they do not fester and become toxic.

Importantly, practices like these do not have with it a goal that the organization becomes some soft, feely place. I don't believe it's practical to walk around on a cloud at the office in a state of joy and Zen. But organizations should not be full of a bunch of stressed-out and unhealthy people. It is our responsibility to do better as leaders. Understanding how our thoughts and words impact others and ourselves is a basic step to managing stress, elevating your leadership, and connecting better with your team.

Cultivating Equanimity

Once you are more intimate with your unique ways of being, you can begin the practice of cultivating equanimity in your efforts at work. *Equanimity* means a state of composure, even-temperedness, stability, and calmness that one can psychologically maintain. It is undisturbed by our own emotions or those of others. Equanimity is a stress-free state of mind, and mind–body research demonstrates that our hormone levels are indicative of this state.[113] How we are being is actually imprinted into our physical being. In the frenzy at the office, amidst a work crisis, or when encountering challenging personalities, as a leader it is particularly important to keep your cool. This is another way to think about maintaining equanimity. This is an essential quality through which trust and connection can be built.

There are ways to maintain this state in your working day, in particular when you interact with others. These are particularly helpful during tough times and when working with difficult personalities. During intense times at work my mother liked to call on the expression *this too will pass* to maintain her composure and get through the project. Karen, a yogi who leads large commercial real estate transactions, shared with me the approach she takes to prepare and participate in important meetings. Her objective is to cultivate an equanimous state of mind, particularly when the meeting involves important transactions and challenging personalities.

Equanimity at the Office

1. Create a list of words or phrases that you can use to elevate your thinking. Have the list handy and add to it overtime. Phrases such as "live into the questions of life," "it depends," or "I don't know" may remind you to see the views of others. Phrases such as "everything is as it should be," "life is a series of teaching moments," or "everything happens in its own perfect way at its own perfect time" may remind you to recognize that things happen for a reason and settle into the understanding that you may never know why. Finally, phrases including "life goes on and it is good" or "I will be fine no matter what happens" may remind you to see that this is just one moment in the grand scheme of things and is not as important as it seems.
2. Prior to the meeting, pick one phrase that resonates with you. Sit tall, close your eyes, and consciously repeat the statement in your mind as you inhale slowly and exhale fully. Continue to repeat the statement until you feel calm and possess an attitude of neutrality, so you can see each person's remarks in the meeting clearly. With practice, this will become more effective.
3. While in the meeting, maintain a baseline presence that is composed, kind, and objective, and unbiased. Approach listening as an art form. Listen to each person with your fullest attention, making eye contact, respecting his or her words as you would like yours to also be honored. Give space to each person and allow for discussion, having each person speak his or her mind. Give balanced attention to the parts of the argument you consider good and bad.
4. When it is time to make a point or take a stand, assert yourself in an honest yet virtuous manner, keeping with your principles. It is possible to be kind while asserting yourself and making a firm decision based on your principles.
5. After you have spoken, do your best to revert back to a composed, kind, objective, and unbiased state.

You can consider using this approach to help you engage with others in a more open-minded and connected manner. An ongoing commitment to this approach offers a way to assert yourself while staying true to your principles. You will also build trust through the reputation you develop as an objective, composed, and polite leader. All of this while still adding value.

Cultivating Openness and Objectivity

Many of our strongly-held beliefs stem from two of the five kleshas or mental blocks that serve as obstacles to growth: attachments and aversions.

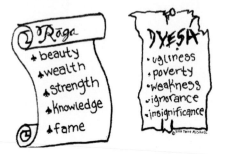

Attachment (raga)

Raga means *coloring* or *mood* and refers to something we are attracted to, have affection for, or find pleasant. *Any* attraction is an attachment, a desire or longing for things and aspects of life that we like and give us pleasure. Attachments can be helpful and elevate us, or unhelpful and degrade us. Dependency, possessiveness, and controlling behaviors are forms of attachment, as is relying on others for our own happiness and well-being.

We can be attached to nearly anything, such as our youth, dreams, work, opportunities, wealth, people, jobs, projects, clients, income, power, responsibility, our house, vacations, our kids, our spouses, our friends, free time, exercise, shopping, eating, or objects of pleasure. Of course, it is only natural and healthy to be attached to some things, our loved ones in particular. A longing for things we are attracted to or like, however, can become an obsession that causes us persistent anguish, worry, suffering, and distress. We can develop an unhealthy obsession with any of our attachments and then worry and force things—and worry and control some more—until we think we are seeing the result that our mind believes is consistent with our worldview. Cultivating healthy relationships with our attachments supports our well-being and our ability to connect with and engage our teams.

For most of my career, advancement served as an unhealthy attachment (and probably still does!). At one point, my career became such a source of focus and attention that it was all I thought about and all I wanted to talk about. Advancement, power, achievement, and wealth were what I coveted and wanted more of. A friend once told me I was obsessed with work. I now see that I was obsessed, addicted even. At dinner with friends, emotionally-charged discussions about my work would always come up. During calls with my mother, work was often the subject of discussion. The higher I rose, the more I longed for; I kept raising the bar. I remember telling an equally ambitious lawyer friend that I felt that I lost myself somewhere along the way.

I was now a different person—less fun, too serious. So many interests and hobbies were no longer part of my life. I told her that I was once the dancing-on-tables, free-spirited soul who was artistic, creative, and funny. She said I'd simply matured. Maybe she was right. But that didn't satisfy me. I felt that parts of myself were missing in action, so overtaken by my focus on career and advancement that they were disempowered and stuffed deep enough into my being that they didn't surface anymore. When work or any one attachment is your singular focus and of utmost importance, it becomes more difficult to maintain healthy relationships with others, life is less enjoyable, and you can become a pretty dull person. I put up walls and was guarded, fearful that someone would get in the way of my ever-expanding goals. It would have benefited my leadership and I would have been more satisfied with work in general if I had been more lighthearted, less fearful, and more open. I would have engaged with colleagues in a healthier way, opening up about my life and my interests. The things that people find most interesting about a person typically involves how they spend their free time, their passions, and their hobbies.

Although my attachment story pertains to work, you can be attached in an unhealthy way to many things. It is hard to foster healthy relationships and connect with people who are consumed with any of their attachments in an unhealthy way. Obsession is a dark, deep, heavy emotion, whereas healthy attachments are light and balanced. The best leaders have a balanced view of life. They are strong and courageous, because they are open and vulnerable. They don't hide away bits of themselves; rather, they are often self-deprecating and funny. Great leaders manage to retain some of their healthy attachments, their lifelong hobbies and interests, and can even—at times—leverage them in their work. A person enthusiastic about something other than work is more interesting and natural to speak with and, consequently, connects and establishes trust more easily with others. What are your attachments? Write them down.

Aversion (dvesa)

Dvesa, aversion to things we dislike, is the opposite of raga. Aversion is avoidance of things we find unattractive, unpleasant, sorrowful, or painful. Like attraction, aversion can be helpful or unhelpful; unhealthy aversions are the ones to observe and begin to change.

We often label things we do not favor as evil, wrong, painful, or dishonorable. Activities some may consider burdens, such as chores, paperwork, marketing, fundraising, traveling, bookkeeping, expenses, or budgeting, are aversions to some of us. Sitting in traffic, noise, people with poor hygiene, condescending people, or unkempt houses can irritate, disgust, or repulse us. Confrontation for some of us may be an aversion and we become attached to the idea that we don't want to confront anyone. Rather than leaning into and learning from the things that make us uncomfortable in our lives, we recoil from them, which can be problematic. I generally dislike public speaking, confrontation, and being questioned. Those are some of my aversions. If I consume myself with these dislikes and avoid doing them, I will severely impede my ability to promote this book (unhelpful)! If I welcome my aversions considering them necessary and embrace them head on as part of my experience (thus disempowering them some) I will have a great opportunity to move toward a more neutral view of them while promoting the book with more success (helpful). Sometimes letting go of an aversion means taking a risk and being vulnerable.

Our distaste for things we dislike in others can also serve as a window into that which we dislike in ourselves. Aversions breed negative attitudes and disdain for others. When we consume our thoughts with all the external things we dislike, they become bigger in our minds and can make us unhappy or even overwhelm us. We can lose ourselves in the list of things we are trying to avoid in order to create our imagined life. We even try to avoid parts of ourselves we do not like and wish no one to see. We lose our way, lose track of ourselves, and tuck pieces of ourselves away, hiding them from others. Aversion inhibits our growth. By accepting all of ourselves, just the way we are, and cultivating an attitude of fearlessness through vulnerability, we grow more accepting and move forward with our lives unimpeded by our aversions. What are your aversions? Write them down.

Likes and Dislikes: Leadership Commentary

If we divide our work into things we like and things we don't like, we don't do a great job at the things we don't like because of our chosen attitude. For example, we can decide in the morning that work is awful and dread going, and this attitude will help us to see work as awful all day long. Likely, when we go to bed at night, we will still feel that work is awful. If we try to have a more neutral attitude all the time and try to temper the highs of our likes and lows of our dislikes, we begin to see things as more balanced overall. We become able to celebrate a big win or mourn a big loss quickly, but then move on. When we transcend our attachments (and aversions), we begin to possess an attitude of neutrality focused simply on doing what needs to be done. When we are no longer shackled by attachments and aversions we gain resilience and strength. This helps us stay open to, yet unaffected by, criticisms and accolades too; we simply know that sometimes people will be pleased, and other times they will not. Escape your attachments and take a long-term view of your work and yourself.

Often, we categorize and label things in the extreme rather than considering the possibility of a middle ground, and when we label things as likes and dislikes, it inadvertently sets a bad tone for the team. We aren't always aware of our tendency to separate and divide and then favor and treat differently, but as a result of our labels, even if they are just in our minds, we tend to look down upon things we don't like, and this separation serves to marginalize work that falls into the realm of things *we* don't like. Accordingly, the type of work we *do* like is favored in importance, both in our minds as leaders and in our actions. These opinions trickle down to our team. We don't have to actively dislike things that we aren't naturally drawn to or for which we do not have natural talents. Through awareness, we can learn to change our thoughts and recognize, respect, and even honor that all work is an important component to the daily functioning and success of any project, whether personal or professional. Transcending our natural tendency to label and divide allows us to develop leadership qualities like openness and objectivity allowing us to bring together and unite the team.

Philosophy: Manifesting More from Less

> Be at least as interested in what goes on inside you as what happens
> outside. If you get the inside right, the outside will fall into place.
> —Eckhart Tolle

Social Principle 4: Temperance – Moderation – Discretion (brahmacarya)

Brahmacarya is the principle of temperance, moderation, and discretion, one of the five *yamas*. It involves the sensual pleasures, life choices, and, ultimately, behavior. The traditional yogic interpretation involves continence, most associated with our own sexuality, but this is not to be mistaken with abstaining; it's merely controlling. In a modern day context, brahmacarya is most applicable with regard to our desire to please our senses and how this impacts our well-being and our actions.

We may not be able to work *less*, but we can work *well*.

Overindulgence[114]

We enjoy a life of indulgence, of immoderation, often indulging to excess in any assortment of the things we believe will satisfy our senses— the food we eat, the drinks we consume, the intense exercises that we do, the activities for our kids, the money and power we seek, the entertainment we require, the television, the news, the degrees, the home(s), the projects, the car(s), the clothes, the electronics, and so on. Addiction sets in from overindulgence, and suddenly we lose control. There is a shift of power, and the food, drinks, exercise, activities, money, power, and belongings are now in control of us. We live for *them*. A host of unhelpful byproducts appears as the shadow side of immoderation, including guilt, shame, obsession, regret, lack, fear, negative self-talk, disconnection, and confusion.[115]

Excess

Its easy to see how we go over-the-top with many things in our lives. We may choose exercise programs we're not conditioned to do, leaving us injured and depleted. We may carry our diets too far in nonsensical ways, leaving us malnourished, tired, and unhealthy. We may consume many supplements and vitamins, not knowing exactly if our bodies are actually deficient in what we are consuming. We may carry our spirituality too far in ways that do not cultivate peace or harmony, instead leading to separation and division. We overindulge when we lounge, too: on television, snacks, and sugary soda or alcoholic beverages. We need bigger houses with bigger spaces to store the excesses we forget we own and seldom use.

Our Lavish Lives

Our overindulgence, overdoing, and over-the-top desire for excess or a *magnification of experience* has now become a societal habit, and it is addictive. As addicts, we become emotionally attached to our jammed full, overindulgent lives. This emotional attachment makes it very difficult to give up this life, and it becomes part of our story. It feels wrong to change, in fact. Slowing down—and doing or having less—makes us feel inferior in some way, or guilty and ashamed, as though we are not doing our jobs, not being good parents, not keeping up. This societal condition is evidenced by our trash problem, our obesity problem, our pharmaceutical drug problem, our debt problem, and our stress problem.

Office Indigestion

We are used to jamming our lives full, overdoing everything, and always looking for ways to be more efficient, to streamline, and to optimize. So we indulge, in a different way, at work, in the number of hours we spend working, airline miles we clock, tasks we complete, phone calls we make, and meetings we schedule. We choose our driving routes and our departure times so we can pack more into our days and then get angry or stressed when we encounter traffic. We are so full and over stimulated that we feel tired, so we try to find ways to *create energy* to do even more and feel better while doing it. The mere idea of being less available and less accessible promotes anxiety and stress in many of us, stemming from fear.

The Point of Diminishing Returns

The principle of brahmacarya requires us to spend the time to find the point of diminishing returns in everything we do. Overindulging always leaves us feeling worse in the end; it taps our bliss and takes away from our vibrancy. When we overindulge in experiences, happenings, and events, we take them in very fast, giving us no time to savor and appreciate them. Our uncomfortably full lives cause us indigestion.[116] We are packed full with so much stimulation that we can't even process our lives fully, let alone notice, appreciate, and be grateful for our abundance. When our lives become too full and busy, we also find that everyday tasks become very dull and mundane. Lethargy and boredom set in as we become disconnected from the very basics of life. In a leadership context overindulging at work ultimately decreases our productivity and encumbers our ability to connect with and engage our teams. This doesn't necessarily mean you should work fewer hours, unless you are clearly overworking to begin with. Rather, begin to work *well*, so you can engage better.

Savoring Life

This principle asks us to respect and honor every moment and to seek to find the goodness in all aspects of our lives. When we practice moderation, we create space in our lives to notice, to *savor*, and to live fully. This principle establishes that all duties have some meaning, and when we spend time in appreciation of all of the tasks and people in our lives, they will seem less mundane. We instead will begin to find them interesting and nuanced. It is through this awareness and noticing that we can choose to practice moderation.

Discretion at Work

The principle of brahmacarya also involves discretion, which is particularly important at work. As a leader, this would involve making sure that our communications and actions are in good taste and polite. Dysfunctional behaviors begin with poor hiring choices, starting with the leadership. Dysfunctional personalities can damage entire teams and even organizations taking years to repair. Seriously negative behaviors like harassment stem from a long series of other dysfunctional behaviors that happen well before the actual harassment incident. Behaviors to pay attention to include massive egos, verbal abuse, hostile communication, open signs of disrespect toward others, and negative talk about others. As an enlightened leader, take care in your hiring choices and remedy dysfunctional behaviors by leaders quickly before they disengage the team and escalate into serious violations.

Well-being in life can only be achieved through a felt sense of balance, a felt sense of enough. Employing brahmacarya in life involves taming our addiction to overdoing and excess and moving toward recognizing *enough* and *just right.*[117] Brahmacarya involves a personal responsibility to choosing balance in life. By letting our cravings and addictions go, we reverse a downward spiral and find freedom in a light heart, healthy relationships with people, and a restored sense of wonder and delight.

Questions for Leaders: Temperance, Moderation, and Discretion

1. Do you measure performance based upon face time or on merit? Do you measure performance using broad and principled measures that also serve to unite the team? Is that made clear to your team?
2. Can you remember the details of what you did yesterday? What did you enjoy about your day?
3. Do you appreciate, notice, and attempt to discover the nuances in your work, even the most mundane of activities?
4. Do you have a racing mind? Is your life too full? Are you experiencing *life indigestion*? Do you mostly react to life or respond to life?
5. Is your life so full that you feel bored at times? Are you forcing life or experiencing life? Do you have time to appreciate your life so that it has the opportunity to become amazing and interesting to you?
6. Do you frequently miss your children's activities or plans with your spouse when you have told them you will attend?
7. Do you find that you must cancel vacations or plans with friends? Do you have a difficult time committing to time with friends?
8. Is psychological abuse tolerated at the office?

9. Have any members of your team expressed concern about how they were being treated, either to you or to others? Did you do anything about it? Do you have a clear process for handling incidents of mistreatment?
10. Are you emotionally controlled and seen as realistic, pragmatic, open-minded, and receptive to differing opinions? Do you expect the same of your team?
11. Are office behaviors discreet, inclusive, and respectful to every member of the team?
12. Do team members dress professionally? Have examples of professional dress been made clear to the team?
13. Does your team make it home for dinner with family?
14. Does the team behave as professionals at company events?
15. Are you a reliable leader, parent, spouse, or friend?

Concluding Statement

Focusing on the dimension of the mind, you will see how self-awareness and self-reflection allow you to get to know yourself in ways that can help you cultivate emotional control and equipoise, steadiness and ease. Being present and conscious in our lives by creating space and reducing distraction minimizes anxiety, stress, and negativity and promotes clear thinking and pragmatism. Conscious awareness furthermore supports satisfaction and happiness. Understanding your perspectives and beliefs and distinguishing them from pure facts helps you become more open-minded, receptive, empathetic, objective, and unbiased—supporting your ability to engage and inspire more people. Changing your speech can promote self esteem, determination, inner strength and positivity. Reflecting on your attention to this layer, you will notice a lightness and ease in your days as people respond to you better and life flows more simply, because you've lightened the load by removing some of the mental baggage that otherwise weighs heavy.

Chapter 7
Yogi Secret #5: Knowledge

Old Maxim
Life happens to me.

New Maxim
I make my life happen.

Resolve: I possess the locus of control of my life experience. By staying grounded in my values, honoring the intelligence of an open mind, and allowing my intellectual muscle, my brain, some rest, I manifest my life and leadership on my own terms.

Yogi Secret #5 allows me to develop or maintain personal qualities inherent in inspiring leaders including: discernment and clear judgment ~ healthy ego ~ good listening skills and trust ~ adaptability and resilience ~ intelligence and clear perception ~ strong concentration and focus ~ good memory ~ intuition

Learn to be silent. Let your quiet mind listen, and absorb.
—Pythagoras

The fourth layer is the knowledge dimension called the *vijnanamaya kosha* and involves our intellect, knowledge, and intuition. *Vijnana* means knowledge or intellect, representing the part of us that allows us to discriminate (*viveka*) and engage in higher thought, intuition, and creativity. This dimension is a deeper fine-tuning of its predecessor, the mind layer, as it involves our higher mind, residing in the subtle, subconscious realm where the things we think, do, and say are habituated and embodied as part of our inner knowing and intuition. It is sometimes called the layer of personality and is where our sense of self and our individuality, called the *I-maker* or *ego* in yoga, are shaped. Our insights into the world around us are deepened by time spent supporting this dimension, as are our connection to nature and to faith and, in turn, to hope. This dimension allows us to apply intellect, discernment, and rational thought so that we may see events in our lives with clarity; when we become aware of and use it wisely, this dimension allows us to make rational decisions and have vision.

This is the most important chapter for leaders and will allow you to evolve your thinking, so you are free to act in a way that is healthy and empowering. It is possible to move through life with little attention to the dimension of knowledge, but given its role and function, you will soon see how authentic, connected, and inspiring leaders use it.

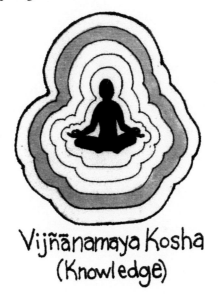

Vijñānamaya Kosha
(Knowledge)

Harnessing Our Human Potential

The Mind–Body Link

As has been covered, yoga is grounded in the understanding that we are holistic and our body and mind are linked. Modern science continues to validate this belief. We now also see how our emotions are tightly integrated with our mind-stuff—our beliefs, perspectives, and worldview. We are highly complex and fascinating creatures. Debate continues among scientists about the differences between emotions and senses, about which comes first, and about where emotions originate; nonetheless, science continues to demonstrate a clear interconnectedness that goes from body to mind and/or mind to body and/or body to body, which is simply fascinating. Studies have demonstrated that when we experience different emotions, chemicals are secreted from the brain and/or from other parts of the body. These chemicals then lock onto receptors found on cell membranes all over the body, not just in the brain as you might expect. [118] The receptor is akin to a keyhole, the chemical the key. The right chemical key opens the "door" to certain behaviors of the cell. In other words, an emotion can make a cell activate in a way that causes physical or physiological reactions consistent with the emotional state we are experiencing. For example, the effects on the body of the emotion of anger might include a tightening of the jaw, an increase in blood pressure, or sweating. This explains the notion that we can think ourselves sick. This is also why, as children, when we were cold we were told to think of a warm beach. By doing the latter, we could increase our body temperature. Doing the former, we may get sick.

What this means is that our mental and emotional being literally changes and influences our physical being. Our emotional state has a lot to do with our mind and how we see the world (our perspectives, beliefs, and worldview) based upon what we've learned and experienced (our mind-stuff). We've already seen how exercise (physical), breathing practices (energy), and an expansion of perception (conscious mind) can affect our mental and emotional being. Now we will come to understand how we can create space and tap into our subconscious mind in the knowledge dimension, which is an extremely powerful way to positively affect our holistic well-being. What it also means is that, with attention and awareness, we can change ourselves at the cellular level as we move beyond unhelpful emotions, beliefs, perspectives, and worldviews. Imagine the positive impact when an intention to change is directed at the many unhelpful states—like stress, anxiety, depression, anger, hostility, defensiveness, fear, or insecurity.

The truth is that most of us already knew this, at least a little. We've already felt our bodies respond to emotions. Every time we make an important decision, our body reacts. If we pay attention, we can feel the sensation, often in the heart, gut, or throat. The heart may flutter or feel as though it is brimming when you feel truly joyful. Your heart, chest, gut, or throat may feel constricted or tight when something you are doing, saying, or thinking is unsettling to you. As you begin to notice these sensations, you will notice when your body is uncomfortable and when it is pleased. You have probably also noticed that when you intentionally change the physical body by getting a massage to release tension or by exercising for example, you impact your physical body, your energy, and your state of mind.

Begin to notice and understand what it means to be guided by the intelligence of the mind-body. This will serve you well in all decisions.

The Field of Consciousness

In order to better understand why and how we tend to think and act in certain ways, it is helpful to understand a bit about what Hari-kirtana das calls the *field of consciousness*, the part of us that includes both the conscious and subconscious minds.[119] Modern researchers and experts continue to study and evolve their thinking about consciousness and psychology, and every school of thought has a different approach. Yoga's approach sees the field of consciousness as being made up of four aspects of the mind: *manas* (sensory mind), *chitta* (storehouse of memories), *ahamkara* (ego or I-maker), and *buddhi* (intellect). Our sensory mind, ego, and intellect perform functions; the data warehouse stores information gathered from the past. Our relationship with these aspects of the mind helps shape our personalities.

Once you have an understanding of the field of consciousness, you can begin to pay attention to the functions at work as you move through your life. This awareness alone will allow you to exercise free will by liberating you from the quick reactions that stem from the subconscious. When you are able to recognize the functions of the field of consciousness that lead you in thought and action, you will soon be able to observe these functions at work in others. It becomes a game of logic, which is helpful in the leadership context, as you begin to see clearly how others come to certain ideas, beliefs, attitudes, and decisions. This *inside* information can help you not only connect better with others but also guide you to ask the questions that will allow you to build rapport, position your ideas, and establish buy-in.

You can begin to observe the functions of the mind during discussions with people. Discussions about unpopular office decisions or somewhat controversial news events offer a particularly easy way to observe the functions at work and to learn about a person's temperament. Note whether the person is able to engage in a healthy dialogue, listen, and consider all sides of an issue while being relatively calm, even if he or she has a strong opinion. How they approach this can serve as an indicator as to whether they are seeking to understand, and as such using intelligence (higher mind), or simply being reactionary (lower mind). If they maintain some level of equipoise, you know they have the capacity to be discerning, open-minded, and clear. If they constantly want to challenge, debate, or become defensive, it is evident they are allowing their ego and emotion to overshadow the higher mind. If they don't ask your opinion and have no interest in entertaining another view, they could be stuck in a black-and-white world led by what they have learned in the past, rather than *feeding their knowledge* and using their intelligence to be discerning in the present. Understanding this helps you know if your conversation will support a healthy debate, conducive to learning, sharing, and creating. Do you use intelligence (higher mind)? When might you tend to be reactionary and close-minded (lower mind)?

This doesn't mean we don't have preferences or take sides. But when a person's ego has them clinging to his or her perspectives so strongly, they often cannot be reasoned with, can easily be unkind, hurtful, or even hostile toward others, and, likely, have little control over their emotions. These are not the traits of inspiring leaders that elevate their teams to be more engaged in their work. As a leader, these traits are important and helpful to recognize when hiring new employees and even when working with your team. Let's delve a little deeper and look at another example.

Thought Patterns and Potential

In yoga, *vrittis* refer to the whirling sea of thought waves, including old thoughts, images, and senses that we have in our conscious minds. When we're done using or creating a specific thought wave, when an experience (anything we feel, think, do, say, witness, read) is over, the vritti slowly subsides and deposits itself in the depths of our subconscious mind (*chitta*) for later recall. These old thoughts, images, and senses sitting in the data warehouse of our subconscious mind (mind-stuff or memory bank) are called *samskaras* (impressions). Each samskara holds a certain amount of *potential*, or the energy that pushes it back into our conscious awareness, making it a thought wave in the whirling sea again. A passing notion or thoughts about something of which we have little interest will have less potential than something we feel strongly about for example. This exchange of thought wave to impression, and impression back to thought wave, relays continuously between the conscious and subconscious minds. This is one way to imagine how we form habits and how we can consider changing them.

The Path of a Pizza Habit

Here's a personal and silly example, but it illustrates well how this works. My whole family likes pizza, so we tend to eat it often. Practically every time I have pizza, I like it. In my subconscious awareness I have many favorable impressions of pizza; consequently, its potential is strong and it easily makes its way into my conscious awareness as a thought-wave. In other words, each subsequent time I need to plan a family dinner, the chances become greater that I think of pizza. If I continue to make a regular choice to eat pizza, you can see how I am creating and strengthening a pizza habit. This is the path of a habit of thought that leads to a habit of action. The less I choose pizza and the more I ignore my desire for pizza and focus on other options, the less strong the pizza habit becomes via its weakened potential in my mind. In this case, pizza represents *raga*, an attachment, of mine.

Adding a bit more yoga terminology, I can also choose to be discerning about my pizza and pick a healthier, organic version loaded with vegetables (a sattvic choice). I can also be pulled by my desire to be in the good graces of a family who owns a pizza shop and order from there (feeding my ego).

Deepen the Right Roots

This segment is about becoming aware of *how* your mind works and *how* you come to create thoughts and make decisions, not to be confused with the idea of right and wrong choice-making. Here is the important point: we have the power to change our habits of thought, which will strengthen other habits and consequently change what thoughts surface in our conscious awareness. The first step is awareness, recognizing what part is at play in your life and whether or not this supports your well-being. The more we participate in certain habits of thought, habits of words, and habits of actions, the deeper and more powerful their roots in our subconscious awareness. As we evolve our thinking, we can choose to deepen the right roots.

Removing the Coloring

> That which feels like poison at the start but tastes like nectar
> in the end is said to be happiness in the mode of goodness,
> which arises from the serenity of self-knowledge.
> —Bhagavad Gita. 18.37

Imagine a big pot of stew. Imagine all your memories and experiences as a variety of vegetables in the pot, each bouncing about and scrambling for attention. Some vegetables you favor quite a lot, others you actually think taste awful, and then the rest are in between. The vegetables you really like and those that you think taste awful will be louder—and therefore get more attention from—your mind. When left unchecked, the mind and ego will guide us to avoid the vegetables we have disliked in the past and load up on those we know we have liked, even though our intellect tells us that eating all the vegetables offers a variety of nutrients that are good for our bodies. We often ignore our level-headed intellect and make habitual decisions predicated on the past and not the present moment, in this example completely ignoring the fact that the vegetables will taste different when all blended together, and not even considering that we should try to eat them because they are good for us.

Now, instead of stew, think of a pipeline full of projects. You can imagine how our mind can easily draw us to prioritize our past preferences (depicted by the light bulb in the illustration below) and can take us away from being open to other opportunities. Yet, nothing can ever be exactly repeated in life. This time it may be different. Or consider a personnel problem, which is rarely something anyone likes to deal with, an aversion. You can see that if we allow our ego to push us to resist dealing with the problem, we will be jaded from the beginning and will not be able to see the problem clearly. Understanding the aspects of the mind and our habits help us make intelligent choices with a clear perception.

A Leader's Mind

The Seeds We Plant

All of these impressions, which include past memories, feelings, and images recorded by the sensory mind, reside in our data warehouse, and we deposit new impressions all the time. Subconsciously, we draw upon this gigantic data warehouse to perceive and process new information, informing our real-time thoughts and behaviors. These impressions act as *seeds*, as they are what we plant in our minds that form habits, opinions, beliefs, perspectives, and ideas. The seeds that we plant will affect our current reality, including our ability to be intelligent, discerning, and perceptive leaders.

Like mental gardening, we plant seeds every day. As in any garden, from time to time we need to pull out weeds. We want only those seeds that serve our health, well-being, and our leadership to root and grow into lush plants and trees. We must consciously rid ourselves of seeds that are not helpful to us so they don't root, become prolific, and take over. Through mental gardening, we can grow a lush garden free of weeds and damaging substances that contradict our well-being and our growth as leaders.

We can make choices about how we spend our time, with whom we interact, how we speak, and what we choose to think, so that we can feed our mind positive and uplifting images that serve our ability to be discerning and clear, and to connect with our teams. We can also make choices as to the pace at which we feed our field of consciousness. When we make a habit of feeding our field too many inputs at one time, our mind races, and we all know a racing mind makes it difficult to connect to ourselves, let alone others. When we consciously moderate the pace of inputs so our mind is not stirred up, we connect better with our teams and respond more reasonably to leadership situations.

Conscious Living

Conscious living involves the layer of knowledge. The two go hand in hand. You can't live consciously without seeking knowledge and using the intelligence of the higher mind. In Sanskrit, long-term, goal-directed intelligence—also called intellect—is *buddhi*. The root *budh* means *to be awake*, and buddhi can be thought of as the intuitive faculty that leads to our higher intelligence, our awakened self, our spiritual awareness. It can discern what is the best course of action. Buddhi is like the wise elder, responsible for knowing the truth, making the highest decisions, and guiding the other aspects of mind. Figuratively speaking, another way to consider buddhi is like the boss who sends the mind clear guidance based on intelligence. The mind then acts as middle management, in charge of directing the workers of thought, words, and action.

But sometimes buddhi becomes clouded, and we all know what can happen when we do not have clear guidance from our leader. If you are overtired, your intellectual capacity is clouded and you cannot reason as well, so your judgment is impaired and your actions will be based upon a less useful set of information. If you are operating at too quick a pace, your intellect doesn't have time to work things out, and you make impulsive decisions. If buddhi is cloudy or unclear or you don't give it that moment to work, the mind and ego will try to work out the answer on their own, without clear guidance and discernment from your intellect. If you are unclear or cloudy, do what you need to do: ask more questions, slow down, calm yourself, or get more sleep. You always want to think and make decisions from a fully informed and clear place. Seeking to understand through questioning creates clarity, allowing you to function with knowledge and intelligence.

Disobeying the Boss

Of course, we are not perfect, and we don't always obey the boss, even if guidance is clear. The same is true of the mind. It doesn't always listen.

We can choose to ignore intelligence and often do, even though we are quite aware of the better choice. Oftentimes our decision to ignore intellect is driven by our egos, which influence the mind to base a decision that feeds our cravings and desires and/or moves us away from things we dislike, regardless of whether they are good for us or not. Like a student in a yoga movement class who pushes into poses before the body is ready and then hurts the body in the process, we allow our ego to trump intelligence. Ego can disempower or weaken our function of intelligence, if we let it. Our ego tends to align itself with impressions in our data repository that it finds satisfying too, like a business alliance that the ego wants to keep alive past its useful life. Remember this scenario when deciding whether to expand into a new market niche, for example. If you are too eager to expand and allow ego to prevail, you may prematurely enter the market. Or when you hold onto a client, vendor, or even an employee simply because you *like* them long past their benefit to the company. When we can release the grip of the ego, we can allow ourselves to lead with clarity and intelligence.

Distortion of Reality

Tumultuous and distracting fluctuations of the sensory mind (a barrage of thought waves), can distort reality like a ripple in a clear lake distorts the reflection of pristine mountains. We need good knowledge and information for our intelligence to function clearly, but we also need *space*. The space needed varies from one person to the next. Only you know when your mind is too full of uncontrolled racing thoughts. The state of your nervous system is a good indicator. Allowing time to pause and the space to clear the mind will let us recognize good knowledge and information. Pauses matter. Space matters.

When my mind is racing, I know I am not going to pay attention to the person speaking before me, so I need to make the effort to look them directly in the eye and take a few breaths to move from busy mind to one that is paying attention to the person speaking. The pause is the moment when I choose to take a breath and look the person in the eye. I then became more present to their needs. This is an example of how, in one moment, I can make a choice to live more consciously. Another choice would be to not genuinely listen and react by giving a disconnected response. In those instances, the other person usually knows they were not fully heard, which is unsettling to them. Obviously, this is not a way to support your team; nor is it a way to foster engagement and connection.

As we begin to understand ourselves better, pause, and see things more clearly, we can tap into intelligence, reasoning, and discernment. When we allow our intellect to do its work, we are present, connected, and engaged. This is the place where perception and judgment are clear and we are wise and discerning. We ultimately want to have control of our mind and senses and respond with equipoise in our days. This control allows us to be adaptable and resilient, qualities essential to managing change and navigating uncertainty. Without adaptability and resilience we will not be inclined to embrace change and manage through chaos. Resilience strengthens and helps us to overcome resistance and handle negative reactions with grace and control. The layer of knowledge is what differentiates us from other species. Focus on this layer allows us to transform our leadership.

Mind Awareness Training

Thought Awareness

As leaders with long to-do lists and too many responsibilities, most of us never stop thinking. When we begin to notice our racing and spinning minds, we realize how challenging it can be to focus and still the mind. We first need to become aware of and appreciate the various thoughts that circulate through our minds every day. Then we can choose on which thoughts we want to focus and on which we do not.

Learning to intentionally choose which thoughts we want to pay attention to—giving attention to those that serve us and no attention to those that do not—supports well-being and great leadership. This is mind-awareness training. By making a conscious choice to focus on certain thoughts and not others, the thoughts that do not serve us slowly fade away and become less powerful. This is the beauty of our ever-changing brains: they adapt. If we cognitively reinforce a stimulus (a thought), the cortical regions of the brain will strengthen accordingly, and vice versa. Through conscious awareness practices like this, we are directly influencing how we think.

The Energy of Attention

> Where attention goes, energy flows.
>
> —Rolf Gates

The phrase, *energy flows where attention goes* is fairly common. I like the way Rolf Gates phrases it better, as he leads with attention. We have control over our attention and where we place it. We choose whether to offer attention to certain activities and people in the form of the actions we take, the words we use, the e-mails we write, and the thoughts that consume our minds. If we offer attention to negative things, those things will, by default, become energized, bigger, and more impactful. If we offer attention to things we consider positive, they too will become larger. In this way, through the thoughts we choose to send energy toward, we manifest much of our everyday life experience.

Categories of Thought

The thoughts we play over and over tend to follow patterns and be lumped into a handful of categories, such as thoughts about controlling things, planning, relationships, self-judgment, family, work, or important conversations. It is a practice in awareness training to notice and consider our particular patterns of thought. When we begin to understand our patterns, we can begin to transform them by offering attention to those that serve us and ignoring those that do not. This is not easy. It is hard to overcome our habits of mind, but understanding your own unique patterns of thought will enhance your perception, allowing you to be more open-minded, discerning, and clear.

We can also dissect our patterns and try to recognize which aspects of the mind are at play. Are they patterns based upon emotions from past experiences that may not be relevant today? While having realistic expectations is important, agonizing about or clinging to something unknown—based upon emotions, experiences, and events of the past—is neither helpful nor constructive. This is a function of the lower sensory mind drawing on past impressions, which will never be exactly the same again. Is there a pattern that has you clinging to what you want or avoiding things you don't want in an unhealthy way? Clinging to an attachment to things we like or dislike is an obstacle that tethers us, thus preventing us from being open to something new.

The Trails We Lay

Rolf Gates once suggested that we visualize the mind as a ski slope, with each pattern of thought a different trail. If we stop using the trails that do not serve us, they will fade over time as the snow shifts and new powder covers them. Then, instead of retracing old trails, we can choose to carve new ones. When we are no longer wasting our precious time on trails that don't serve us, we have more time and energy to carve out new ones that do. And every subsequent season, more life-serving trails of thought will emerge, physically changing the structure of our brains.

Neuroplasticity

The scientific term relating to the ability of our brains to change is *neuroplasticity*.[120] Our understanding of this is fairly recent, replacing the long-held belief that our brains are static. Our brains actually have the capacity to create new neural networks based upon new

> Our brains are malleable and can change—at any age.

information that we give it—at any age, not only as children. We can retrain our brains in how we think and, correspondingly, retrain how our bodies react. We merely need to notice our patterns of thought, move away from those that don't serve us, and spend our energy on those that do. Simply noticing and choosing to move on weakens the energy of the thought that does not serve us and, in time, those thoughts will fade until they have little bearing on our lives.

Thought Awareness Practice

An exercise like the one that follows allows you to think about how you are energetically influencing your life through your attention. You can then work to give less energy toward thinking that does not serve your growth as a leader. For example, if you are constantly stressed about work, then you are making work a big negative, since stress isn't constructive. So, whatever occupies your mind in an unhelpful way, try to move into the mindset that everything will work out the way it is supposed to, recognizing that so many things are completely out of your control. Every time your mind wants to worry, pause and think *everything is working out just the way it is meant to*. Or *life happens in its own perfect way at its own perfect time without brute force of will*. Each time you do this practice, give even less energy to the trails that don't serve you.

Thought Awareness Practice

1. Find a comfortable seated position where you can remain without moving for five to ten minutes. Set a timer. You may choose to be cross-legged, perched on a couple blocks, on a pillow, or perhaps in a chair. If you choose a chair, sit on the edge of the seat with feet flat on the ground. Make sure you are warm and the room is quiet. Make sure you are not overly hungry or thirsty. We are attempting to remove any possible distractions.
2. Rest the backs of your hands on your thighs, with palms open. Close your eyes. Sit up tall. Find length in the spine as the crown of the head draws toward the ceiling and the abdomen tones. Notice your breath. Breathe softly through your nose. Notice the soft rise and fall of your chest. Still the eyes behind closed lids.
3. As thoughts arise, let them pass by, and notice your inhale and exhale.

4. After your timer goes off, open your journal and list every thought you can remember that came into your mind during the practice. This could include: planning, your to-do list, conversations you had or have yet to have, judgments you made about yourself or others, criticisms, contemplations, e-mails you need to send, calls you need to make, emotions, a deadline, someone's health, parents, kids, worry, a promotion for which you were passed over, work, research, etc.

5. If you don't remember most of your thoughts, do the meditation a couple more times over the next few days and add to your list.

6. After you have a list that you feel is representative of the sorts of things you expect to come up in your thinking mind, see if you can group them into three to five corresponding categories or themes. You may be able to group them a couple of different ways. Categories or themes might include: kids, work, house, difficult conversations, to-do list, planning, worrying, organizing, and controlling.

7. Self-reflection: How do these groups of thought influence your state of mind? How do they influence your perceived level of stress? Do they contribute to your stress? Should you give certain thoughts less attention or energy? Which trails do you wish to be less prominent? Which trails are not supporting you?

Cultivating a Strong Sense of Self

Obstacle to Growth: Mistaken Identity (asmita)

Mistaken Identity

In yoga, an obstacle to authentic, inspiring leadership and self-realization is called *asmita* and is one of the five *kleshas,* or veils. Asmita is like a

case of mistaken identity or I-ness, where we falsely define ourselves in terms of labels and then desperately cling to those definitions of ourselves. The I-ness refers to a mind that says *I am this* and *I am that.* It is our *false ego.* Some labels for myself could be: yoga teacher, investment professional, wine enthusiast, foodie, world traveler, entrepreneur, writer etc. What does it really all mean? It can be fun to describe ourselves in various ways, but in the end it is an illusion. They represent things I have done and like to do. They are not the permanent part of me. Labels are impermanent. Under the influence of illusion (*maya*), directed by the false ego, we live a life of futility. In yoga, we believe that the core of what we are is naked of labels. We are that unchanging and permanent part of our core essence, our spirit. It is our clinging to our false ego and identification with labels that cause us to reduce and limit ourselves and miss out on broader possibilities. Reductionist thinking limits and confines us to our chosen labels and establishes expectations. We typically think labels build us up in some way, but consider instead how they serve as boundaries that wall off something more and block us from other opportunities. Consider how they set us up for disappointment and suffering when we don't live up to our labels. In fact, leaders who feel the need to continually refer to their strengths and accomplishments are often less strong and competent than leaders who have a quiet confidence and lead instead with a cheerful demeanor and skillful processes.

The Opposite Is True

What we at first see as true may in fact be the opposite. Vulnerability, for example, is the key to unlocking droves of strength and power. Accordingly, the softest spoken or the kindest should not be mistaken as the weakest. The loudest person in the room often has the weakest inner strength, and so must make efforts to prove and overpower. It is often the leaders who can sit contentedly, saying nothing at all unless asked, who have the strongest constitution. Strong leaders are

> The leaders with the biggest mouths in the room are often not the strongest or the smartest, simply the loudest.

humble and with healthy egos lead by example. We need ego, a healthy ego. A healthy ego is our internal power that holds us together when the world around us is falling apart. It fortifies our inner structure and protects us from harm. It makes us resilient and strong. A healthy ego helps us clarify boundaries, pursue goals, and persevere. A healthy ego empowers our pursuits and fuels our motivation. A leader's ego is healthy when he or she believes in him or her self and consequently prioritizes his or her needs. A healthy ego has transcended attachments and does what is *necessary*, grounded in principle, without guilt or remorse. Leaders with healthy egos don't need to show their strength, power, or control. They simply do their work and assert themselves when they need to. They are likeable, and people naturally follow them. Their inner strength is steadfast. They express an abundance of gratitude, appreciating the small stuff, like a sunny day, a good run, or a favorite lunch.

The False Ego Is Fragile

If we cling desperately to external aspects of ourselves like our image it can make us miserable as it *falsely* fuels our identity and self-esteem. When that image is altered in some manner, we feel lost and even terrified. If a label we cling to goes away our self-esteem is shattered. A maligned (false) ego can be self-righteous, but is actually fragile and overly concerned about what others think. It wants desperately to be accepted. When left unchecked, false ego can make some of us believe that everything we have ever come to learn is right. Our false egos can be absolutist and live in a black-and-white world, but such a world is a fantasy of mind and fueled by fear. When the bottom falls out, a good measure of the false ego's role in your life can be found in the extent of your struggle with the aftermath.

A person with a healthy ego can take risks and rebound easily from failures. A healthy form of ego has everything to do with being secure in our self, exactly as we are in this moment, accepting and honoring all of our qualities, whether we consider them good, bad, or neutral. A healthy ego offers us the strength to show up authentically and wholeheartedly. A healthy ego supports our ability to function as wise, discerning, rational, fair, neutral, open, and clear-seeing leaders. It also allows us to appropriately leverage necessary leadership qualities like decisiveness, conviction, strength, courage, assertiveness, and tenacity. A healthy ego offers a person the confidence to go after dreams and try new things yet understands balance and takes care not to tip into excess. With a healthy ego we are seen as reliable and responsible. Led by the false ego a person will pursue every next opportunity always seeking more, while destabilizing the bodies and minds of everyone in their lives. Are you always raising the bar and sacrificing yourself in the process? If so, where are you trying to get to and will it lead to happiness, health, and inspiring leadership? A healthy ego knows when to say no and harbors no regret.

Enlightened Ego

In this book, I detour from the traditional interpretation of liberating ourselves from ego completely, by distinguishing between the false ego and a healthy ego and advocating a practical way of thinking about ego in a modern context. The word enlightened elevates the healthy ego as oriented toward something greater, a fundamental yogic principle. We skillfully harness and use the ego by becoming aware of our own ego at play, working to function with enough ego that we can participate fully in life and effectively at work, yet always allowing our intelligence and principles to prevail. This also involves humility. The humility in knowing that we do not have all the answers nor will we ever, and so we proactively leverage the expertise of others the best we can then settle on faith. With humility we know we are dependent upon others and are not going it alone. An enlightened ego is where we have the right amount of ego to fulfill our unique purpose, yet we are conscious of our impact on ourselves, on humanity, and on the world around us. Using our enlightened ego we serve as the caretakers of ourselves and of others in pursuit of noble goals.

> No one is useless in this world who lightens the burdens of another.
> —Charles Dickens

It is important to clarify that pursuing a higher truth or orienting your life toward noble goals, is different from being an egalitarian. An egalitarian by some definitions would be an idealist who believes that we can and should impose all of our own self-created ideals on others to resolve all of the world's problems. In an ideal world, while such intentions may help people they may not be realistic; further, egalitarians can be quite outspoken, rarely humble, and their false egos can be enormous—gigantic even.

In *I Can See Clearly Now*, the late Dr. Wayne W. Dyer shares that we teach our kids that it is important to live to satisfy their (false) ego, to accumulate stuff, to win, to compare favorably against others, to ascribe value in life through the eyes of all things monetary. He furthers that we often pressure our children in the opposite direction of the tip of Maslow's pyramid of needs, in the opposite direction of self-actualization, leading to emotional and personality disorders, anxiety and stress and physical illness.[121] This is a natural way of parenting as it stems from the underpinnings of our great society; we understand it well because we pressure ourselves in this way, too. There is a tipping point to everything, in this case it is to our health and well-being and our evolution as humans and leaders.

When we choose to become aware of our ego and leverage it in a positive way that supports our well-being, we can make principled choices in service of ourselves, our teams, our families, and our society. An enlightened ego is used for our own growth and development as a human as well. *Knowing* that we can be better and leveraging our ego to improve and to grow in a helpful way is a healthy use of the ego.

Lessons and Mistakes

> In life, you always serve as a lesson or a mistake to others.
> —Coelli Marsh

I first heard this quote in a yoga class. As the teacher described what she meant by this quote, I came to appreciate the breadth of the responsibility in my day. Everything I do in every moment reflects out to others and serves as a lesson or a mistake. Everything I say and everything I write matters. My facial expressions have a big impact on others. My behavior and tone of voice make a real difference. My appearance affects others, too. I am constantly sending messages to others, acting either as a teacher or as the type of person to avoid being. Everything that I choose to do or not do in my life matters and serves as a teaching moment to others. Every moment of every day presents an opportunity. Wow, that's a big responsibility.

Having the role of a leader is an honor. Leaders who serve as mistakes are counterproductive to corporate culture, and their toxic byproducts spread quickly and multiply. If we hold ourselves to high standards, we will know that every moment of the day we are serving as a lesson, a teacher. Good leaders set examples in everything they do and people look up to them as mentors and role models. Good companies and good societies can be considered in this way too. Leading through your own example allows you to see your leadership in this way, as a service to the benefit of others. This involves keeping your ego in check. A healthy ego gives us our sense of self, of worth and individuality, but too much ego moves us into the false ego territory and blinds us into thinking we have control over things that are beyond our control, which is most of life. False ego puts us in a perpetual state of chasing and coveting the next shiny object, taking us away from the present moment and away from authentic and wholehearted living. False ego has us checking off the next box of yet another accomplishment we've made as the discerning stand by shaking their heads, neither inspired nor impressed. And so we try even harder to do even more. Can you see the parallels between this way of being and our stress and lifestyle drug problems?

Good Listening and Building Trust

Leaders who use their dimension of knowledge and have healthy egos tend to be really good in business meetings. Through good listening and paying attention, they can easily discern how to navigate the dialogue. They are excellent at noticing body language, are sensitive to the energy of the others in the room, and are better able to perceive whether they are getting the messages conveyed. Above all, they are great listeners, and great listeners are patient, can offer helpful feedback, and can make dialogue inclusive.

Client, customer, and employee relationships are deepened through good listening practices.

Vomiting on the Audience

On the contrary, those who operate in their own false ego-dominant world often, what I call, *vomit on their audience*. These meetings are never as effective as they could be, as these leaders simply communicate whatever they want to say without regard for what the recipients want to hear or whether they actually understand what has been said. The false ego-led leader fills the room with their voice without allowing others to speak very much. They see things through the lens of their own eye, unable to see things from all sides. If you asked them if the audience got the message, of course their often too-dominant ego would think so, but really they do not have a clue; nor do such leaders typically care one way or the other as they are quick to find fault and will easily place blame on others for anything that goes wrong.

Holding Space

It is very difficult to simply sit and listen to someone speak without interjecting, especially in a fast-paced environment. Because of this, many of us feel we aren't fully heard. Holding space for another person to communicate openly and honestly is one of the best ways to establish trust. A listening practice will help you connect better and establish healthy, trusting relationships with your teams. Through listening you will better discern what truly motivates each individual. It is also important to observe to whom you choose to listen, and to recognize that this too is your choice. Two people can say the exact same thing, and many of us would find that we would listen to one person and not the other. When you begin to be honest about this truth, perhaps you will become more open to others.

Building Trust

Healthy feedback with your team is fostered through good listening skills. In fact, effective communication is only possible when you become very good at listening. When people feel listened to, they feel secure and supported, making them less anxious or stressed and accordingly able to function at work without damaging their health. Trust is borne out of feeling supported. When you learn to listen, you build trust with your team. Building trust is an essential quality of a leader and necessary to instill a shared purpose amongst the team. Mentor and coach your team to build trust and allow yourself to be vulnerable. With trust comes honesty and openness, both necessary to establish buy-in. Healthy and clear communication begins with good listening and will enhance team engagement. In order to improve your listening skills, you have to practice. Consider the exercise below; you can also try this at home with a family member or with a friend.

Listening Practice

1. Schedule fifteen-minute one-on-one meetings with key members of your team.
2. At the start of the meeting, turn off all gadgets, sounds, and beeps that may disrupt the meeting. Have the team member do the same.
3. Tell the team member that you are working on being a better listener to support your skills as a leader. Before he or she starts to speak, set a timer for five minutes, explain that you will nod your head and use facial expressions but otherwise *you will not respond for five minutes.*
4. Ask the team member for a report on how things are going overall. Ask him or her to be as open and honest as possible and to speak about whatever comes to mind.
5. Look directly into his or her eyes. Listen attentively to every single word. You may think of solutions, fixes, or answers as they speak, but try not to allow your mind to wander from what the person is saying until the timer goes off. Do not even take notes. Just listen as deeply as you can.
6. After the timer goes off, finish your meeting as you ordinarily would. Ask for feedback about the listening part of the meeting.
7. Reflect upon how that meeting went and what you learned. Consider scheduling fifteen-minute listening meetings every month or two with your key team members. Or make it a natural start to every meeting.

Meditation

Meditation, *dhyana,* is the seventh of the eight limbs of yoga. Meditation is a tool to access our higher self and drop into the depths of our imagination and intuition. Patanjali states in the *Yoga Sutras* that it is through meditation that one begins to overcome the obstacles to growth. This ancient yogic practice dates back thousands of years and is now widely known to help people experience better lives in many ways pertinent to leadership.

Traditional yogic meditation involves repetition of a mantra aloud or recited in the mind. A mantra is a time-honored Sanskrit word or phrase derived from the ancient Vedic texts that is repetitively chanted as an object of meditation. A mantra is traditionally given to a practitioner by a wisdom teacher. Sanskrit mantras have a special resonance that facilitates progress in one's meditation practice.

When we think of meditation, an image of a person sitting upright with crossed legs and closed eyes may come to mind. This is a common way to meditate, although some people prefer to keep their eyes open (eyes open may be the only way a person who has experienced some forms of trauma can meditate). There are also forms of meditation that are done lying down and some people can have a meditative experience while taking a yoga movement class. You do not have to be in a quiet place to practice meditation; it just makes it easier for most of us. Experienced meditators can meditate alongside dozens of people who are talking.

Research-Based Benefits of Meditation

Supports Mental Health

Modern science has been studying meditation more closely for some time now, and the findings are astonishing. The research primarily focuses on practices involving a seated meditation. The same benefits may not be the case in a walking meditation for example. The health benefits have been shown to be numerous, ranging from reducing heart attacks amongst heart patients[122] to reducing anxiety.[123] Daily meditation practice has proven to reduce symptoms of depression and stress as well.[124] Researchers can now measure impacts on the brain using Magnetic Resonance Imaging (MRI) technology. Regular practice of meditation appears to change the physical structure of the brain, too, mitigating the thinning of the prefrontal cortex as we age and, as such, enhancing neural structure associated with cognitive and emotional processing.[125] A thicker prefrontal cortex lessens anxiety and depression as it allows us to see things more clearly and helps us modulate our limbic system's natural tendencies toward negative emotion.

Better Attention Span and Focus

Sustained meditation is like boot camp for our brains. It's a training regimen. Meditation improves attention span. Using diffuse tensor imaging (DTI), researchers found that regular practice of meditation appears to minimize the aging process of the brain, essentially keeping the brain younger by preserving its white matter. So, a meditation practice may help to maintain vibrant neural functioning as well as brain health.[126] Especially important to leaders, the sustained practice of meditation has also been shown to improve attention span and focus.[127] Improved attention allows us to be more decisive and clear in our work. This is particularly helpful as we get older, since our ability to pay attention degrades as we age.[128] Meditation may also help to stave off mental illness, as a hallmark of many forms of mental illness is the lack of a sustained attention span.[129]

Improved Memory

Meditation also improves memory. Mindfulness research confirmed increases in the concentration of the brain's grey matter within the left hippocampus, the region of the brain that plays a role in memory formation, learning, and emotions.[130] The degrading function of the hippocampus as we age is what results in declining memory. Meditation literally increases the density of the good stuff in our brain.

In time, our meditation practice exercises our brain, hones our concentration abilities, teaches our nervous system to relax, and allows us to drop more quickly into deeper meditative states. With a regular practice of seated meditation, we can remain in a deeper state of meditation for longer and longer increments. A yoga movement practice allows for the release of tension in the physical body and a deep relaxation that supports a seated meditation practice.

The Mind—Body Connection

The Relaxation Response

While meditation itself is an ancient practice that has benefited people for thousands of years, it was not until relatively recently that a relationship between the mind and body was contemplated and researched in the West. In 1968, in the days of The Beatles (who were known to be yogi's and meditators), a group of meditators stopped by a lab at the Harvard Medical School, where researchers—Herbert Benson, MD among them—were studying blood pressure. These practitioners told the researchers that they could alter their blood pressure through meditation. The researchers were not interested and probably didn't believe them anyway. After a great deal of persistence, the researchers eventually conducted a variety of experiments on the practitioners measuring bodily functions during meditation. Their findings were beyond dispute, demonstrating a rapid decrease in oxygen consumption, heart rate, metabolism, blood lactate levels, and respiratory rate. A decrease in blood lactate levels is consistent with someone who has moved into the restful side of their nervous system and, as such, is directly linked to a decrease in anxiety and panic attacks as well as an increase in feelings of well-being.[131] Such rapid decreases in these bodily functions could not be repeated in any other manner, *even during sleep*, and such rapid decreases in oxygen consumption could likewise not be repeated even if one held one's breath.[132] Benson later deemed this entire set of symptoms the *Relaxation Response*.[133]

Western Medicine Proves Mind-Body Connection

The importance of this work cannot be overstated. For the first time ever, these findings proved to the western medical community that there was a connection between body and mind.[134] This was a fundamental advancement; up until this point, the western medical establishment did not believe that our minds could influence our physiology or vice versa. Centuries prior, there were many claims coming from the East of the benefits of meditation and other practices; these claims were deemed by the western medical establishment to have been based on misinformation or erroneous conclusions.[135] It was unconventional and professionally risky, not to mention a leap of faith, to even postulate that simply sitting and keeping your mind fixed on one thing with your eyes closed (aka meditation) could actually alter the physical body. Thank you for your courage, Dr. Benson!

Invoking the Relaxation Response

Through further studies, Dr. Benson demonstrated that certain techniques elicit the Relaxation Response, including the practices of meditation and yoga movement and found that regular practice could even lower blood pressure to the normal range for people with high blood pressure.[136] We can elicit this set of conditions any moment of the day to find calm in rough times. We simply need to find a quiet (or even not-so-quiet) place to sit in a comfortable position for a while with our eyes closed, and then redirect our attention to a single thing, like a special word or the breath. Anytime our mind wanders, we draw it back to this thing. All the while, we must maintain a passive attitude, not caring whether we are doing it right, not trying to accomplish anything. Then the Relaxation Response happens *all by itself.*

That's it. Simply sit, close your eyes, anchor your mind, do not judge yourself, and soak it in.

> Sitting quietly, doing nothing,
> spring comes,
> and the grass grows all by itself.
>
> —Zen Proverb

Brain Frequency

Our brain activity is measured and categorized in four bands of frequencies within which we tend to exist, typically broken down as beta (14 to 30 cycles per second, or cps), alpha (8 to 13 cps), theta (4 to 8 cps) and delta (up to 4 cps). Beta is our normal waking state, our rapid-fire, activity-based thinking state. Alpha is a relaxation state, often achieved during a yoga movement class, passive activities like listening to music with eyes closed, or active relaxation such as meditation and calming breathing practices. Theta is the brain state of early sleep, a lucid dreaming state where we are drifting off but the mind is still thinking, fading in and out. It is possible—and desirable—to move into a theta state during deeper meditation practices, including meditative yoga movement classes, particularly during the minutes of rest at the end of class. Delta is the least active brain state, like being in a deep, dreamless sleep. We initially enter the world in delta; newborn babies are in this state all the time. Delta is a high-quality, regenerative state of growth. In the relaxation states of alpha, theta, and delta, the activity of our limbic system (seat of emotions) in the center of the brain slows down.

Alpha➔Theta➔Delta

Meditation allows us to drop into our slower-functioning brain, certainly into alpha, but even into theta or delta. Yoga communities around the world know that a practice of yoga and meditation leads to direct increases in feelings of well-being. Using an electroencephalogram (a device that measures brain waves), researchers confirmed that certain activities like yoga and meditation change the electrical activity in our brains.[137] In 2009, researchers used an EEG to measure the brain waves of experienced meditators, both during meditation and while relaxing. They found significant increases in theta during meditation, even more than from relaxation techniques alone.[138] In another yogic meditation practice called yoga nidra or yogic sleep it is possible to be consciously aware while producing delta waves. This state lets us tap deep into our latent subconscious awareness, the place of supreme internal knowing (*prajna*) and pure potential. Advanced yoga meditators may seek to access this place. For most of us during a meditation practice, we typically find ourselves shifting back and forth between brain states which is why our meditation practice may feel fleeting. We go into and out of it in waves and we may wonder whether we are actually meditating. I found that with experience overtime, the longer one can reside in the deeper brain states and time seems to pass more quickly.

Executives Who Meditate

There are many highly successful executives who practice meditation. Here is a list of some of them, gathered from *The Huffington Post*,[139] Arianna Huffington's book *Thrive*,[140] and *Business Insider*.[141]

- John Mackey, Co-Founder & CEO, Whole Foods Market
- Mark Bertolini, Chairman & CEO, Aetna
- Bill George, Former Chairman & CEO, Medtronic
- Bill Ford, Executive Chairman, Ford Motor Company
- Oprah Winfrey, Chairwoman & CEO, Harpo Productions, Inc.
- Arianna Huffington, President, Huffington Post Media Group
- Jeff Weiner, CEO, LinkedIn
- Padmasree Warrior, Former CTO, Cisco Systems
- Ray Dalio, Founder & Co-CIO, Bridgewater Associates
- Larry Brilliant, acting Chairman, Skoll Global Threats Fund
- Russell Simmons, Chairman & CEO, Rush Communications
- Robert Stiller, Founder, Keurig Green Mountain
- Marc Benioff, Chairman & CEO, Salesforce
- Roger Berkowitz, President & CEO, Legal Sea Foods
- Ramani Ayer, Former Chairman & CEO, The Hartford
- Evan Williams, coFounder & Former Chairman & CEO, Twitter
- George Stephanopoulos, Chief Anchor & Chief Political Correspondent, ABC News

Stilling the Body and Centering the Mind

A Little Indian Restaurant

With the smell of curry in the air, there I was in Florida at 6 a.m., sitting in the middle of an Indian restaurant on a rug. Before me was a man I barely knew who invited people to come to his restaurant at dawn to learn to meditate. He gave very limited instruction; instead, he just sat and meditated, and we were supposed to follow along. I was twenty-seven years old and in the middle of a really intense, three-month training program for the management consulting firm with which I had just started working. I was really stressed, curious about meditation, and thought it might help. I think I failed this Indian man, because all he said was "Be still." A few minutes later, he said, "Be *still*." And then soon after, "*Be still*." He sounded irritated. I was sitting there with my eyes closed and legs crossed on the floor. I thought I *was* still, but by the third time he said something, I felt that perhaps I didn't even know what it meant to be still.

Movement and Vibration

We never are really still, after all. Our heart continues to pump blood, our organs continue to function, our circulatory system continues to move nutrients around the body, and our digestive and elimination systems continue to do their jobs. At a cellular level, every one of our cells has a life of its own and is constantly busy, performing its function. Our bodies are predominantly water and fluids, which easily move along with us. And, at an even smaller scale, our bodies are molecules and atoms. Our bodies are in a constant state of vibration. The frequency at which we vibrate is impacted by the frequencies all around us from the energy in our environment—including music, phones ringing, people, voices, hum of the lights, temperature, traffic outside, and even the weather. There is nothing ever still about our bodies, even as we sleep.

Dropping Into Meditation

So, what does it mean to *move into stillness*, to *drop into* meditation, and how do we get there? Let's back into that answer. Our intention in yogic meditation is to allow our minds to take a break from the chaos through single-pointed concentration. Many people want to learn to meditate because they have heard that it will help them manage their levels of stress—and this is true. However, it is not possible to manage your stress and drop into meditation unless, at some basic level, you can learn to relax and be still.

Our breath is one tool that can help to move us into a calm place where we can sit silently, concentrate, and be still as we meditate. If we have a lot of stuck tension, the tension may distract us; a little stretching may also help us sit comfortably. Yoga movement practice is a great way to release tension, relax your body, and calm your mind, so that you can begin to cultivate a practice of meditation. Many people find that mantra meditation is the best way for them to move out of the racing mind and begin to find calm.

When our nervous system is relaxed, we can learn to concentrate on one thing, and over time—with practice and without judgment—we simply drop into the less active brain states.

Centering

Centering is a good practice that can help you learn to control the mind and senses and is a way to calm yourself during your day when you don't have a lot of time. You can practice centering your mind at work before transitioning from one thing to the next, such as before starting a new work task, a meeting, or a conference call. You can also guide everyone to center before the start of a meeting or even in the middle of a meeting that is trending in a not-so-helpful direction.

Five-Minute At-the-Desk Centering Practice

1. Sit upright in your chair.
2. Place your feet flat on the floor.
3. Knees should be in a 90-degree angle and comfortable. Sit toward the edge of the seat, but feel comfortable and supported.
4. Draw the belly in. Lengthen your spine. Sit tall.
5. Place your hands on your thighs or knees, wherever comfortable, palms facing up or down.
6. Relax the shoulders. Relax your jaw.
7. Close your eyes and make them still.
8. Bring your attention to your relaxed inhales and exhales.
9. Maintain a passive attitude, letting thoughts pass by.
10. Stay for five minutes. Return your attention to the relaxed inhales and exhales when the mind wants to wander.

Noticing is a form of self-awareness. Notice how your body feels. Notice your mind. Notice the difference in your state of mind and in the sensations in your body from the beginning to the end of the practice.

Yoking the Mind

Everything we do is infused with the energy with which we do it. If we're frantic, life will be frantic. If we're peaceful, life will be peaceful. And so our goal in any situation becomes inner peace.

—Marianne Williamson

Turning Inward

The practice of noticing the monkey mind and drawing the mind back from the mayhem in order to concentrate is often called *turning inward* and is another way to think about *pratyahara*, the fifth limb of classical yoga. Pratyahara is traditionally considered to be the action or process of withdrawing or *yoking* the senses inward, a step necessary for the concentration required for meditation. What this means is that we slowly start to move our attention away from what we perceive through our senses of vision, hearing, touch, taste, or smell, toward a still, internal place that exists separate from any sensory experience. Reducing distraction in all forms in our lives is likewise a practice in pratyahara in life. Simplifying life is an easy way to get rid of some of the noise that otherwise distracts the mind and senses.

Yoking the Senses

The process of yoking the senses in preparation for meditation can begin by sitting quietly, noticing each of your senses, and then choosing one on which to focus, allowing the others to fade into the background. For example, if you choose to focus on your sense of hearing, focus *all* your attention on hearing. Try not to notice input from the eyes, nose, mouth, or skin. You might listen, for example, to the hum of the air conditioner rather than paying attention to the cool air it blows. Through this practice, we can begin to still the racing mind and relax the body, through concentration on a single thing.

When we withdraw from or yoke the senses, we eventually don't notice them as much and begin to have better control of the senses. Turning inward offers a path of coming to center, so that we can go with the flow at work and in life rather than fighting against it.

Sense Withdrawal

We have all had the experience of concentrating so hard on something that we didn't even hear a person come into our office and speak to us. Meditation and sense withdrawal may feel a bit like that, but we do it intentionally. There could be sound in the room but we don't hear it, because we're concentrating so much on the practice that we've yoked our hearing. We could be cold, but we don't feel cold, because we've yoked our sense of touch. There could be a lot of visual stimulation in the room, but we've closed or softened our eyes, thus yoking our sight. Or we could have a critical deadline to meet at work, but we don't give energy to this thought as we sit. Our thoughts appear, but with practice, we can allow them to float away, because we've yoked the thinking mind through sensory withdrawal. Over time, thoughts don't come as strongly as we sit.

Do Not Judge Yourself

Once we yoke the senses inward, we can concentrate fully on our meditation practice. Yoking our senses is a way to control your mind and senses so you can concentrate. It is not easy to do it. It is important *not to judge yourself*. You are not doing it wrong when the mind moves back to noticing senses or thoughts. With any kind of concentration practice, our minds often move away from the point of focus. The mind does not ask permission from us; it just moves. That is natural, and the fleeting nature of the practice is actually part of the practice. Noticing what your mind tends to move toward, or when it wanders, is a discovery in and of itself, a gate to deep levels of self-awareness and self-reflection. We are honing our powers of concentration along the way, practicing compassion and non-judgment toward ourselves by reminding our inner voice to stop interfering with the process by telling us we are doing it wrong. Yoking the senses can be thought of as a prequel to concentration, and concentration itself a prequel to meditation.

Concentration

Single-Pointed Attention

Concentration or *dharana* is the sixth limb of classical yoga and has to do with focusing on one thing for a period of time. In the yoga meditation tradition, this kind of focus is called *single-pointed attention*. Yogic meditation requires the practitioner to begin by turning his or her attention to an object of meditation. The object can be one's breath, a visual reference to a sacred principle or, most often, a mantra. Patanjali describes numerous possible objects of meditation in his Yoga-sutras. Next, one concentrates on the object by repeatedly returning one's attention to it. By practicing concentration on an object over a long period of time, one develops the ability to keep one's attention focused on the object. This is the stage of meditation. When meditation reaches a point where complete absorption in the object of meditation is effortless, one has attained the state of samadhi. At that point, the subject and object are said to merge, to unite, to become one.

The practice of concentration allows you to learn to control your conscious mind and senses, so they do not control you. As leaders, it is common and often necessary to have overbooked schedules and multi-tasking minds. This works only when you also have the ability to snap back to a singularly focused mind, concentrate fully, and get things done well. Concentration practice helps us harness our awareness on the present, so we are less likely to succumb to preoccupation and distraction. When our minds move too quickly and in ways that cause us to feel heightened or anxious and degrade our attention span, our minds are controlling us. Practices in concentration can help us regain control of the moving mind and maintain our powers of concentration as we age.

The Gaze

There are other ways to practice concentration that will help you access the stage of meditation. In a yoga asana class we may direct students to concentrate their gaze, or *dristi*, on a single point like a spot on the wall. This helps students to stop moving and to concentrate. Advanced students have trained their minds and can control their breath with ease, so that they move through the flow in a controlled pace, always in concentration and in a very calm, meditative-like state. Balancing postures are a good indicator as to whether students are in their thinking minds or in concentration; if we do not concentrate on a single point of focus in a balancing posture, we cannot balance. It is not possible to be still in a balancing posture if our minds are racing, if we are looking around the room, if we are planning for the future, or if we are judging ourselves. Even a mental pat-on-the-back for striking a beautiful balancing pose will take you out of concentration and throw you off balance. Maintaining complete focus on being in the pose for the full duration of the pose is the key to dynamically holding a balancing posture. Concentration and focus requires complete control of the conscious mind and senses.

Object of Focus

At work, you can practice dharana by selecting any object of your choosing, such as a picture frame or paperweight, and then giving it all of your attention, uninterrupted, for several minutes straight. Keep the gaze relaxed, and blink as little as possible. Concentrate only on the object. Notice every characteristic of its shape, movement, and color as relevant. Harnessing the wandering mind will build strength of concentration.

The Anchor

In meditation, this single point of concentration can be referred to as an *anchor*, the thing we return to and concentrate on when our mind inevitably wants to wander. As already mentioned, traditionally the anchor is a mantra. There are many meditation techniques and consequently options for anchoring your meditation practice: an anchor can be your breath, an image of a beautiful scene, an emotion, a question with which you are wrestling, a mantra, a word, a prayer, or an affirmation. The mind always wants to waver; this practice involves the continual effort of bringing it back.

Anchor Meditation: Visualization[142]

1. Find a comfortable seated position where you can remain without moving for ten minutes. You may choose to be cross-legged, perched on a couple blocks, on a meditation cushion, or perhaps in a chair. If you choose a chair, sit on the edge of the seat with feet flat on the ground. Make sure you are warm and the room is quiet. Make sure you are not overly hungry or thirsty. We are attempting to remove any possible distractions.
2. Rest the backs of your hands on your thighs, with palms open. Close your eyes. Sit up tall. Find length in the spine as the crown of the head draws toward the ceiling and the abdomen tones. Notice your breath. Breathe softly through your nose. Notice the soft rise and fall of your chest. Still the eyes behind closed lids.
3. Visualize a beach. Visualize a clear, calm, bright blue ocean.
4. Visualize a clear glass sitting on the beach in front of where you are seated. Watch as you pick up the glass and walk into the water up to your ankles. Scoop up some sand and water with the glass. Walk back onto the beach and sit down. Place the glass on the sand in front of you.

5. Focus on the glass. Notice the sand floating around in the water. Now begin to notice the sand settling and the water becoming clear.
6. Repeat this mantra in your mind through the meditation practice: Let the sand settle and the water become clear.
7. As thoughts arise, return to the image of the sand in the glass settling and the water becoming clear.

Over time, you will be able to return to the anchor and stay for a while. Perhaps you will reach a point where you are so calm and deep into your meditation that you will not notice anything else. Some call this a *complete sensory withdrawal* or *dissolving into space*, because that's somewhat how it feels. Over time, this withdrawal from the senses while sitting for longer and longer periods allows one to access deeper and deeper states of meditation.

Meditation Techniques

Begin With A Five-Minute Daily Meditation Practice

You don't require a guru to learn to meditate but a teacher might be helpful. You may find that you prefer to practice different techniques at different times of day or different times in your life. Most of us will require a quiet room. There are many ways to approach a meditation practice. You can invite positive feelings that you need more of, such as peace, joy, and love—or characteristics you wish to embody, such as equanimity and strength. You can use mantra, affirmations, prayers or new beliefs on which you want to do inner work. You can drop in a word, a question, or something around which you would like clarity. When you begin a practice of sitting, don't judge yourself. Just be aware, kind, and committed. In time, you will start to notice subtle differences on days when you meditate and on days when you do not. Then you will begin to appreciate the importance of a regular practice. Get curious about experimenting.

It's better to practice daily for a short amount of time than once or twice a week for longer. Set yourself up for success. Choose a length of time that feels doable and commit to it. This can be as short as five minutes a day. Yes, that will still make a difference because it will start to cement a sitting habit. This is the most important first step.

Try Several Techniques

Each individual will find his or her own unique path to meditation. Some may prefer group meditation, others may like to be guided by a recording or a live person, and still others will want complete silence in a room by themselves. While sitting is the more traditional position for extended meditation, meditation can be practiced sitting, lying, or even walking. Lying is a good starting point for beginner meditators, as many people find it easier to put their mind at ease in a reclined position. A walking meditation typically involves a back and forth or circular pattern that one follows repetitively as they try to find a serene mental state. Beginner meditators who simply cannot sit still, who fidget constantly no matter how hard they try not to, may feel better in group meditation that is led or even better by participating in yoga movement classes as a means to learn how to use their breath and how to relax first.

Cheer Yourself On

The deeper the meditation, the closer we are to a sleep state without being asleep. Still, sometimes we may fall asleep—and that's part of the process. Accept it with non-judgment and detachment and just keep practicing. Regular uninterrupted practice requires that you invoke that inner cheerleader, cheering you on, never giving up even if you sat for a week straight and felt that all you did was think with your eyes closed. More than likely that was actually not the case and next week might feel different. As the cliché goes, if you fall off the horse, get back on the saddle. With practice you will begin to notice the sometimes-subtle benefits of a sitting practice in your life. In all aspects of yoga, and certainly in meditation, we are asked to allow and let go. Allow whatever is coming up in your mind, without judgment. Your job is to passively sit, concentrate on your chosen anchor, and just be. The rest will come.

Morning Meditation

I like to meditate first thing in the morning. It's easier for me to take that time before the excitement of the day begins. I just sit up in bed, prop a pillow under me, roll my shoulders a little, close my eyes, and go. Sometimes I don't even set a timer, but when I do it's typically for twenty minutes. It is also nice to simply come out of meditation when the time seems right or when something in my house—such as the sound of a child coming into my bedroom—brings me out. Some days, thirty minutes disappear and it feels like five. Many days, I'm interrupted at five minutes, reminding me that acceptance and unconditional love are part of my yoga practice, too. Do what fits best into your life. With serenity enter into the wild unknown revealing more joy along the journey.

Eight Steps to Meditate in Bed

1. Upon waking, sit up in bed and work out the kinks in your body if needed with ten to thirty seconds of simple bed stretches and shoulder rolls.
2. Prop your butt up on the edge of a pillow.
3. Cross your legs in a comfortable way.
4. Sit up very tall. Lengthen your spine including your neck.
5. Close your eyes and relax your eyeballs, fixing them on a point behind closed lids like the tip of your nose.
6. Draw your belly in and take a few deep breaths, becoming aware of your inhales and exhales.
7. Begin to breathe naturally, but maintain the breath awareness.
8. As thoughts arise, let them go and bring your attention back to your inhale and exhale, repeating softly and slowly in your mind: *I inhale, I exhale.*

You can meditate like this for the rest of your life; there is no need to make it any fancier. But if you want to get fancier, you can create a little meditation corner and sit on a little meditation cushion. You can also take a meditation class and even hire a meditation coach.

Group Meditation

If you'd like to meditate with a group, some forms of meditation have special centers that one can join to learn to meditate in that tradition. Many yoga studios offer free meditation *sits*. Research your area, and do not feel intimidated about walking into the new setting. There is no way to do it wrong. Everyone there was a beginner once, too.

Paths to Meditation

This section offers several ways people seek to have a meditative experience. I have found them to be useful in their own way. You may want to try them all.

Ways of Finding a Meditative Experience

1. **Mantra:** A mantra repeated out loud or in ones mind, which has meaning or is a seed sound called bija mantra in yoga. Many yogis believe there is meaning in everything including the ancient bija mantras. Bija mantras are single syllable sounds that formed the basis of primordial language. *(Om*—a bija mantra representing the universal sound connecting us all; Lokah Samastah Sukhino Bhavantu – may all beings be happy and free from suffering and may I contribute to the happiness and freedom of all; Ong Namo Guru Dev Namo – I bow to the divine teacher within; there are countless other mantras that have meaning from which to choose)

2. **Affirmation.** Silently or sometimes audibly repeat a positive statement that represents what you would like to devote yourself to or what you would like to cultivate more of in your life. (I embrace and accept the differences in all human beings; I am beautiful, bountiful and blissful; I am filled with joy) Or repeat a single word or pair of words (love, ease, courage, strength, hope)

3. **Prayer.** A general prayer or a prayer offered toward another. (May I be an instrument of peace; send blessings and healing to a loved one or to all people around the world)

4. **Object.** Choose an object on which to concentrate your attention. This can be something physical, like the flame of a candle, a statue, a stone, a flower, a lava lamp, a snow globe, or your breath. When thoughts arise, bring your attention back to this object of concentration. Use it as a touchstone. If you are using your breath as an anchor, for example, notice the breath and return to the feeling of each inhale and each exhale when the mind wanders. If you want to cultivate strength, you may choose a stone and focus your meditation on its properties. If cultivating softness use a feather, beauty a flower, confidence a flame. With practice, thoughts will begin to pass by without much effort on your part. You may have a sensation of dissolving or blending into your object of concentration. If you are holding an object, you may choose to put it down after awhile. If you have your eyes open as you are looking at an object, you may choose to close them after awhile.

5. **Counting.** Maintaining a rhythmic pace for a period of time can support a meditation practice. Using counting tools like the beads on a mala or a metronome helps to associate with the rhythm of the breath. Practitioners also count the number of times they have repeated a mantra using a mala.

6. **Visualization.** A guided or self-created visualization of a place that is very peaceful and harmonious is a helpful anchor. Common visualization practices include a beach, mountaintop, meadow, or the galaxy.

7. **Body scan.** Certain meditation practices bring attention to a specific body part, such as the crown of the head, or to canvassing the body and bringing attention to each body part, inviting it to relax. The feel and weight of the body and each body part becomes the anchor, allowing the practitioner to drop into awareness and out of distraction. This is particularly conducive to a supine (lying down) meditation.

8. **Yogic sleep (yoga nidra).** Often thought of as one of the most restorative forms of meditation, yoga nidra is a long, deep meditation practice done lying down with eyes closed while listening to a teacher who is guiding you. The purpose is to slow the brain waves to a sleep state while remaining conscious. Because each session tends to be at least thirty minutes long, it is easy to fall asleep during the session. Many people do a yoga nidra practice at night in bed for this reason; it is excellent for people with insomnia and burdensome levels of stress. This is a guided practice, so if you're not participating in a group class, find a yoga nidra audio class online, put on headphones, and listen to the recorded session. Allow it to lull you to a sleep state or at least to put your mind to rest. If you fall asleep, great, take the headphones off when you wake up. With practice, it becomes easier to remain awake yet relaxed for longer periods, enjoying the benefits of this deep meditation.

The Uncharted Territory

The IMAX film called *The Universe* showed original footage of the universe captured through massive telescopes seated in the darkest and most deserted parts of the earth. At many times, the footage panned out from a single star to its galaxy and then to the many, many galaxies nearby. By the end of the film, we really understand the mind-blowing fact that our planet and the other planets orbiting our sun are just one galaxy of a *billion* other galaxies in the universe. Our minds are much like this: one vast universe of which we see or utilize very little.

Meditation is a practice of consciously moving into the vast, uncharted territory of our minds. We do this by becoming still, fixing our attention on something, and settling into ourselves. Every time the mind wanders we bring our attention back to our object of focus thus training the mind and developing mastery overtime. Through deep states of meditation and self-awareness practices, a matrix of possibilities emerge for our lives like a spectrum of color. We *expand* our consciousness and move about our days with a broader sense of ourselves and of the world around us. With an expanded consciousness, it becomes difficult for us to go back to believing that there is only one way. Seeing events through a prism commits us to grand visions and limitless possibilities.

Philosophy: Manifesting Authenticity and Abundance

Social Principle 2: Truth—Integrity (satya)

> Before you speak, ask yourself—is it kind, is it necessary,
> is it true, does it improve on the silence?
>
> —Sai Baba

Truth (satya) is one of the five yogic social principles. It has within it honesty, integrity, and being grounded in truthfulness. This is a profound virtue that helps you to be authentic, real, and true to yourself.

Truth and Fact vs. Opinion and Perspective

The principle of integrity states that communication should be as exacting as possible, preventing any deception. Don Miguel Ruiz captures the essence of satya in his widely read book, *The Four Agreements*, in his chapter called "Be impeccable with your word."[143] Attempt to remove all hidden agendas and share all agendas openly and with clarity. Resolve is good, but recognizing the difference between truth and perspective and truth and opinion takes wisdom and practice. If something stated in a meeting is opinion or based on one's own life experiences without consideration of the views of others, then it is not truth. A commitment to the truth is a commitment to a big-picture view.

When discussing products and services, acting with integrity involves speaking the truth based upon fact. Facts are not perspectives. Treading the line makes us appear insincere and untrustworthy to others. Treading the line invites risk into the organization and at some point backfires.

Speaking the truth and living from truth exist beyond the level of the story. We often tell ourselves that things must, should, or have to be done a certain way. The next time you feel this way, ask yourself why. Is it an ego-based identification, part of your story rather than truth itself? It's normal to feel we have to do and accomplish a lot of things; in reality, there is very little we *have to* or *must* do in life. As a leader, exist above the level of the story and lead from truth. Assess your use of *have tos*, *musts*, and *shoulds* in the context of your own well-being and that of the team.

Integrity

Leaders who claim to be filled with integrity can often be void of it entirely. Integrity is a way of life, not a label. Think about people who guard their words or actions. If we are authentic and speak from truth, firmly grounded in the intention of being supportive and kind toward others, there is very little need to be so guarded.

> If something cannot be explained in a succinct manner, it is likely based on non-truths and is not honest.

Saying one thing to one person and something different to another is not acting with integrity. Saying one thing and thinking another is not truth and is not honest. Integrity and truth come only from leaders who have a healthy dose of humility and intelligence, through which they are able to operate from a clear place that is naturally open to all views. Admit your own mistakes and acknowledge your limitations. Give the benefit of the doubt to others. Supposition, gossip, hearsay, or erroneous conclusions are not truth. Truth is more often succinct and directly-stated than not.

Small white lies or painstaking reporting adjustments begin to create an environment of questionable performance and questionable integrity, which create doubts about performance and the future. While using data in a way that presents a positive marketing message is a normal operating procedure, if it deceives someone into believing something that is not true, then it is void of integrity. Make it a practice to leverage multiple sources to assure the accuracy and appropriateness of your marketing messages.

Integrity at the office importantly involves reliability, punctuality, and honoring commitments. We have a habit of continually breaking promises and commitments with no regard for the consequences of such actions. This degrades relationships and connection to others, which is counterproductive to growth and development as a human being. Regularly cancelling appointments or showing up late for meetings with others is disrespectful of their time, puts your reliability and time-management skills in question, and will not support your ability to connect or engage with others.

If you are unsure if you are acting in integrity or not, ask a random and wide-ranging selection of people how they perceive you and see what adjectives come up. This will tell you how your actions are seen in the world.

Be Real, Reasonable, and Reliable

Be real, reasonable, and reliable. Overcommitting and under-delivering leads to dissatisfaction and disappointment. Allowing every member of your team to live their own truth through their own identity will spur creativity. If your team must pretend their way through the day—being forced to adhere to rules that conflict with organizational principles or even their own principles—they will be discontent. If there is a situation where it seems that the principles of the business seem to be in contradiction to those of an employee, it is probably just a misunderstanding. If you discuss this situation openly and seek to understand in detail the specifics of the person's belief, common ground should arise. And if a conflict in foundational principles does persist, then perhaps that person is not a fit for the team—even if that person is you. Everyone's performance will suffer when rogue employees are allowed to act out of accordance with fundamental principles shared commonly among the rest of the team.

Questions for Leaders: Integrity and Truth

1. Do you have a tendency to speak about the performance of competitors or peers without direct, firsthand knowledge and understanding?
2. Are your alliances, ventures, and partnerships committed to truth, thus providing a healthy ecosystem in which to operate?
3. Are you very clear on the specifics of the law and regulations in your field? Do you seek to understand and explain legal statutes to the team? Do you explain the consequences of violation? If the law involves interpretation do you guide the team to operate a clear distance from the line or to operate as close to the line as possible without treading over?

4. Are you very clear on what you are asking of your team? Do you listen to your team?

5. Do you find your staff quick to make excuses about their work? If so, have you fully heard why?

6. Is it clear to the team that they are expected to communicate in an honest yet kind manner? Is it clear that such discourse helps to form the identity of the team and shape the culture of the organization?

7. Are your meetings full of healthy debate or full of inflexible opinions and confrontation? Do people talk over one another?

8. Do employees feel comfortable offering their opinion? Do they have the opportunity to share? Do you encourage them to share?

9. Do you break commitments in your life and blame it on self-identified higher-priority things?

10. Do you display a courageous commitment to integrity?

11. Do all people in your life find you reliable?

12. Do you repay all your debts of service?

13. Do you compensate people appropriately?

Social Principle 5: Non-possessiveness—Gratitude (aparigraha)

Non-possessiveness, non-hoarding or *aparigraha* is the one of the five social principles or yamas. More subtly, it involves not holding onto that which can be let go. A positive equivalent of non-hoarding is gratitude and appreciation.

Non-Possessiveness

From the perspective of a leader this involves not holding onto every work product. Let go of the need to own and micromanage every written report and project your team puts together. Allow your team freedom of expression and ownership. Guide, facilitate, encourage, and teach your team. If you don't have meaningful value to contribute, and you have assessed the work as accurate and in keeping with the desired objective, let go of the need to put your signature on it. Let go of the need to take credit for your teams work and instead give credit to them. Give credit to your team while knowing that you are ultimately responsible. Enlightened leaders never throw subordinates under the bus and always take full responsibility.

Things

Non-possessiveness doesn't mean we shouldn't own things but when we seek to possess and own a lot of things, each one occupies a little bit of our mind-space, which is already full of both essential and nonessential thoughts. Our goal should be to free up space in our mind, not to fill it by giving it more things to think about. We need to maintain our things, organize our things, find a place to store our things, and then of course we must remember to use our things. We have so many things that we need professional organizers to organize our things, and we often do not use our things because we do not remember we own them, which for some can create guilt. I have a motto that reads *know what you own*. Most of us don't know what exists deep in drawers, desks, closets, pantries, or storage areas. When you offer gifts to your team or clients for special occasions, consider not adding to their inventory of things by gifting them services or products they will consume.

Non-Coveting

The social principle of non-possessiveness is also described as non-coveting, or trying not to desire what others have. Examples include not coveting another team member's salary, bonus, office, clients, projects, or travel opportunities. This can be quite a challenge in an office environment where we seek fairness and growth opportunities. As leaders, we have the opportunity to help change that dynamic simply by being good communicators of expectations, good listeners to our teams, and openly appreciating the unique talents and efforts of all team members. You can help each team member clearly see his or her path of growth. Continue to challenge your team while helping them work through their own insecurities and setbacks along the way.

Saying Good-bye

Let go of those things you are holding onto *just in case* and *for a rainy day*. If you like to hold onto things at home you probably hold onto things that you don't really need at the office, too. You can start this practice at work by creating a little more space on your desk and in your filing cabinets, which lightens your mental load, too.

Importantly, we hold onto much more than just things. We hold onto worn-out beliefs about others or ourselves, worn-out ideas, worn-out opinions, worn-out pre-programming, worn-out ideology, worn-out resentments, and worn-out grievances. We often hold onto what we feel we *need* to hold onto for security or we simply have held on so long that we never thought about letting it go. Like standing in a line at a grocery store, you become more committed to the line you chose the longer you stand in it. The longer we hold onto patterns, the more we feel a part of them, an ownership, and over time it becomes more difficult to say goodbye. We may feel afraid, remorseful, or just stubborn about saying goodbye. So we hold on, we possess them, and they possess us. Aparigraha is *non*-possessiveness. Take a chance, let go of the outdated and worn-out to allow space for something new.[144]

Gratitude and Appreciation

Gratitude and appreciation tends to be scarce in highly competitive office environments. In cultures where every member of the team is openly and honestly appreciated and supported, people will not feel the need to be in an ongoing state of competition against one another seeking ownership and possession. At some level, competition is healthy and necessary, such as the competitive spirit that helps motivate and inspire. Healthy competition feeds the soul and is fun and energizing. When competition is borne out of a sense of resource constraint and lack, like a need to fight for scarce resources (a job, a promotion, a raise, a bonus), it becomes unhealthy. Unhealthy competition is counterproductive to performance and exhausting to work in. An office environment where the team is constantly competing against one another keeps the team in a perpetual state of stress, tapping vibrancy and fueling discontent. Highly competitive environments foster contentious divisions full of resentment and conflict impeding productivity and creativity. Grateful environments instead foster the desire to work in cooperation, supporting one another for the good of the company and its broader ecosystem.

Changing Scarcity to Abundance

Leaders can change the perception of scarcity of resources, time, and to some degree income, to a perception of abundance by allowing this principle to guide communications and decisions. Afford every team member equal and ample growth and development opportunities. Help the team to understand one another's unique contribution by showcasing skills and talents at meetings and in other forms of communication. Make it known that everyone shares in excess return and spread it as broadly as possible. Regularly and openly express appreciation for work efforts. Create a *thank you* culture.

> Kind words can be short and easy to speak,
> but their echoes are truly endless.
>
> —Mother Theresa

Create a *Thank You* Culture

Create a thank you culture that embodies appreciation and support toward one another. Working in cooperation rather than isolation is scalable. If we thank people more regularly, acknowledging the value in what each person offers each day, we can help them to exist each day with satisfaction in their work. Move your team beyond a negative place where they focus on deprivation, what they do not have today. Help them connect to their work so they feel positive and content about their current situation, yet excited about what tomorrow brings. Team members need to feel connected to their work in order to motivate themselves to do the work well. Tell them that you want them to feel positive and excited about their work directly. Ask them how you can help to achieve that goal. Spread kind words. They are little gifts.

Allow Good Expressions to Circulate

To truly appreciate yourself, your life, and your team, you must allow space in your life to feel appreciation and gratefulness. After you feel it, express it. Allow these good expressions to circulate in all areas of your life. Keeping positive expressions bottled up because of lack of time creates a negative undercurrent of stagnation and heaviness in the work environment. A healthy environment allows for the circulation of good verbal expressions. Environments filled with mutual respect and appreciation are vibrant, alive, productive, and positive. You can feel this. Giving appreciation is good for others, feels good to us, and helps us connect with our team. Take note of your employee who always seems to fix the printer problems for the team and thank them. Learn the names of the cleaning crew and the security guards and thank them. Don't hold back. Give good expressions freely every day.

The Small Stuff

Appreciation involves noticing the small stuff, too. After business school, I flew to Costa Rica for a month to learn Spanish. I was paired with a family that included a mother, two daughters, and a son. I did not start off knowing any Spanish, and the mother did not speak English, so communication involved a lot of gestures. The home was middle class by Costa Rican standards of living. Still, they had only cold water in the house. They lived amicably with insects, the host mom regularly ushering bugs out of the kitchen rather than stomping on them. Showering with spiders in cold water took some getting used to. Their plumbing couldn't handle toilet paper. Throwing my used toilet paper in the trashcan beside me took quite a lot of getting used to. This experience made me realize how many of our riches and simple comforts we take for granted. So don't forget the little things, such as appreciating the warm water when washing your hands in the office on a cold winter day or the abundance of food we enjoy at mealtimes. An internal *thank you* builds awareness and fills our internal stores of gratitude.

Questions for Leaders: Non-Possessiveness and Gratitude

1. Do you regularly extend appreciation for the hard work efforts of every member of the team? Do you expect appreciation in return? Do you feel slighted if you don't receive appreciation?

2. Does every member of the team feel supported? Do you feel supported?

3. Do you hold grudges about past performance? Does your team?

4. Do all of your team members feel they have ample opportunities for growth?

5. Do all of your team members understand each other's roles, contributions, and competencies? Have you worked toward funneling each individual toward specifics at work that he or she is really good at? Do you learn from your team?

6. Are all good events and performance appropriately recognized and rewarded, even the seemingly mundane and small?

7. Do the team members work in harmony with or in competition with one another? Do they believe the work environment is fair?

8. Do you employ policies of financial prudence that allow for long-term employment even in the downtimes?

9. Do you compensate partners and vendors fairly and in a timely manner? What do you do to help them over and above contracting for their services and products?

10. Do you block off adequate time in your calendar each day so that you can maintain connection with your team members and address their needs and concerns? Are you a bottleneck?

11. Do you create space in your calendar to allow for the unexpected? Are you always putting out fires?

12. Is your office cluttered with things you are holding on to unnecessarily? Do you take time to unclutter your life, including your material possessions?

13. Does the enterprise have a strong program for community and philanthropy, allowing the team and leaders to put their skills and money to good use?

14. Do you know the names of the cleaning crew, security guards, and cafeteria staff in your building?

Concluding Statement

The knowledge dimension takes you from fighting with your life to allowing your life to *move through you*. Working to improve the quality of the present moment, by improving the quality of our interactions and thoughts, enlightens our lives. This is a deep human layer allowing us as humans to function as intelligent and enlightened beings. Working to understand how our complex minds work helps us to live consciously, responding to every moment with discernment and clear judgment, intelligence and clear perception. Spending time truly listening to others establishes trust and improves your ability to connect and engage your team and consequently motivate and inspire them. Exercising yet relaxing your brain by removing distraction and focusing on a single point of concentration in a meditation practice builds helpful neural structure. The quiet of a meditation practice also promotes vision, insight, intuition and innovation. Reflecting upon your attention to this layer, you will find you have improved your concentration, attention span, and memory, and you have an enhanced ability to find calm in the chaos. You will find that you have enhanced your capacity for handling stress and controlling your emotions. Your team will find you more fair, open, and easier to connect with. They will feel listened to and consequently more trusting and willing to support you too. The team will work harder and better together as well.

Chapter 8
Yogi Secret #6: Bliss

Old Maxim
My experience is dictated and limited by external conditions.

New Maxim
My inner freedom creates a condition for unlimited potential.

Resolve: I choose an unbounded and joyful life experience. I direct my choices in consideration of my unique purpose, honoring what I'm meant to be doing right now. By prioritizing strong connections to others, appreciating my own gifts and all of the abundance in my life, I will find joy and peace in each of my days.

Yogi Secret #6 allows me to develop or maintain personal qualities inherent in inspiring leaders, including: meaningful engagement through purposeful living and leadership ⁓ vision ⁓ connection and healthy personal relationships ⁓ clarity and balance ⁓ joy and happiness ⁓ contentment and peace

Some men see things as they are and ask why; I dare to
dream of things that never were and ask, why not?
—George Bernard Shaw

The fifth and final layer in the Pancha Maya Kosha model is the dimension of bliss and joy called the *anandamaya kosha*. Don't you want to feel joyful most of the time? A healthy layer of bliss supports our likability quotient, which we all know is necessary for leadership success. I have an American friend named Ananda. Her name is a testament to a young mother's enduring love for her newborn baby because her name means *bliss*. Those with children can certainly imagine the sensation of first seeing your baby, the feelings of love and delight that rush through your body. It is a blissful experience.

This dimension is of particular importance, as our bodies and minds can be harmonized only if we are in touch with our layer of bliss. When our bliss dimension is full, we feel good; we are vital, connected and happy. A healthy dimension of bliss allows us to walk through life with ease. We become free of the baggage that weighs many of us down, free of the things in life that consume and overwhelm us. This doesn't just help us; it helps others, for just being in the presence of someone who is free in this way makes us feel more calm and secure. Someone who is free is energetically full yet steady and he or she shares that positive energy with others. In some way, he or she has connected to meaning and purpose in life and finds satisfaction through that connection. His or her eyes appear bright and face content. A person who can find freedom and contentment with most everything that arrives in his or her path is just right in body and mind, continuously tapping into great stores of bliss and joy. As with any dimension, life has a way of altering our balance of bliss. It is difficult to feel connected to that joyful part of us all the time. So we have to intentionally bring our attention back to it and tap into this important part of ourselves.

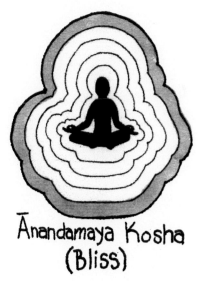

Ānandamaya Kosha
(Bliss)

How to Be Free

Finding Freedom

Freedom

We all have internal stores of bliss. When we take measures to uplift ourselves, we can then reside in the freedom found there. A good connection to our bliss dimension allows us to notice times when it seems as though everything in our lives is in sync and we feel great. This involves a positive connection to the present moment. When we do things that lift us up and give us joy, and we pay attention to the feelings that accompany those things and offer gratitude for them, we access and nurture this dimension.

Samadhi Moments

Samadhi, the eighth limb of yoga, will be discussed in the context of bliss. The traditional understanding is that samadhi is experienced when the practitioner, through deep concentration, spontaneously and effortlessly mentally absorbs into an object of meditation, experiencing the oneness of all. This is an experience of pure awareness. Meditative absorption where one settles into pure awareness can be thought of as a state of being deeply connected to our inner self, united with the spirit, which feels illuminated and expansive. Samadhi is a spiritual experience of union. In a more contemporary interpretation, we can think of samadhi moments as moments that feel just right, when everything seems perfect in a positive and healthy kind of way. My samadhi moments are often coupled with bliss so full that I tear up from happiness, such as when my son, not so many years ago, had his Kindergarten moving-up ceremony and I watched his little self, gleaming as the crowd of parents clapped. It was a moment of such deep, intimate connection that it was spiritual. Or as I summit a big peak and look out at the beautiful mountain range before me, and the unified oneness of it all, the vast glory of the landscape, the exhilaration of the climb, make for me a samadhi moment. These are places of reflection, where I can sit back and see my life with a huge amount of gratitude and love. It involves a deep connection to the inner self.

Expand Your Heart

Find some time in your busy schedule to do things that expand your heart and make you feel happy and peaceful. When we feel this way, all the other dimensions are in relative harmony. You might experience these expansive moments while kayaking in the Pacific, summiting a mountain peak, or looking into a loved one's eyes. Others may feel it when they sing or listen to music. Some of us may be able to identify times in our lives we refer to as *Zen-filled* or *samadhi moments* or recall the feeling of being *in the zone*. These moments are places of refuge, where everything—if even for just a few moments—is just right. They are expansive and wonderful, but can be difficult to access in modern life.

Soak in Bliss

We can tend to our bliss dimension by soaking in every detail of these special moments when we feel very alive and vibrant so that we may recall them as often as possible. Then we can practice visualizing them even when we are not in the actual moment itself. When we close our eyes for a moment and access our place of refuge, we have an immediate energetic shift. We feel very clear and decisive and happy. The more we can create positive imprints in our mind, the more our bodies will remember how it feels, and the easier it will be to return to those sensations again.

Cultivate Everyday Bliss

Think about cultivating everyday bliss in your life. This brings us true freedom from the clutches of expectation, from the pace of life, from judgment, from racing thoughts. Everyday bliss lets us soak our soul in wonder and pleasure. With a contented mind and a grateful heart, we can feel the appreciation that comes from simply being alive another day to explore and experience the richness of life. Can you imagine the benefits—to yourself and to others—of spending some of your time at the office blissed out instead of stressed out? As leaders, we want to feel happy and vital, connected to the people in our lives and the world around us. This is what differentiates true leaders from people in leadership roles. We cannot inspire others when we are depleted, stressed, negative, fearful, angry, lethargic, and/or disconnected. Lead from a place where you feel happy, balanced, and vibrant.

Filling Your Bliss Cup

This dimension cannot be described too specifically, because it is an integrated sense unique to each of us. We nurture this dimension by doing things that cause us to be full of joy and happiness—I refer to this as *filling our bliss cup*. You can't be full of bliss when your cup is bone dry. With a bone-dry bliss cup we are disconnected and consequently unmotivated and uninspired. Cultivating strong relationships with other people is an important way to fill your bliss cup. We need connection with other people, including healthy support systems and social networks. Let those in your inner circle know how important they are to you. Make sure you have chosen to spend most of your time with people who fill your bliss cup, and spend time honoring the needs of others in your bliss-filling circle. Establish boundaries, and minimize time spent with those who drain your bliss cup and deplete your spirit. A person filled with bliss has a magnetic quality about them. Other people are attracted to happy people. Fill your bliss cup to support your ability to connect with and motivate your team.

You can use the following list to help you focus on activities that fill your bliss cup, ideally so much that the cup is overflowing and spilling out to fill the cups of others. Try an assortment of activities to see what really makes you feel high on life. Figure out what makes your heart sing in a healthy and good way.

Twenty-Five Ways to Fill Your Bliss Cup

1. Smile and say hello to every person you see in a day, looking into their eyes.
2. Compliment a stranger.
3. Help a friend, or anyone, without being asked.
4. Pay for the coffee of the person behind you in line.
5. Summit a mountain and soak in the view.
6. Cradle a newborn child.
7. Play with your children with 100 percent of your attention for thirty minutes.
8. Admire the details of your children's facial expressions as they play or accomplish. (Get off your smartphone while you do this!)
9. Hug your loved ones until you feel the beat of their hearts.
10. Frolic with your pet outdoors.
11. Sing as loudly as your voice will allow.
12. Listen to a song that fills you up.
13. Attend an opera or symphony that moves you.
14. Dance the night away in complete abandon.
15. Spend quality time with old friends.
16. Call positive friends and family members who uplift you.
17. Go on a retreat with your partner or a good friend.
18. Travel to an exotic location and pamper yourself.
19. Spend time at an amazingly beautiful place.
20. Relish how you feel at the end of a long, breath-based yoga practice.
21. Lock arms with your partner as you walk down the street.
22. Silently soak in the very moments after an endorphin-pumping race.
23. Attend a house of worship alone.
24. Read a spiritual text or a book of poetry that moves you.
25. Spend a long time in deep meditation and appreciate your state of mind for the rest of the day.

Bliss at Work

Here are a few simple things you can do at work that take very little time or effort.

Ten Ways to Connect to Your Bliss Dimension at Work

1. Make others laugh. Tell a self-deprecating story.
2. Go out of your way to help a colleague.
3. Give a coworker an unprompted compliment.
4. Invite levity and lightness into all interactions you have with others, particularly when times are tough taking notice of how this lifts up those around you.
5. Every time someone asks how you are, give him or her a positive and enthusiastic answer, and delight in his or her reaction.
6. Admire pictures of your children or your spouse.
7. Relish in beautiful photos related to an upcoming or past vacation destination.

8. Exchange a fun or loving text or e-mail with a dear friend or family member.
9. Listen to a special song.
10. Smell an uplifting essential oil.

Search for what you need right now that will give you that deeply uplifted and peaceful feeling. Widen your vision of what it means to be full of vitality, full of bliss, and let your path be an individual and personal choice. When you commit to finding bliss in your days, things will reveal themselves that you may never have imagined. With a surplus of bliss you will uplift those around you.

Purposeful Living and Purposeful Leadership

> Acting in accordance with one's own nature, even when
> such actions appear riddled with fault, is far better
> than perfectly executing duties prescribed for others. It is better
> to die in the course of performing your own duty than
> to risk the peril of following the path of another.
> —Bhagavad Gita 3.35

The Bigger Picture

As a leader, you expect a lot of yourself, or you wouldn't have found your way into your role to begin with. We typically measure how we are doing at work based primarily upon short-term results. Many of us like our work, work very hard, and are promoted accordingly. But at some point, we may find ourselves wondering why we're doing what we're doing. To stay connected to our work and our leadership and to inspire our teams, it is helpful to feel that our work has meaning to us.

> With a healthy layer of bliss we are smiling and vibrant and become that leader for whom everyone wants to work.

I'm sure you can think of inspiring leaders who have remarkable energy and vibrancy and appear to be really happy. Such leaders seem to be content with the today yet know precisely the direction in which they are heading and can see the pot of gold at the end of the rainbow—their dream for themselves often grounded in something greater. A dream that is both appropriate and realistic. Great leaders are consummate learners, always seeking to enhance their physical and mental vigor. Setting and being clear on your personal purpose and overall vision for your work offers meaning to your efforts and is one way to feel you are heading in a positive forward direction.

Most of us have goals but perhaps not a broader personal vision around what we do. Creating a personal vision means seeking out our own *north star*, something we care about, something that inspires us and can guide us through work and/or life on a day-to-day basis. A vision is an important way to direct our work and/or personal lives toward something that we find meaningful.

This often starts with recognizing our own unique gifts and talents, what it is we were born to do. In yoga, this is called *dharma*. Understanding our dharma can also help us create a personal mission statement. Unlike a vision, which is long-term and broad, a personal mission statement is short-term and specific. It lists what we are currently doing or what we are planning to do, for whom or what, and how, all based upon our unique purpose (dharma) and overarching personal vision.

The self-introspection needed to uncover your dharma and how to reflect it in your personal mission and vision will help you align your life and discover your potential. Each offers a slightly different vantage point about your life, and together they make a powerful whole.

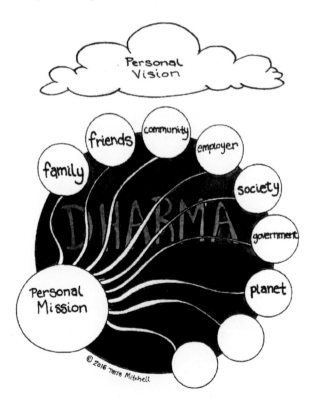

Purpose (Dharma)

Your dharma is your purpose and helps to inform what you are meant to be doing in this life. Yoga believes that the essential nature of all humans is to be of service in some way. So your purpose is oriented toward something higher. Dharma answers the questions, "Why am I here?" and "What am I uniquely meant to do right now in this life?" and "What are my special gifts?" It's important to note that your purpose is not necessarily flashy and extraordinary; for many of us, it will appear quite simple. On the flip side, many of us may not believe that our work or personal lives have the potential of grand, even world-changing impact, and yet we affect an ecosystem of people everyday. Touching the lives of others in a positive and encouraging way *is* impact. When we understand our unique talents and use them in our days we find life more enjoyable.

Your purpose might be teaching, innovating, envisioning new ways, leading, managing people, managing projects, connecting people, coaching, communicating, designing, creating, healing, parenting, working with numbers, or working with your hands. Keep in mind you may have several special gifts. At the most basic level, your purpose is that which you are very naturally skilled. You have probably been drawn to doing it, over and over again, your whole life, even as a child. In the words of Hari-kirtana das, "Dharma is not something we create or make up; it's something already there that we discover. It's a constant around which our lives revolve." While a statement of vision or mission may evolve and morph every handful of years along with your intelligence, maturity, or life changes, the essential nature of your dharma is unchanging, like a watermark in your life.

Being honest about what you are not is also important. A handful of months into motherhood, I discerned that I would be unfulfilled as a stay-at-home mom. My kids are great. Their happiness and well-being are appropriately a top priority in my life. I am dedicated to them and love them dearly. In spite of this, I know that my purpose involves something else. It is my duty as a parent to care for my children to the very best of my ability but it is not my dharma.

Personal Vision

A personal vision has to do with what matters to us, what we are inspired by and drawn toward to make a positive contribution to others, humanity, society, or on the world around us in some way. It is a longer term and broad view and tends to flow naturally out of our purpose. Consider your vision as applied directly to your current field of work. What does the future at work look like in your vision? Perhaps your vision is one where people are healthier, happier, and more engaged in their work? As a talented leader, you may have seen and understand more of the world than many of your employees and much of society. You are well aware of how things function, both good and bad. At the end of the day, the end of your career, at the end of your life, you want to feel that your time was well spent. We all need this to satisfy the dimension of bliss.

You can think about your personal vision in terms of the impact you wish to make over a three or five year period. Or you may wish to think more in terms of what you would like to be remembered by at your retirement party or at the end of life. Having a personal vision to use as a guide is one way to feel as though you are spending your time meaningfully.

Personal Mission

A personal mission, much like a business mission, is a declaration of your short-term goals, objectives, and intentions that embodies your purpose and vision. This is a good way to see how your purpose might play out right now, in your current work and life. A work-related mission may help you connect with your team in a whole new way, shift the corporate culture, innovate a product or service, navigate the next market, move into the next product or service, or start a new company. It may be helpful to share your dharma with others, describing what you believe your unique contributions are in the context of your role in the next big decision you must make and then letting the feedback help shape your mission.

Discerning Your Unique Purpose, Vision, and Mission

Allowing space in your life to follow and reflect upon your curiosities will go a long way toward discerning your unique purpose, vision, and mission. Armed with them, you can make choices that fully leverage your special skills while staying true to your principles. Taking roads that seem less traveled has meaning. All that you do in your work and personal life has meaning. You are disciplined and strong. You have the opportunity to live a meaningful life. Connect to that meaning. Do not sleepwalk through your life at work or at home. Don't sell your soul; *nourish* it.

Creating Your Roadmap

As a leader who has a desire to be better and a longing for meaning and purpose, you will likely enjoy contemplating your dharma, vision, and mission. As you work through this exercise, consider that the happiest people in the world are those who live their lives in service to others. They have a deep connection to other human beings. The vision they hold dear involves helping others, and that is how they carry out their daily lives. When you simply identify with your personal purpose as a leader in service to your team and use it as a guide along your career path, it gives your work meaning. When you embrace and embody the belief that you are in service to your team, you realize that you are incredibly important to the lives of others, and you no longer lose yourself or your sense of meaning along the way.

Write your dharma, your vision, and your personal mission statement in the present tense and make them positive. Use words that are more of a felt sense rather than logical and results-oriented. For example, consider using *higher* instead of *greater* and *serve* instead of *act*. If you are comfortable, share what you have written with others and discuss it with your team. Encourage your team members to think about their personal purpose in the context of the broader organizational goals.

Finally, recognize that your personal mission statement and the way your dharma is reflected in it will evolve over time. Allow for iterations and drafts. Dharma is like the watermark in the background, but your mission in the foreground changes overtime.

Step 1: Uncovering Your Dharma

To discover your dharma, envision the life you've led until now. From that vantage point, reflect upon and write down the special skills and talents that have emerged again and again at different times in your life. Then look for through-lines, categories, and patterns. Really examine the role that you wind up playing again and again in work, play, and other activities. See if you can gather this into a single sentence encapsulating your unique skills that can be called upon to serve others.

Step 2: Writing a Personal Vision

To write your personal vision, it may be helpful to begin with the end in mind. Envision yourself in the later years of your life. How do you want people to remember you? What accomplishments have you made? What were your societal contributions? How would a person you respect and admire describe your life at your retirement party or at a post-retirement birthday celebration? Write this down in a few sentences, using the present tense and positive language. Alternatively, think of your vision in terms of the broader impact you wish to make in a handful of years.

Step 3: Writing a Personal Mission Statement

When considering your mission it's helpful to reflect upon your ecosystem and acknowledge your place in the larger web of life. Consider how you are involved with each member of your ecosystem and your sphere of influence. As you contemplate the relative importance of each ecosystem member to your organization and to your life, consider what you would do if a certain member suddenly went away or changed significantly. What would change? How would your organization be impacted? How would you be impacted?

Now that you have a good idea of your personal ecosystem, reflect on what you can do currently that aligns your unique talents with your personal vision. It may help to discuss this with others you trust and ask for their feedback. In writing a personal mission statement, assume anything is possible. While we do not live in an ideological world, consider that even small steps in a direction can cumulatively make an enormous difference. Where attention goes, energy flows. Make your personal mission statement no more than a short paragraph

Philosophy: Manifesting a Peaceful Life

Personal Principle 2: Contentment (santosa)

Contentment is a Virtue

Contentment or santosa is the second of the five personal principles or niyamas. To be content is to be at peace with the here and now, with where you are on your journey. Contentment is a virtue worthy of cultivation. Contented leaders are satisfied with their team, even in times when things do not go as planned.

> Contented people are happy, and happy people work hard, work well together, and are easy to work with.

Contented teams feel satisfied with their compensation, work environment, and team interactions. Outdated thinking suggests that when we pressure people a lot, we optimize performance. Now we know this way of thinking is wrong. People who are happily engaged in their work, work harder. Killing the human spirit will never result in better performance and studies have shown this. Contented people enjoy their work and are happier. People who are happily engaged in their work, work harder, work well together and are easy to work with, a trifecta of superb team traits.

The Dalai Lama

At a wonderful discussion, the very funny, Boston-born GuruGanesha of the yoga rock band by the same name said that true contentment is radiated the way the Dalai Lama radiates *santosa* wherever he goes. The contentment of the Dalai Lama permeates everyone around him, making them feel more calm and peaceful. We can all make efforts to live in our own version of a contented state. It's not a gift given only to one man. It is a choice we make when we decide to live in the flow of life.

Interdependence of Life

Yogis see all parts of life as interdependent. We see how one part affects another and where apparent boundaries are actually permeable and in constant exchange. Even so, there are unexplained parts of life, things we cannot analyze or assign a cause-effect relationship to and so we accept them as our karma, as our deck of cards, and see them as teachers knowing that whatever we do affects this interdependent web of which we are all a part. The world exists for us to enjoy and learn from. The most significant and seemingly unexplainable events offer the richest opportunities for growth.

Karma and Responsibility

Yoga follows a *karma* precept. The law of karma, as it is sometimes called, offers us the opportunity to take responsibility for the state of our lives. Like paying it forward, it serves us in the long run to do our best in all ways possible today. Contentment is found when we begin to consider that everything that happens in our lives happens in the grand scheme to teach us something; they are teaching opportunities. Sometimes we will never understand why certain incidents happen, but contentment says that there is some universal grand plan at work that we can choose to learn from and learn to accept. Our levels of acceptance and contentment are variables within our own control that allow us to be a party to manifesting our lives overall.

The Vast Sea

A commonly used analogy says that we are all but a wave in the ocean. We can imagine that every leader and every enterprise is also a wave in the ocean. We have a choice whether to cause waves that will settle into the expansiveness or instead create torrents, leaving behind large wakes that rock the entire sea and cause destruction. In which visualization would one find comfort and contentment? Our focus is on humanity. Things like breaking down barriers, creating new markets and new innovations will cause waves and dislocation. But if efforts are oriented toward positive change in keeping with the preservation and protection of humanity, those waves will settle back into the vast sea.

Be the Calm in the Rough

It's true that leaders must wield an axe from time to time. In reality, it is very difficult to always be the calm in the rough, and rocking the boat might be necessary to right the ship. Yoga is an ongoing and conscious practice that begins with awareness. Awareness allows us to properly assess the current of the ocean and the wake we are leaving so we can do what is necessary while keeping with principle. Using the axe to slice off someone's limb is much different from using it to untether a rope from the dock, thus sending someone off to his or her next journey. Through the desire to live consciously, our yoga practice helps us figure out ways to bring back the calm sea when a storm does unleash its fury, mitigate future storms from manifesting, and accept those that happen as part of life.

Gratefulness

Freedom from attachment and acceptance of one's current life are the best ways to access ultimate satisfaction and contentment. When we take time to inventory, contemplate, and feel grateful for our bounty, we begin to find contentment, peace, and happiness. When we spend time sitting in silence, reflecting, and breathing fully each day, we will find ourselves walking differently, with an open heart, more often greeting others with eye contact and a smile. From a contented and grateful place, we can foster a deeper connection with others, which supports positivity, motivation, inspiration, and is good for our health. These feelings and emotions become imprinted and are more easily accessed the more we cultivate them. When we are not at work, if we spend our time noticing more, connecting more, feeling more, and doing a little less, we will be able to access those feeling spaces during the frenzy at the office. We can then bring those positive feelings back when we are doing things we don't enjoy or when things do not go as planned, and feel more contented regardless.

The Middle Path

Not everything in life will always be pleasant. Not everything will always be unpleasant. These feelings and their intensity are within your control. Working toward seeing most of life in the middle, a bit more neutral, helps to cultivate contentment. The middle path is a more centered and calm way of handling the ups and downs of the rollercoaster in our lives. Importantly, a contented state is very different from an *emotionless* state. At the extreme, a contented life could be one that is married to the energy of a whirling dervish, spinning ecstatically through life, powerfully taking in and welcoming anything that comes with a zealous thirst and love of life— while being absolutely okay with whatever happens along the way. We always *go all in* and we always *let go*. The letting go is, for most of us, the most challenging part.

Letting Go

Let the Dice Land

Being grateful for all aspects of your work and life as they are today and living for *today*, in the present moment, is the best way to foster contentment. Things happen, and there is a point at which we have to be okay with letting the dice land as they may. Working harder at rolling the dice does not increase the likelihood that we will throw a deuce the next roll; nor does working less hard diminish that likelihood. In that same way, the result of our efforts are very often not indicative of the amount of effort we put in. We work very hard for some things that don't work out while many other things seem effortless. We tend to underappreciate or ignore the effortless and cling tightly to the effortful. We seem to believe that we have quite a bit of control over the everyday but we don't. What we do have control over is showing up, being prepared, and doing our very best all the time with a heart full of gratitude—then letting the dice land.

Obsession and Contentment

Obsessing over the next deal, customer, or project won or lost is not a settling experience, nor one that is helpful to cultivating contentment. You can work with zeal to achieve improved outcomes while still practicing being content with your best efforts. Focusing on the efforts made by the team along the way rather than the result is one way you can maintain the feeling of contentment, no matter what the result. As a leader, you can take time with your team each month or quarter to reflect upon the team's progress at work and personal accomplishments beyond work.

It is important to understand that letting go of results does not equal indifference. We care, but we seek to not cling to the results and, as such, are emotionally detached from the results. The results do not own or control our state of being, our emotions, or our experience in life. From this vantage point, it is much easier to live lightheartedly and wholeheartedly, allowing us to move fluidly through the ebb and flow of life and work.

Questions for Leaders: Contentment

1. Are you content with your work and life? Do you take all the ups and downs with stride and poise?
2. Is an open communication policy in place and adhered to, such that the team feels comfortable expressing their feelings and resolving issues?

3. Is there a lot of internal discussion about compensation and work opportunities that is fostering discontent in the office?

4. Is compensation clear and fair and based upon merit, teamwork, and a commitment to organizational growth?

5. Are incentives directed toward employees, embodying the principles of the organization?

6. Do you frequently praise performance, uplift others, and genuinely appreciate efforts made by staff and the team as a whole?

7. Does the team move on from challenging times? Do you stew over lost customers, projects, clients, or transactions for months or years?

8. Do you take time to contemplate and reflect upon your successes and abundance? Do you encourage team members to reflect upon their successes? Have you aligned your life toward meaning and purpose? Do you know your purpose? Do you live intentionally?

9. Are you empathetic to the needs of your team members? Do you spend time with them? Do you ask them if they are satisfied with their work?

10. Do people make eye contact, smile, and greet one another politely?

11. Is the enterprise like a calm sea or a stormy one? Do you know how to manage the team to return to a calm sea?

12. Do you make such efforts keep yourself balanced by cultivating moments of joy in your days?

Set Your Start Point

An Attitude Habit

Your attitude is your start point for how you are choosing to be in that moment. Choosing your attitude for each day, event, or job will go a long way to keeping your bliss cup filled. It's a way to focus and develop an *attitude habit*, or perhaps adjust a bad attitude if you have an attitude problem! It does take some desire and willingness to set (or reset) your start point, so use your discipline and will power if you need to. I try to set mine every day as I step out of bed each morning, repeating the same affirmation in my head until my groggy brain absorbs it somewhat. The affirmation I typically use is a very abbreviated form of this Dalai Lama XIV quote:

> Every day, think as you wake up, today I am fortunate to be alive, I have a precious human life, I am not going to waste it. I am going to use all my energies to develop myself, to expand my heart out to others, to achieve enlightenment for the benefit of all beings. I am going to have kind thoughts towards others, I am not going to get angry or think badly about others. I am going to benefit others as much as I can.
>
> —Dalai Lama XIV

This reminds me to start the day with an attitude of bettering myself in a way that is also helpful to others, which is definitely not always the way I feel when I wake up, especially if a child crept into my bed and flip flopped all night long!

How do you want to set your start point? Write down some ideas until one resonates. Then say it to yourself each day. Post it in a visible location or carry it with you. At work, your affirmation could make for a good conversation starter and may set a nice tone for meetings. Having your affirmation visible in a public location may also encourage others to think about how they want to set their start-point each day.

Bliss Surplus

> The Divine is the Only Comedian, playing to an
> audience who has forgotten how to laugh.
>
> —Voltaire

Visualization

Visualization is a very helpful, bliss-filling practice that can calm the mind and serve as a prequel to deep meditation. In and of itself, visualization is a powerful exercise that can enhance mood and general well-being.

A Fall Hike

I am ascending one of the Green Mountains in Vermont on a beautiful autumn day. The air is crisp and cool. In my fleece and hiking boots, my body begins to warm with each step. I smell the wonderful damp scent of the woods in fall, the leaves now carpeting the trail, initiating the cycle of death and rebirth—the scent fills me; it is sweet, familiar, and liberating.

The crunch of fallen leaves beneath my boots and the click of my hiking poles against the rock remind me that I am moving forward. I feel my heart pumping, my thighs warming with each step, my lungs filling with pure, clean air. The sun peeks through the remaining canopy of leaves, illuminating a path of color in its wake.

I ascend. My nostrils flare taking in more air and filling the lungs to capacity; the sinuses are clearing, the body opening. That exhilarating feeling sets in from the inside out; my lungs are wide open now. My thoughts are acute, clear, alive. I feel relaxed but working.

At the summit, my eyes feast on the cornucopia of colors, like a bag of jellybeans against a backdrop of rich forest green. Pops of red, orange, and yellow, accented by deep and full evergreen trees. I inhale. That chill, that full-body feeling of aliveness, of contentment and euphoria, rushes through the body.

I close my eyes. I pause. I notice. I savor this feeling of bliss in the stores of my memory so that I may invite it to emerge another day.

This full-sensory visualization comes from a hike amidst the colorful splendor of a Vermont fall. When you read this, did you feel the heart beating, witness the eyes feasting, notice the breath rich and full, smell the woods and the fresh crisp air, and soak in the subtle silence, the peace? Such is the power of visualization, and it can help us have a feeling of fullness, of vibrancy.

Of course, if you don't appreciate nature, or hiking, or sweating, then this Vermont hiking visualization is not going to do it for you. Spend time reflecting upon what actually fills *you* up, your places of refuge, and then go there often—in your mind. Beloved Yoga studio owner Maryam Ovissi once referred to her studio as a "refuge for thirsty souls to be uplifted and inspired so they too may serve to uplift and inspire others." Find your place(s) of refuge that uplift and inspire you, so that you may uplift and inspire others.

Four Visualizations for Bliss or Meditation

1. Reclining on an ocean beach. Feeling the sun on your skin, the breeze in your hair. Watching the waves lapping against the shore. The wind fills your nostrils with the smell of salt air. Listening to the sound of the surf.
2. Lying in the grass in a wide-open field at night. Watching the stars twinkle in the sky. Seeing the darkness, the expansiveness as far as the eye can see. Noticing the millions of stars in the sky. The big and the small. Appreciating the vastness of the unknown.
3. Sitting on top of a mountain vista. Gazing out across the pointed, snow-capped range. Noticing the bright pops of green in the valleys below. Feeling the bright sun on your cheeks. Noticing the dark evergreen trees, spotted with snow.
4. Walking through a meadow. Seeing the colorful wildflowers with the forest edge in the distance. Feeling the soft caress of tall grasses on your knees. Smelling the sweet scent of the field. Feeling the sun on your arms.

Visualization can also involve recalling moments that really touched or tickled your heart. It is important to be on the lookout for opportunities to be touched. Things that carry with them strong positive feelings are, for the most part, unexpected or unprompted. Most are expressions that make you feel very loved and/or strongly supported. Listed below are some ideas.

Moments

- When your boss strongly goes to bat for you and helps you secure the budget you need for the next year.
- When a friend tells you for no particular reason what an important part of his or her life you are.
- When an employee expresses his or her appreciation for you and shares that you've had a meaningful influence on his or her work and life.

- When your spouse arranges for a nice evening and lets you know it's because he or she would like to spend some quality time alone with you.
- When your child tells you, out of the blue, that he or she loves you.
- When a peer, unprompted, says very supportive things about your work to a group of coworkers.
- When you hear your spouse whom you love expressing how proud he or she is of you to your family and friends.
- When a coworker surprises you with your favorite drink or lunch, knowing you are swamped.
- When you catch your spouse lovingly watching you interact with the kids (or pets) or when you find yourself watching your spouse lovingly interact with the kids (or pets).
- When people at work voluntarily pitch in to help you get through a deadline.

Connection

Depression and Connection

Connection and healthy personal relationships are critical to our vitality. I was raised in Pittsburgh. I find Pittsburgh to be one of the friendliest cities on the planet. In this town you will find yourself connecting and sharing some aspect of your life with the people in the grocery store, parking lot, coffee shop, or wherever you happen to go. People enthusiastically engage in dialog with strangers for minutes at a time. My Mother and Father have always been chatty in this way too. As a kid this was embarrassing. Now, I find it wonderful.

Connection is a core human requirement and even these small interchanges allow us to cultivate a sense of belonging. If we do not feel connected, we feel emotionally and spiritually unsupported and loneliness and depression can set in. By connection, I mean the kind of meaningful connection that happens in person or on a phone or video call—not to be confused with a quick and superficial hello, text message, or Facebook post. Don't get me wrong; I love technology. It is a very helpful way to keep in touch with distant people especially until you get a chance to see one another again. Then you need to set a priority to foster that deep and loving connection in person or at least via phone. When we lose our abilities to connect deeply because we are running around with our face in our gadgets, we disengage. When we live in a near constant state of sympathetic nervous system activation with a racing mind, we lose our ability to connect with others. When our lives are too jammed full, we don't connect. Disconnection from humanity overtime can lead and has led to disengagement, depression, and even despair.

Disconnection

Think about our habits of life. We sit at desks, staring at a screen all day. We walk through the streets, shoulders slumped over and eyes on a gadget. We come home and sit in front of a light box for entertainment. We have become increasingly disconnected from living things like human beings, pets, and even the wonderful cycles of nature, but we are creatures of connection. It is what makes us feel good as humans. We thrive on it, and it is necessary to survive. Disconnected like this we lose the ability to foster deep relationships with others, to communicate, to cope, and our resilience declines. We need to intentionally and proactively reconnect emotionally to everyone in our lives.

Eye Contact

When you walk down the hallway, do so with chest held high. Make eye contact with or say hello to and smile at everyone you see. In his book, *Yoga: The Spirit and Practice of Moving Into Stillness*, Erich Schiffmann, the globally known yoga teacher, shares the importance of looking right at a person until you can see deeply into his or her eyes. This is not a superficial glance; rather, spend a few brief moments looking back and forth into each of the person's eyes until you feel an energetic engagement with the eyes. At that point he says you are truly seeing the person's real self and not just the outside layers, while releasing your own fears and experiencing a deeper connection with them. When we connect in these ways, we open up our lives, inviting vitality, freedom, and creativity. We invite new dialogue with new people and think of new ideas that we otherwise would not have thought about, opening our minds to new ways of thinking. We invite connection to the world around us, connection to nature, and connection to other people. We receive all this simply by walking down the hallway differently.

Transitions

There are many common events and transitions that understandably cause stress and lack of connection. It is important to recognize these times, anticipate some difficulty, and admit that we are human. Imagine the strain on families during work relocations, where each family member has to create new relationships and become part of a new community again. Think about the demise of the health of a loved one and the stress put upon the family. Think of the many marriages that struggle when newborn children enter the picture, given the onslaught of new responsibility. The impacts of the loss of connection due to life events are significant and ultimately affect both body and mind, yet these life situations are normal parts of life. What is important is recognizing the toll they take on health and well-being and, as leaders, being conscious and helpful to yourselves, your friends or family members, and your team members who are going through life changes. As leaders, we need to notice how we are impacted and take measures to restore connection, while at the same time being patient and allowing the necessary time to work through the ebb and flow of life.

Love

The happiest people in life are in love with everything in their lives and share all of themselves in service to others. When you fall in love with everything, you fall in love with life. One of the best ways to connect is through love; love is a heartfelt connection to other people, nature, or things we are very much drawn to. We overcomplicate love, turning it into a complex and special thing, held onto and saved for special times and special people, when it should be simple and generously offered. Love is vast in its array of possible expression. Consider all of life as special. We can love family. We can love friends. We can love our work. We can love trees, too. We can love football, cooking, painting, vacations, early mornings, birds, music, art, hiking, cars, stars, skiing, movies, Starbucks, shoes, food, snow, flowers—and we should love all of it. Try falling in love with everything in your life but especially to other people through connection.

If you don't already clearly know that love is connection, you can't recognize it at first. People may think they have love but may not be sure why they have this empty place inside where they feel disconnected. They may in fact be witness to love, but unless they are internally awakened to it again, they may not ever recognize it is there. Awaken a love of life and you will find you awaken positive connection with others. Without love in your life, I'm not sure there is anything much at all. Meaningful and deep human connection and interaction is critical to our survival. The more we identify with and give outward expressions of love (kindness) to everything and everyone in our lives, the more we will find it coming back to us.

Kindness

Although we don't typically think of it this way, being kind to others has love behind it. Being kind is an act of love. This is important to leaders. Kindness stems from love and appreciation; unkindness from hate and loathing. When we are firmly rooted in love and connection in our lives, we flourish and naturally erupt with kindness toward others. When we are in states of stress, defensiveness, self-loathing, envy, and fear, it is very challenging to be rooted in love and kindness. When we neglect humanity, we neglect connection, making kindness and love nearly impossible. Bring humanity back into the workplace, into your leadership, and into your life.

Rules of Engagement

Consider adopting some of the rules of engagement listed below and observe how your connection to others changes.

Ten Rules of Engagement

1. No screen time after 9 p.m.
2. No gadgets in the bedroom.
3. Gadget-free weekends once a quarter.
4. No gadgets while consummating a transaction with a human.
5. Pick up the phone instead of texting or e-mailing.
6. Meet for coffee in lieu of speaking on the phone.
7. Socialize regularly with friends.
8. Date nights once a week with your significant other or an evening out with a dear friend.
9. Leverage regular opportunities to be with others at yoga studios, fitness centers, or any other membership clubs.
10. Make monthly calls to distant friend(s) who uplift you.

Cycles of Nature

The Seasons

In the spring and summer, the chlorophyll-filled leaves of a maple tree soak in the sun's energy to create simple sugars we call sap. The tree converts this to starch, uses what it needs, and stores the rest for the winter. The cooler fall season causes the leaves to turn a brilliant color, shrivel, and drop, and the tree becomes dormant for winter, living off its stored starch. When it awakens with the warmth of spring it converts the stored starch back into sap to use for fuel, and sugar makers harvest the rich, sweet nectar and process it into syrup. It also sprouts leaves to provide it with nutrition for the upcoming year.

The maple tree does not forget to care for itself each season. Nature does not become distracted and so busy that she forgets to do her thing. Grass does not forget to grow, nor flowers to blossom, nor trees to sprout leaves. We have a lot to learn about ourselves from the cycles of nature and her ability to remember the changes that she needs to go through with each season.

Noticing and getting in touch with the change of the seasons and appreciating the course of nature and its effects on the environment *and on us* can help us move toward a more connected place where we can tune into our own needs. The change and movement in fall and the cold of winter challenge the body and mind and can be deranging at times tipping us into states of stress or unease. During the transition of seasons noticing, awareness, and self-care become even more important. The morning light on a tree in the summer is just as beautiful in spring, winter, and fall, and yet it is always different. Try to reconnect to nature and her cycles.

Reflections on Creating Space

Leisure Time

Different cultures approach leisure time differently. Europeans put a premium on it. Americans tend to brush it off. A British man once told me that people of the UK and Germany consider vacations as important as any large asset purchase such as a house or car. Many years ago, I worked for Klaus Martini and his team of portfolio managers at Deutsche Bank's mutual fund arm in Frankfurt, where the lead investment managers took one-month vacations—one full month! While they were gone, the rest of the team pitched in and the funds continued to be managed. When leaders actually take their vacations like this, it becomes part of the process to divide up work while folks are away. Month-long vacations did not damage the bank's success in the least. In fact, Deutsche Bank became the largest bank in the world at that time. Perhaps that time off actually allowed the team to decompress and be more effective upon their return. Imagine that.

Spa

In many countries, spas and bathhouses are prevalent and affordable. Participation in them is a cultural norm. Soaking in tubs, steaming, and sitting in saunas for eight hours straight can release every last muscular tension imaginable. Americans have the occasional hot tub at the gym but not really a culture of using them—and it is very difficult to find a bathhouse with large heated pools and soaking tubs. In much of the world, massage is also known to be therapy and is an activity regularly enjoyed by the masses, not simply the people with lots of disposable income.

Evening Time and Overdoing

In many countries, when the day ends, the family arrives home to socialize and converse over a meal. They don't feel the need, after a full day of work and school, to do more work and more schooling or an abundance of activities.

Those who overdo do so out of fear, insecurity, and lack of confidence. These are mental and emotional issues. Many rat racers, sacrificing-their-lifers, have within them deep insecurities that perhaps have haunted them for years. It may not be apparent to even their inner circles because mental challenges these days can be easily masked by an appearance of confidence fueled by a hidden bottle of anti-depressants. Deep-seated fears have a way of possessing and controlling our every decision and damaging our health, well-being, and our ability to connect with others.

Think about creating space in your life for healthy leisure and creating a life of well-being. Be honest about what you are *meant* to do in this lifetime. Don't let the rat race lead your life for you. If you have established trust with your team, you should be able to step away for some R&R.

Concluding Statement

The dimension of bliss is peaceful, happy, and content. In takes effort to maintain and requires that we live a meaningful and connected life. At some point in time, all ambitious leaders want to find meaning in their work. Having a plan, a roadmap, that we are working toward supports our own satisfaction at work. Our roadmap has meaning, because we uniquely and intentionally create it with our deepest desires and abilities in mind. To tap into our stores of bliss we need to rediscover the things that lift us up and then bring them regularly into our lives. Balance your work efforts with sufficient time spent filling your bliss cup. Find ways to connect with others and seek to develop healthy personal relationships in your life. This in turn nurtures the layer of bliss and supports your leadership. Reflecting upon your attention to this layer you discover that you find more happiness in the everyday, you live a meaningful life, and have simplified your life focusing your efforts on what you can honestly handle without taking anti-depressant or anti-anxiety drugs to cope. Your team finds inspiration through your example as a very happy, healthy and connected leader.

People with a surplus of bliss have a glow about them, a light. Their light is infectious. Others love to work or spend time with them because it feels so good just to be in their presence. Happy leaders can more easily connect with, motivate, and inspire other people. Engaged and happy leaders will also more effectively build a shared purpose amongst the team, which helps to retain good talent. Discover the employees in your organization who are bliss-*full*. They are walking gold mines, and will only serve to expand the capabilities of the entire enterprise, driving growth. Spend a lot of time with them. Learn from them, and allow others to spend time with them so they may learn from them, too. Once you find these people, allow their light to spread broad and deep through the organization. Make them your leaders. Become such a leader.

Chapter 9
Yogi Secret #7: From Vision to Action

Old Maxim
Changing my life involves a comprehensive and time-consuming well-being plan.

New Maxim
The smallest shifts in daily habits will have meaningful, positive effects on my well-being.

Resolve: I will commit to a holistic well-being plan beginning with easily achievable daily choices. I will acknowledge my accomplishments and make small, daily, beneficial habit changes a lifelong endeavor.

Moving from trying to undertake a comprehensive well-being plan to instead enacting small incremental changes focused holistically allows me to achieve successes in the direction of health and well-being. Having a practical and sensible well-being plan in my life will allow me to serve as an example to my team members as they begin to see the parallel between my well-being and my performance as a leader.

Be the change that you wish to see in the world.
—Mahatma Gandhi

Yoga practitioners know that the practice is everything. The practice is, in fact, the only thing that matters. And the practice is a process. There is a saying often used in yoga: "How you do *anything* is how you do *everything*." Every thought, word, or action—including the food choices you make, the speed in which you lift your leg in a yoga asana class, the manner in which you handle employee problems, the tone and volume of voice you use, how available you make yourself to your team, and the facial expressions you maintain—tells the world who you are.

Our practice involves going at our processes, at how we do things, and improving upon our processes, again and again and again. When we do this, growth eventually happens. Things shift. We create new, self-serving habits. It is through repetition that we begin to embody the qualities of inspiring leadership. As yoga teachers, we know the objective of yoga movement practice is not achieving a certain pose, shape, goal, or state. It is not born from an ideology of perfection. We are already perfect in our unique and wonderful ways. Rather, the practice is about how we are *being* as we move through life often taught first on a yoga mat. When all focus is directed toward results it serves as a distraction from the process, habits, and practices cultivated along the way. Happiness, health, and team engagement are found through good practices.

Small, subtle shifts will profoundly benefit your work and well-being. It is said to take twenty-one days to cement a habit—although it takes most of us much longer. Go slowly, and give yourself plenty of time so that you can notice and celebrate what you are able to accomplish along the way. One of my favorite songs is Frank Sinatra's "My Way." Do it *your* way. Do it for your family and do it for your team. Blaze a new trail. Be resolute about your well-being. You are worth it.

Where to Begin

It will require a commitment to transformation to move from thinking about yourself as one-dimensional to thinking about all of your layers. Start first with simple things you are most likely to have success with, cement these new habits, and enjoy your success. Then add on from there. Yoga is a very personal practice of living. Through trial and error, you will assess the tools and habit changes that resonate for you.

What might seem the most linear place to start isn't necessarily the only way or the most appropriate. If you are diabetic, you may want to focus on diet and exercise, but you may actually have more success by focusing first on meditation. If you have anger management issues, the mind may be the most linear place to start, but perhaps working on your purpose and principles would be a better place to afford you early success. If you have a racing mind, the mental dimension would again be the most linear place to start, but consider instead starting with your energy dimension through breath regulation. In yoga, we seek sustainable growth and well-being for the rest of our lives, not momentary patches, quick fixes, and numbing agents.

Find a place that challenges you but doesn't feel too threatening. If starting with a certain activity really intimidates you, start somewhere else, or find a partner to work with. This is a process of finding balance and not moving toward pain and suffering. But when you find yourself resisting the process or disinterested in tackling one of the dimensions, explore this resistance and spend some time with the self-awareness exercises in the mind chapter. Why are you resistant? Is there fear lurking behind the resistance? To overcome resistance you must really want to experience a life of well-being and believe that it will positively influence your ability to lead.

Beginning Today: Thirty-Minute Weekday Soul Saver

Many of you are extraordinarily busy. Here is a very simple and straightforward plan that averages about thirty minutes a day during the week and a weekend plan that may take up to one hour each day. It is enough, when done consistently, to send you on path where you are happier, healthier, and better able to connect with and engage your team.

Weekdays

Move your body vigorously a minimum of thirty minutes and/or take yoga movement class for your mind–body. Choose your assortment but at the beginning plan to move your body two to four times during the week.

Throughout the day, begin to notice when you become stirred up. Breathe through the feeling. Write down the nature of the incident for easy recall. Keep a running list and reflect upon this list.

Sit on the bed in the morning, before bed, or both for five to ten minutes with your eyes closed. Practice relaxing every part of your body. Practice centering yourself during transitions in your workday.

Spend ten minutes reflecting on one of your principles each week and the role it plays in your life and leadership today. Alternatively, begin to consider how to find greater purpose and meaning in your work and life by reflecting upon your purpose, vision, and mission. Write your thoughts down in a journal.

Weekends

Plan meals for the upcoming week. Purchase your food and prep for the week, so you can begin to feed your body nutritious and energizing food every single day.

Take a yoga movement class for your mind-body.

Do at least one thing that makes you really happy noticing how great you feel doing it.

Identify Other Possible Starting Points

You can approach your plan like a gap analysis of your life. Inventory where you stand with your five dimensions, and think about where your gaps are and how you can begin to fill them using the ideas in this book. Consider which of the following statements are true for you, and choose a few corresponding starting points then modify the thirty-minute soul saver accordingly:

Going Deeper Start Points

1. If you have trouble concentrating, focusing, or paying attention:
   a. Work on creating space and quiet time.
   b. Cultivate a meditation practice.
   c. Participate in group yoga movement classes.
   d. Listen to some music that really moves you and sing at the top of your lungs. Feel the energy and notice the mental shift that has taken place.
2. If you always respond *stressed* when someone asks how you are:
   a. Focus on meditation or breathing exercises.
   b. Participate in group yoga movement classes.
   c. Set an intention to stop saying you are stressed and instead be honest about what you are actually feeling and why—"I feel anxious because…."
3. If you always characterize your life as busy in a negative sort of way:
   a. Focus on meditation.
   b. Practice the principle of gratitude.
   c. Write down all the list of things you believe you must do from morning to night, in chronological order, without forgetting a single thing. Ask yourself what would happen if you didn't do some of the things. Must you really do them?
      i. Shave the list down. Push some of the must-dos to a later day, shorten the amount of time it takes to do the must-dos, cross them off the list, or delegate them.
      ii. Add different must-dos to your list, including things like quiet time, breathing time, meditation time, journaling time, and a walk in nature.
4. If you suffer from insomnia:
   a. Work on your sleep routine.
   b. Take a bath.
   c. Participate in group yoga movement classes.
   d. Listen to deep meditation practices like yoga nidra as you lie down to rest.
5. If you don't think you are very well-liked by your team:
   a. Study and work on the principle of kindness.
   b. Study your emotions and what stirs you up.
   c. Allow yourself to be vulnerable.
6. If you often feel underappreciated:
   a. Identify your root fears and notice if/how this has become a pattern in your life.
   b. Visualize yourself being appreciated fully. Practice living live as though you are the most appreciated person in the world.

    c.   Express great appreciation toward everyone around you.

    d.   Openly communicate your expectations at all times to as many people as you can. Overly communicate. Clarify often.

    e.   Be honest about your feelings and what you desire at all times. While a base of support won't help you here because it is an inside job, it may be helpful to be reminded of your talents by family and friends or a coach.

    f.   Cultivate empathy and compassion for others.

7.   If you always think you have a terrible team:

    a.   Study perspective and work on expanding your perspective.

    b.   Spend time reflecting on the yoga kleshas, especially ego and ignorance.

    c.   Work on your principles, especially non-harming.

    d.   Practice affirmations of tolerance and acceptance throughout the day.

8.   If you have trouble making friends or developing alliances:

    a.   Work on your principles, especially non-harming and integrity.

    b.   Reflect upon how you feel about yourself, the expectations you set, and the pressures you put upon yourself.

    c.   Seek to understand ego and how ego shows up in your life.

9.   If it does not seem that anyone wants to work for you:

    a.   Work on your principles, especially non-harming and integrity.

    b.   Spend time reflecting on the yoga kleshas, especially ignorance and ego.

    c.   Work on your layer of bliss and consider your likability quotient.

10.   If you feel that you react a lot or are more angry and less kind than you'd like to be:

    a.   Work on lengthening your breath, extending your exhale, and pausing at the end of the exhale.

    b.   Study your feelings and emotions and begin to anticipate your emotions and the state of your nervous system.

    c.   Study your way of breathing and the feelings in your body when you are stirred up, and discipline yourself to take a few breaths before speaking or writing anything.

    d.   Begin to observe your thoughts and evaluate your perspective and worldview.

    e.   Practice seeing, appreciating, and trying to understand both sides of any issue all the time.

11.   If you often feel nervous, agitated, or anxious:

    a.   Work on lengthening your breath, extending your exhale, and pause at the end of your exhale.

    b.   Make it a goal to first notice and then feel your nervous system when heightened, and then notice when the relaxation response is triggered in your body and you calm down. Seek to trigger the relaxation response through your breath throughout the day.

    c.   Discipline yourself to do five-minute centering practices throughout the day.

    d.   Begin to observe your thoughts and self-talk, seeking to remove negativity.

    e.   Focus on being vulnerable by expressing yourself more often.

12.   If you feel like you are often depressed or see work as a burden:

    a.   Seek out more challenging assignments.

    b.   Consider what kind of work you find interesting.

c. Outside of work, focus on your happiness by adding some fun into your life, reengage with close positive friends, and laugh more.

d. Cultivate a gratitude practice.

e. Take measures to make your diet extremely healthy.

f. Bring lightness into your life, consider the friendships you keep, colors you wear, music you listen to, and television programming that you watch.

g. Force a smile all the time, especially when you don't feel like it.

h. Find a supportive community to hang out with.

13. If you think you have mental/emotional challenges and take drugs as the solution without shifting any other parts of your life:

a. Discipline yourself to reset your attitude to believe that you do not need to be permanently medicated.

b. Be honest. Get very clear on who you are and who you are not including all your natural skills and all of your limitations. Acknowledge and appreciate all your perfect imperfections.

c. Reflect upon fear in your life. Replace fear with freedom.

d. Decide where you can compromise and reclaim parts of your life.

e. Study your principles especially non-harming and reflect upon your innermost thoughts.

f. Reflect upon in what ways you harm yourself with negative self-talk and how you then in turn harm others. Turn harmful thoughts into loving and supportive thoughts.

g. Seek to study and understand the role that ego and ignorance play in your life.

h. Reflect upon life's greater meaning and your greater purpose.

i. Instill faith in the journey by continually focusing energies on the process and the intrinsic rewards of simply doing your best and letting go of results, whatever they may be.

j. Practice gratitude and humility all the time.

14. If you are always tired and lack energy even though you believe you eat well, move enough in your day, and sleep pretty well:

a. Work on shifting your movement routine and check in with how you feel along the way.

b. Ask yourself if you are overdoing it in some way, perhaps even obsessing over some element of your life.

c. Cultivate some quiet time in your day.

d. Shift something in your diet.

e. Have a comprehensive diagnostic blood test to make sure you are not nutrient deficient.

f. Use a sleep device to see if perhaps you are rolling around more than you should be.

g. Tap into yourself a bit more deeply through meditation or yoga.

h. If these shifts aren't helping, consider whether you are unsatisfied with some element of your life.

i. Consider your purpose and what lifts you up and energizes you. Visualize that fully. Set an intention to make small shifts to adjust your current path so you may begin to move toward one that allows you to feel vibrant.

15. If you can't seem to motivate yourself:
    a. Contemplate how you are aligning your life with your dharma, personal vision and personal mission.
    b. Study and practice the yoga of action and duty, called kriya yoga, by working on discipline in your life.
    c. Study and practice the yoga of selfless service, called karma yoga, by reframing your life as a service to others.
    d. Practice gratitude and spend time on your vision and purpose.
    e. Cultivate a meditation practice to help you find clarity.
    f. Exercise vigorously.
    g. Seek to be inspired by others (Ted Talks).
16. If you have a tough time being confident about your decisions or how to set boundaries:
    a. Focus on distilling your vision and understanding your purpose.
    b. Establish a realistic path to achieving your vision and get clear on who supports that path and who does not. Limit time with those who do not support your path.
    c. Cultivate a base of support that will help you manifest your vision. If you have no base of support, consider whether your vision is realistic.
    d. Practice being vulnerable, taking risks to boost your self-esteem.
    e. Study fact-based and positive speech in your life.
    f. Make a study of strength and courage in life. Say affirmations of strength throughout the day. Meditate using affirmations of strength.
    g. Do strength-building exercise.
17. If you feel that you are always consumed with maintaining your weight:
    a. Ask yourself if your vision for yourself is reasonable and possible.
    b. If so, focus on diet. Kick it into gear by disciplining yourself with a twenty-one-day group detox/cleanse diet where you spend three weeks on a strict program, breaking down bad habits, cultivating new habits, making friends, noticing how you feel, and learning about yourself.
    c. Commit to eating only that which nourishes the mind and sustains the vitality of the body.
    d. Find an exercise group that you like and will keep you committed. Rigorously move your body several times a week.
    e. Write in a journal all the things you have in your life for which you feel grateful.
    f. Write down all the reasons that you are talented and special.
18. If you still aren't sure where to begin:
    a. Seek to gather information—from family members, friends, or members of your team—that may help you guide your priorities.
    b. Pay someone with the expertise to help you formulate a plan.

Create Your Holistic Well-being Action Plan

Once the thirty-minute soul saver becomes part of your life, your resistance to taking time for your own well-being will fade even more. Tapping into yourself and your life will become a habit, and this entire process simply becomes a natural way for you to organize your days, weeks, months, and years. Reorienting your life in this way will require time, dedication, and patience. It will not happen overnight and nor should you try. The mere exercise of putting together a longer-term plan and setting one-, three-, and five-year goals could be quite exciting and/or daunting.

There are many ways to customize a plan. Consider once again targeting one or several of your starting point activities. These may be things that you have felt you've needed to do for a long time. Keep it simple, and celebrate small successes. Begin to recognize that even subtle shifts can have profound effects. Even this initial plan may take years to fully manifest and you may find yourself changing it along the way.

Sample Personal Holistic Well-being Action Plan

Fictional Case Study:

This is a one-year plan for a typical leader who is forty-five years old in the prime of his career. This leader has, by most accounts, been extremely successful in his field. He has a high income and is in a position of power, managing many people. He would like to lose thirty pounds, has been on blood pressure medication since the age of forty-two, and often suffers from insomnia, because his mind is always thinking about work. He would like to feel more energetic each day. He sees any downtime as unproductive time that could be spent working, so his days are jammed full with work.

When he is with his wife and kids, he is often checking his e-mail and, as a result, is becoming increasingly disengaged from their lives. This bothers him, but he doesn't know what to do about it. He is easily agitated, very ambitious, and feels stressed at times. His results at work are quite good, and he has been working extra hard of late since he is up for a meaningful promotion that he didn't get the last time an appropriate position came available. While this leader pays some attention to food, trying to follow various diets that are popular, he hasn't stuck with any one way of eating and eats a lot on the run while traveling. His awareness of nutritional content and portion sizes is limited. This leader has never thought about paying attention to how food affects his mood.

This leader tries to exercise a few days a week at the gym and hires a personal trainer to try to get his weight in check. He misses fairly often, though, and so it hasn't helped him lose the weight his doctor suggested he lose. He does not know how to meditate, the benefits of meditation or breath work, or the health benefits of emotional control. He feels the whole idea of mindfulness is a fad and instead believes that his fast-paced, results-focused way of living is the right way for a leader to operate. He considers himself successful based on his income and title.

He does not think about principles in life or how they help his ability to lead and engage his team, thus influencing performance and productivity. Focused only on top and bottom-line metrics of performance, his perspective is that he does a great job. Yet, according to his team, he isn't the most inspiring leader, and his lack of emotional control at times hasn't helped foster a following. He is quick to judge and quick to blame employees. He believes in on-the-job training and he neither has the time nor the patience to connect with, empower, or leverage the potential of his team. His actions foster an environment of fear, resource constraint, and competition, leaving little room for cooperation and cohesion. Until now, he has not considered how his way of being a leader impacts his own health and well-being as well as that of his team. He has not considered that his way of being a leader may actually degrade productivity, morale, creativity, and innovation.

This leader, after recognizing the merits of a holistic well-being program, might write an initial plan such as the following to address all his dimensions:

Holistic Well-Being Action Plan	
Physical	Focus on increasing my daily vegetable consumption and decreasing my carbohydrate consumption through reduced portion sizes. Make healthy food choices every day. Eat more slowly. Commit to moving my body vigorously at least three times a week. Commit to doing yoga movement classes to learn to relax and become self-aware. Develop a sleep routine.
Energy	Practice inhaling and exhaling for two minutes before meetings. Practice smiling all the time and looking people directly in the eye. Discuss guidelines for effective communication openly with my team. Cocreate solutions as appropriate. Consider how fear may be driving some of my interactions and decisions.
Mind	Consider whether expanding my perspective will make me more open-minded and might be the best solution to better connecting with and engaging my team. Develop a relationship with my breath and the state of my nervous system. Become very clear on the details of the times in which I feel stirred-up and when I feel calm. Drive home from work in silence. Have technology-free dinners with family.
Knowledge	Sit in bed for ten minutes each morning with my eyes closed and breathe into my inner stillness. Engage in the listening practice with my team. Pause before answering questions at work. Ask more questions before answering questions. Study whether my ego is getting in the way of discernment.
Bliss	Inventory in writing the things that have always given me the greatest joy and do one of them each week. Write down my personal purpose, vision and mission and notice how orienting my life toward them promotes satisfaction and meaning. Practice being grateful and content.

Connection	Consider the way I could bring the principle of kindness and non-harming into my every thought, word, and action to connect better with my team and my family. Spend time studying and adhering to my own set of principles overtime.

Visualize Your Ideal Daily Routine

Consider the ideas in your holistic well-being action plan and write out your ideal daily routine from morning to night according to your workday. Recognize that this is an ideal that may never fully materialize. Expect, though, to incorporate some of the elements of your plan into your daily routine at any given time. Your ideal plan may look something like this:

Morning Ritual

5–6:00 a.m.: Wake up early. Sit on your pillow. Meditate for ten to twenty minutes. Drink eight ounces of water with lemon or Braggs Apple Cider Vinegar. Practice yoga asana or exercise if you have time for thirty to sixty minutes. Shower. Eat a healthy breakfast: steel cut oats, eggs, a low-sugar breakfast bar, yogurt. Go to work.

Work Ritual

Upon Arrival

Focus on the most important/difficult items first for the first two to three hours of your morning. If absolutely necessary, scan your e-mail briefly, identifying any truly urgent messages; otherwise wait until mid-morning. If you have spent the time to agree upon a communication plan with your team and establish boundaries, you will begin to not feel that every e-mail is urgent. Drink fluids: purified water, green tea, or ginger tea. Make conscious choices around caffeine intake as the day goes on.

Mid-morning

Check e-mail for the first time. Breathe fully and consciously, not allowing any e-mail, meeting, or work task to change your nervous system. In meetings, practice listening better, looking people in the eye, and smiling. Stand up once an hour and do some mid-morning stretches, leveraging your chair, desk, or doorway. Drink fluids: purified water, green tea, or ginger tea. If you exercise in the morning and/or didn't eat enough for breakfast you may feel the need to eat a nourishing snack: hummus and carrots, a hard boiled egg, apple and peanut butter, a protein and vegetable based smoothie.

Lunch

Choose a healthy yet light lunch like a hearty salad that will not cause you to be too tired or too hungry in the afternoon. Drink fluids: purified water, green tea, or ginger tea. If this is the best time to get away and move your body, take a yoga or exercise class or go for a run.

Mid-Afternoon

If you drink a lot of caffeine, cut off your intake in mid-afternoon so it does not interfere with your sleep. Change positions by working at a standing desk for the afternoon and/or sitting on the floor. Carve out a little time each week for self-study, contemplation of principle, and goal-setting oriented toward holistic well-being and the development of essential leadership skills. Choose a nourishing snack if you need one. Take a brief energy walk outside if possible and while meeting with a colleague. Drink fluids: purified water, green tea, or ginger tea.

Evening Ritual

If you weren't able to move your body much during the day, take a yoga class, a brisk walk, or go to the gym, taking care to wind down to relax the nervous system before bed.

5–7:00 p.m.: Drive home from work. Drink fluids: purified water, ginger tea, or another herbal tea.

Before 7:00 p.m.: Eat a healthy dinner that is either simple to prepare, prepared by someone else, or that you made on the weekend. Catch up with family.

Until 9:00 p.m.: After dinner, clean up, dim the lights, enjoy some family time, watch the news, wrap-up any absolutely necessary work, drink purified water or chamomile tea.

9:00–10:00 p.m.: Thirty minutes to one hour before bed begin a sleep ritual. Turn off all devices. Pick some of the following to do each night: read an inspiring book, write in your journal, review your vision and intentions, take an Epsom salt bath, massage your body with a relaxing oil like sesame oil, get intimate with your partner, practice yoga asana, or meditate for twenty minutes. It is important to not judge yourself if you cannot attain what you envision to be a perfect sleep ritual every night.

9:30–10:00 p.m.: Lights out. Sleep until 5–6:00 a.m.

Establish a base of support, and involve others who also want to embark on a path of holistic well-being that supports their lives and their leadership. Share your plan and the material you have learned in this book with interested friends or colleagues. Or, if you want to influence the culture at work, share this framework with the top executives, the director of human resources, and your peers, soliciting their support and feedback. Seek to make sticking to your respective plans a point of discussion each week.

If you like doing things with other people, recruit a friend or family member to create his or her own plan, and then help one another along the way. Having a partner on this path can be extraordinarily helpful. Carry a copy of your plan with you. Put a summary of your current goals in your notebook, your briefcase, or your purse, so you always have them with you to reflect upon. Invite new health-supporting conversations into your life by discussing your plan with your family, friends, healthcare providers, and other leaders.

Concluding Statement

Design your own plan but start with a simple and achievable one. Once you have created it honor that it is probably too much for one time and don't feel as though you have to start with all of it at once. In time, move through all of the dimensions and invite small shifts until you have a plan in place that works for you. Be patient with your progress. After some time, life will change and you will need to amend your plan, just as you amend and revise your financial plan. Your holistic well-being plan is always there to remind you stay on track and care for all of your dimensions so that you may develop qualities essential to leadership success. Upon reflection, you will find yourself happier and healthier and better able to connect with, engage, and inspire your team.

Chapter 10
Leaving a Legacy

Old Maxim
I am a conventional leader.

New Maxim
I am a conscious leader.

Resolve: I will acknowledge the greater good that every person and every leader and every organization can offer to society and humanity. I will support and showcase the contributions that others are making. I will serve as an example and do my part to leave a legacy that inspires future generations.

Honoring my life and the opportunities that I have to leave a better world in my wake will allow me to lead a more connected and happy life that likewise inspires future generations.

The road is long and winding. Pave a conscious path.

A New Leadership Paradigm

The road is your life. No matter how long and winding the road, you can choose to make it as pleasurable as possible, or not. You can choose to be a conscious leader, or not. Change is in the air. Leaders are pursuing their work in ways that include altruistic ideals as a measure of their own ideas of success. Executives are beginning to implement conscious measures at their organizations. John Mackey, co-Founder and CEO of Whole Foods Market, cut his pay to $1, donated his stock portfolio to charity, established a fund to help employees going through difficulties, and capped executive pay.[145] Mark Bertolini, Chairman and CEO of Aetna, addresses the well-being of his team with yoga and meditation programs geared toward stress management. He also gave his lowest paid employees a 33 percent raise.[146] Of course, there are many more examples if you just look for them. The Conscious Capitalism organization for example is filled with conscious leaders and noble efforts. You can build the inner skills necessary to lead consciously thus raising the consciousness of your enterprise making it rank as a highly desirable and admirable place of work. With essential leadership skills you will better engage your team guiding them to work together more productively and profitably as well.

When you peel the layers away, you will discover that we are all the same. We have the opportunity to operate in a way that improves upon the lives of others, with a service mentality. If you are in any position that influences others toward a goal, you are in a position of leadership. You can choose to act in service of others and conduct your leadership accordingly. Redefining *power* as the mastery of your mind and senses will allow you to acquire control over your every thought, word, and action, and use them in virtuous ways. With newfound mental strength and vigor, how can you, in your own way, aspire to higher ideals, leaving behind a noble legacy and contributing toward a new leadership paradigm? A leadership paradigm that is healthy, helpful, and inspiring. How can you be the next leader who improves upon the lives of others and the world we live in? How can you, in your own way, directly improve upon the lives of those you influence? How can you bring humanity back?

> Become the master of your mind and senses.

Concluding Statement

Life is fraught with challenge. It certainly hasn't always been a walk in the park for me. I've had a lot of practice in being resilient and bouncing back. An inner knowing had me see that things were not so bad even if my mind was telling me otherwise. Struggle is inevitable but setbacks are temporary and strengthen character. My mother taught me to have the fortitude to carry on no matter what. And she did not cage the bird that really wanted to fly. This tenacity and fortitude or grit, as some now like to call it, remains part of my character because I hold close an impenetrable belief that I have every right to make the most of my abilities in this lifetime, and so I shall. I have never stopped believing in myself. Neither should you.

When the end comes, what impression will you have made on the lives of others, on society, and on the world? What legacy will you leave? Try something. It may not work out—but what if it does? Lean into your strength. Live into the questions of life. This includes the whole idea of how you get your work done each day, how you think we have to be, and who you include in your circles. Take nothing as truth that you cannot understand as rational in your own mind and good in your own heart. There is a beautiful golden thread of yoga that is helpful in living this life. Use its five-layered framework, its tools, techniques, and philosophy and make a plan to lead consciously from a place of holistic well-being. Yoga teaches us that we have the choice to be a soft, rolling wave or a tsunami, leaving damage and carnage in our wake. Choose the path that allows you to maximize your contribution while also elevating others in some way.

One earns the luxury of becoming an engaging and inspiring leader. It is a practice, a life long practice. This journey is your own. Get playful, get curious, explore and find the mix of things to attend to that serve you and your life at this point in time. One thing is for certain, what is right for today isn't right for tomorrow, and will, without a doubt, meaningfully change from one year to the next. In time, this life long practice shifts our perspective and we begin to see that all of this self-care is actually a *service*. It is then that our commitment to the practice becomes *devotion*.

> The journey is vast and varied
> Long and windy,
> Choppy and smooth.
> At each turn my heart bursts.
> I feel it sometimes.
> It lets me know.
> My teacher drums forth, yet with wavering
> Comes discernment.
> The constant beat a friend, a companion
> Leading me on.

About the Author

Tarra Mitchell is incorporating her distinctive background in business and yoga to contribute to the great conversation around leadership and consciousness. *The Yoga of Leadership* is borne out of a desire to inspire and empower leaders to lead healthier, happier lives, and better connect with and engage their teams. *The Yoga of Leadership* demonstrates how personal wellbeing is a key indicator of success and principle is an essential component of inspiring leadership.

Beginning first with the leader's own experience, the systematic program shared in *The Yoga of Leadership* has the promise of catalyzing organizational excellence through conscious leadership and well-being. Tarra's work experience has allowed her to develop relationships with a wide variety of personalities in the global business arena, which was a key to her success. Tarra's highlights include directing billion-dollar fundraising events and ushering in commitments of capital from institutional investors in the private equity investment sector, forging new business ventures and relationships in Asia and Europe, and advising entrepreneurs and executives on financing and marketing strategies. A twenty-year practitioner of yoga, Tarra is a registered yoga teacher at the five-hundred-hour level and has studied extensively with master teachers and private mentors to support her research. Tarra's fascination with human behavior and culture led her to concentrate her academic studies on international business and explore much of the world for business and pleasure. Global awareness continues to influence her writing.

Tarra lives in Wellesley Hills, Massachusetts with her husband and two children. Connect with Tarra at www.tarramitchell.com.

Notes

Section 1: The Holistic Health of Leadership
Chapter 1—Leadership and Well-Being

1   At a fundamental level: Maryam Ovissi, Founder/Director/Visionary Beloved Yoga, enlightened me to the idea that a basic human need in any society is to feel safe, secure, and supported.

2   **"pure self within":** Nischala Joy Devi, *The Healing Path of Yoga: Time-Honored Wisdom and Scientifically Proven Methods That Alleviate Stress, Open Your Heart, and Enrich Your Life* (New York: Three Rivers Press, 2000), 69.

3   **that which spreads:** Gary Kraftsow, *Yoga For Wellness: Healing With the Timeless Teachings of Viniyoga* (New York: Penguin Compass, 1999), 130.

4   **demonstrated in his cardiovascular studies and term psychosocial support:** Devi, *The Healing Path of Yoga*, Forward XI.

5   **Our lack of movement:** Mark Hyman, *The Blood Sugar Solution: The UltraHealthy Program for Losing Weight, Preventing Disease, and Feeling Great Now!* (New York: Little Brown and Company, 2012), 21–22.

6   **For an extended discussion on tools and modalities that support the dimensions see:** Kraftsow, *Yoga For Wellness*, 130–131; Cyndi Dale, *The Subtle Body: An Encyclopedia of Your Energetic Anatomy* (Boulder: Sounds True, 2009), 282–286; Devi, *The Healing Path of Yoga*, 69–79.

7   **"…refers to the vital metabolic functions that sustain our life and health.":** Kraftsow, *Yoga for Wellness*, 130.

8   **For additional information on tools and modalities that support the dimensions see:** Kraftsow, *Yoga For Wellness*, 130–131; Cyndi Dale, The Subtle Body: *An Encyclopedia of Your Energetic Anatomy* (Boulder: Sounds True, 2009), 282–286; Devi, *The Healing Path of Yoga*, 69–79.

9   **There is an enormous lost cost:** Johns, G. (2010), "Presenteeism in the workplace: A review and research agenda." *J. Organiz. Behav.*, 31: 519–542. doi: 10.1002/job.630.

10   **In a 2010 study by:** Daniel J. DeNoon, "Obesity's Hidden Cost: Lost Productivity at Work," *WebMD*, October 8, 2010, http://www.webmd.com/news/20101008/obesity-hidden-cost-lost-productivity-at-work; Finkelstein, E.A. *Journal of Occupational and Environmental Medicine*, published online ahead of print, Sept. 25, 2010.

11   **some estimates:** "The Cost of Presenteeism," *About*, Retrieved: August 20, 2014, http://jobsearchtech.about.com/od/workplaceissues/a/Presenteeism.htm; Johns, "Presenteeism in the workplace," 519–542.

12   **Their findings:** Johns, "Presenteeism in the workplace," 519–542.

13   **Similarly, still other:** Sandy Smith, "Presenteeism Costs Business 10 Times More than Absenteeism," *EHS Today*, March 16, 2016, http://www.ehstoday.com/safety-leadership/presenteeism-costs-business-10-times-more-absenteeism.

14   **According to:** Centers for Disease Control and Prevention, "Chronic Disease Prevention and Health Promotion," Retrieved February 16, 2016, http://www.cdc.gov/chronicdisease/index.htm.

15   **The CDC indicates:** Centers for Disease Control and Prevention, "Chronic Disease Prevention and Health Promotion," Retrieved February 16, 2016, http://www.cdc.gov/chronicdisease/about/prevention.htm.

16   **The Journal of the American Medical Association:** C.L. Ogden, M.D. Carroll, B.K. Kit, K.M. Flegal, "Prevalence of Childhood and Adult Obesity in the United States, 2011–2012," *JAMA*, (February 26, 2014): 311(8), 806–814, doi:10.1001/jama.2014.732.

17   **According to:** Centers for Disease Control and Prevention, "Prevalence of Self-Reported Obesity Among U.S. Adults by State and Territory", *BRFSS*, 2014, http://www.cdc.gov/obesity/data/prevalence-maps.html.

18 **Although stress levels:** American Psychological Association, "American Psychological Association Survey Shows Money Stress Weighing on Americans' Health Nationwide," *American Stress in America™: Paying With Our Health*, February 14, 2015, http://www.apa.org/news/press/releases/2015/02/money-stress.aspx.

19 **According to the CDC:** Tatiana Nwankwo, M.S.; Sung Sug (Sarah) Yoon, Ph.D., R.N.; Vicki Burt, Sc.M., R.N.; and Qiuping Gu, "National Health and Nutrition Examination Survey, 2011–2012," *NCHS Data Brief*, No. 133, October 2013, http://www.cdc.gov/nchs/data/databriefs/db133.htm#x2013;2012</a>.

20 **It is the most:** Paul Heidenreich et al., "Forecasting the future of cardiovascular disease in the United States: a policy statement from the American Heart Association," *Circulation*, 2011; 123:933–44, Published online before print January 24, 2011, doi: 10.1161/CIR.0b013e31820a55f5.

21 **Notably:** Go AS, Mozaffarian D, Roger VL, et al, "Heart disease and stroke statistics—2013 update: a report from the American Heart Association," *Circulation*, 2013; 127:e6–245, Published online before print December 12, 2012, doi: 10.1161/CIR.0b013e31828124ad.

22 **According to the Mayo Clinic:** Mayo Clinic Staff, "Chronic Stress Puts Your Health at Risk," *Mayo Clinic*, July 11, 2013, http://www.mayoclinic.org/healthy-living/stress-management/in-depth/stress/art-20046037?footprints=mine.

23 **While many stressors:** the concept of improving our capacity for managing stress came out of private discussions with Maryam Ovissi.

24 **The CDC reports:** "Therapeutic Drug Use", *Centers for Disease Control and Prevention*, 2009–2012, http://www.cdc.gov/nchs/fastats/drug-use-therapeutic.htm.

25 **"the third leg of the stool":** Herbert Benson, *The Relaxation Response* (HarperTorch: New York, 2000), 4.

Chapter 2—Yoga: The Science of Consciousness

26 The "2016 Yoga in America Study": Ipsos Public Affairs: The Social Research and Corporate Reputation Specialists, "2016 Yoga in America Study," commissioned study, Yoga Journal and Yoga Alliance, January 2016, 4. http://www.yogajournal.com/uncategorized/new-study-finds-20-million-yogis-u-s/ Retrieved October 2014.

27 **Vivekananda also democratized:** Carol A. Horton, *Yoga Ph.D.: Integrating the Life of the Mind and the Wisdom of the Body* (Chicago: Kleio Books, 2012), 43–50.

28 **Seals found:** Edwin F. Bryant, *the Yoga Sutras of Patanjali* (New York: North Point Press, 2009), xx.

29 **Surviving the oral:** Ibid., xxiii.

30 **The Mahabharata:** Ibid., xxviii.

31 **Yet, Patanjali's:** Ibid., xxxiii.

32 **The cryptic:** Ibid., xxxv.

33 **A science that holds:** Hari-kirtana das (yoga scholar, philosopher, and theologian), informed through discussions with scholar throughout 2015.

34 **reference to psychological techniques:** Bryant, *the Yoga Sutras of Patanjali*, xxx.

35 **It allows leaders:** Daniel Goleman, *Emotional Intelligence: Why It Can Matter More Than IQ* (New York: Bantam Dell, 1995), 43.

36 **false ego:** Hari-kirtana das, his term shared in discussions throughout 2015.

37 **We are neither:** Hari-kirtana das, language clarified with him in 2016.

38 **Other translations:** Salvatore Zambito, *The Unadorned Thread of Yoga: The Yoga-Sutra of Patanjali in English* (Paulsbo, WA: The Yoga-Sutras Institute Press, 1992), 124.

Section 2: 7 Yogi Secrets for Leadership Success
Chapter 3—Yogi Secret #1: Aligned Intention

39 In yoga, sankalpa is: Rod Stryker, The Four Desires: Creating a Life of Purpose, Happiness, Prosperity, and Freedom (New York: Delacorte Press, 2011), 83.

40 **They are consummate:** Ibid.

Chapter 4—Yogi Secret #2: Physical

41   **When our sympathetic:** Timothy McCall, Yoga as Medicine: The Yogic Prescription for Health and Healing (New York: Bantam Dell, 2007), 48.

42   **In fact:** Ibid., 49.

43   **Eventually, when left:** Adapted from The Stress Solution by Lyle H. Miller and Alma Dell Smith, "Stress: The different kinds of stress," *American Psychological Association*, Retrieved: February 14, 2016, http://www.apa.org/helpcenter/stress-kinds.aspx.

44   **Empirical evidence:** Timothy McCall, *Yoga as Medicine: The Yogic Prescription for Health and Healing* (New York: Bantam Dell, 2007), 49.

45   **A 2013 survey:** "Workplace Stress on the Rise With 83% of Americans Frazzled by Something at Work," survey conducted by Harris Interactive and commissioned by Everest College, 2013, Retrieved: February 24, 2016, http://globenewswire.com/news-release/2013/04/09/536945/10027728/en/Workplace-Stress-on-the-Rise-With-83-of-Americans-Frazzled-by-Something-at-Work.html.

46   **The American Institute of Stress:** "Workplace Stress", The American Institute of Stress, Retrieved: February 24, 2016, http://www.stress.org/workplace-stress/.

47   **The curious question:** "Definitions: Stress," The American Institute of Stress, Retrieved February 24, 2016, http://www.stress.org/daily-life/.

48   **Further, when we don't:** Michael D. Gershon, *The Second Brain: A Groundbreaking New Understanding of Nervous Disorders of the Stomach and Intestine* (New York: HarperCollins, 1998), 86.

49   **10 Steps to Conscious Eating:** influenced by a cleanse led by Carolyn Weininger, a leading yoga teacher in Northern, VA.

50   **If you're going to eat:** David Servan-Schreiber, Anticancer: A New Way of Life (New York: Viking, 2009), 73.

51   **It is commonly known:** Hyman, *The Blood Sugar Solution*, 79.

52   **Choose pure:** Wee Peng Ho, "Anti-Inflammatory Diet: How to Choose the Right Cooking Oil," *the conscious life*, https://theconsciouslife.com/omega-3-6-9-ratio-cooking-oils.htm.

53   **Dr. Michael Gershon:** Harriett Brown, "The *Other* Brain Also Deals With Many Woes," *The New York Times*, August 23, 2005, http://www.nytimes.com/2005/08/23/health/the-other-brain-also-deals-with-many-woes.html?_r=0.

54   **Twenty percent of:** Michael D. Gershon, *The Second Brain: A Groundbreaking New Understanding of Nervous Disorders of the Stomach and Intestine* (New York: HarperCollins, 1998), 179–180.

55   **SSRI Medications:** Ibid., 223.

56   **The National Sleep Foundation:** Max Hirshkowitz et al., "National Sleep Foundation's sleep time duration recommendations: methodology and results summary", *Sleep Health: Journal of the National Sleep Foundation,* Volume 1, Issue 1, 40–43, doi: http://dx.doi.org/10.1016/j.sleh.2014.12.010.

57   **Researchers at Berkeley:** Rick Nauert, "Sleep Loss Challenges Emotional Control", PsychCentral, 1, Retrieved February 25, 2016, http://psychcentral.com/news/2007/10/23/sleep-loss-challenges-emotional-control/1443.html.

58   **Our amygdala:** Ibid., 1.

59   **When impaired:** Public Affairs, UC Berkeley, "Sleep loss leads to anxiety, poor food choices," *Berkeley News*, June 12, 2012, http://newscenter.berkeley.edu/2012/06/12/sleep-loss-studies/.

60   **Those who slept:** Camille Peri, "Coping With Excessive Sleepiness," *WebMD*, February 13, 2014, http://www.webmd.com/sleep-disorders/excessive-sleepiness-10/10-results-sleep-loss?page=2.

61   **We may think:** Ibid.

62   **Chronic sleep:** Ibid.

63   **It is part of our:** R. Bowen, "The Pineal Gland and Melatonin," Colorado State, March 17, 2003, http://www.vivo.colostate.edu/hbooks/pathphys/endocrine/otherendo/pineal.html.

64   **Our melatonin:** R.J. Reiter, "The pineal gland and melatonin in relation to aging: a summary of the theories and of the data." *Exp Gerontol.* 1995 May-Aug;30(3-4):199–212, http://www.ncbi.nlm.nih.gov/pubmed/7556503.

65 **Due to its:** Ibid.

66 **It peaks:** Atul Khullar, "The Role of Melatonin in the Circadian Rhythm Sleep-Wake Cycle," *Psychiatric Times*, July 09, 2012, http://www.psychiatrictimes.com/sleep-disorders/role-melatonin-circadian-rhythm-sleep-wake-cycle.

67 **Make sure:** "What temperature should your bedroom be?" National Sleep Foundation, Retrieved February 25, 2016, https://sleepfoundation.org/bedroom/touch.php.

Chapter 5—Yogi Secret #3: Energy

68 **Prana is called:** Devi, *The Healing Path of Yoga,* 73.

69 **For additional detail about the many energetic and chakra systems around the world:** Cyndi Dale, *The Subtle Body: An Encyclopedia of Your Energetic Anatomy* (Boulder, CO: Sounds True, Inc., 2009), 287–321.

70 **One cannot see:** Mark Stephens, *Teaching Yoga: Essential Foundations and Techniques* (Berkeley, CA: North Atlantic Books, 2010), 49.

71 **Riding the Wave:** subsection inspired by a workshop led by Rolf Gates and private discussions with Marni Sclaroff, a leading yoga teacher in Northern, VA.

72 **8 tips for keeping:** Information regarding energy use in various types of meetings influenced by conversations with Marni Sclaroff.

73 **Proper breathing:** Doug Keller, *Refining the Breath: Pranayama: The Art of the Awakened Breath* (Self Published: Fifth Edition), 8.

74 **That, in turn:** B.K.S. Iyengar, *Light On Pranayama: The Yogic Art of Breathing* (New York: The Crossroad Publishing Company, 2011), 17.

75 **People with emotional:** Ibid.

76 **From a biochemical:** Candace B. Pert, *Molecules of Emotion: The Science Behind Mind-Body Medicine* (New York: Scribner, 1997), 186–187.

77 **Some examples of:** Keller, *Refining the Breath: Pranayama,* 20.

78 **Elite athletes:** Iyengar, *Light on Pranayama,* 20.

79 **"dome shaped muscle":** Keller, *Refining the Breath: Pranayama,* 40.

80 **"brings the breath…":** Keller, *Refining the Breath: Pranayama,* 40.

81 **contributing to their optimal functioning:** Donna Farhi, *The Breathing Book: Good Health and Vitality Through Essential Breath Work* (New York: St. Martin's Press, 1996), 53.

82 **Most of us are either:** Iyengar, *Light on Pranayama,* 21.

83 **Poor breathing:** Ibid., 31.

84 **There are four stages:** Iyengar, *Light On Pranayama,* 99–111. This was further a detailed subject of study during advanced teacher training led by Maryam Ovissi and Julia Kalish.

85 **How you address:** Farhi, *The Breathing Book,* 146.

86 **Lengthening our exhale:** Farhi, *The Breathing Book,* 102.

87 **Traditionally:** Iyengar, *Light on Pranayama,* 55.

88 **This practice is:** Keller, *Refining the Breath: Pranayama,* 61–62.

89 **This vigorous breathing:** Keller, *Refining the Breath: Pranayama,* 121.

Chapter 6—Yogi Secret #4: Mind

90 archaeologist: a similar analogy was used by Jafar Alexander in a group class, a leading yoga teacher in Northern VA.

91 **"thoughts and feelings" (as part of the Mind layer):** Devi, *The Healing Path of Yoga,* 75.

92 **Our prefrontal cortex:** Amy F.T. Arnsten, "Stress signalling pathways that impair prefrontal cortex structure and function," *Nature Reviews Neuroscience* 10 (1 June 2009): 410–422, accessed March 1, 2016, doi:10.1038/nrn2648. Also appearing on Deric's MindBlog; "Stress pathways that impair prefrontal cortex," blog entry by Deric Bownds, June 2, 2009.

93 **In Buddha's Brain:** Rick Hanson and Richard Mendius, *Buddha's Brain: The Practical Neuroscience of Happiness, Love and Wisdom* (Oakland, CA: New Harbinger Publications, Inc, 2009), 41.

94   **Our memory of things:** Hanson and Mendius, *Buddha's Brain*, 53–58.

95   **We have less control:** Ibid.

96   **A weak prefrontal:** wiseGEEK, "What is the prefrontal cortex?" Retrieved March 1, 2016, http://www.wisegeek.org/what-is-the-prefrontal-cortex.htm.

97   **Our brain:** Hanson and Mendius, *Buddha's Brain*, 57.

98   **Directing our energy:** Hanson and Mendius, *Buddha's Brain*, 53.

99   **When we overuse:** Hanson and Mendius, *Buddha's Brain*, 57–58.

100 **Sri Aurobindo:** "Sri Aurobindo," *Wikipedia*, Retrieved March 1, 2016, http://en.wikipedia.org/wiki/Sri_Aurobindo.

101 **He defines:** Sri Aurobindo, *The Integral Yoga: Sri Aurobindo's Teaching and Method of Practice* (Twin Lakes, WI: Lotus Press, 2011), 118–122.

102 **Self awareness is:** Daniel Goleman, *Emotional Intelligence: Why It Can Matter More Than IQ* (New York: Bantam Dell, 1995), 43.

103 **Nine principal:** Peter Marchand, "9 Rasas: The Yoga of Nine Emotions," http://www.rasas.info.

104 **In a discussion:** David Romanelli, *Livin' the Moment: Getting to Esctasy Through Wine, Chocolate and Your iPod Playlist* (New York: Broadway Books, 2009), 13.

105 **As defined by:** "Understanding the Facts of Anxiety Disorders and Depression is the First Step," *Anxiety and Depression Association of America*, Retrieved March 2, 2016, http://www.adaa.org/understanding-anxiety.

106 **According to the CDC:** L.A. Pratt, D. J. Brody, and Q. Gu, "Antidepressant use in persons aged 12 and over: United States, 2005–2008," *NCHS data brief, No. 76, National Center for Health Statistics,* 2011. http://www.cdc.gov/nchs/data/databriefs/db76.htm.

107 **This represents an increase:** Ibid.

108 **Many of the:** Ibid.

109 **Anxiety disorders:** Ronald Kessler et al., "Prevalence, Severity, and Comorbidity of Twelve-Month DSM-IV Disorders in the National Comorbidity Survey Replication (NCS-R)," *Archives of General Psychiatry* 62.6 (2005): 617–627. http://doi.org/10.1001/archpsyc.62.6.617.

110 **The estimated cost:** P.E. Greenberg et al., "The economic burden of anxiety disorders in the 1990s," *J Clin Psychiatry* 1999; 60(7):427–35.

111 **In his book:** Robert Butera, *Meditation for your Life: Creating a Plan that Suits Your Style* (Woodbury, MN: Llewellyn Publications, 2012), 67–77.

112 **Hanson and Mendius:** Hanson and Mendius, *Buddha's Brain*, 62–63.

113 **Equanimity is a stress-free state:** Dr. Claudia Welch, *Balance Your Hormones, Balance Your Life: Achieving Optimal Health and Wellness through Ayurveda, Chinese Medicine, and Western Science* (Da Capo Press, 2011), 2.

114 **The section on brahmacarya is influenced by:** Adele, *The Yamas & Niyamas*, 76–88.

115 **A host of unhelpful:** Rolf Gates and Katrina Kenison, *Meditations From the Mat: Daily Reflections on the Path of Yoga* (New York: Anchor Books, 2002), 50–56.

116 **Our uncomfortably full:** Influenced by an analogy used in a yoga class led by Maryam Ovissi of Beloved Yoga.

117 **Employing brahmacarya, use of the words "just right" and "enough":** Adele, *The Yamas & Niyamas*, 78.

118 **Studies have demonstrated:** Candace B. Pert, Ph.D., *Molecules of Emotion: The Science Behind Mind-Body Medicine* (New York: Scribner, 1997), Chapter 7: 130–149.

119 **"field of consciousness":** Hari-kirtana das, scholar's original term and description shared in discussions in 2015.

120 **The scientific term:** "Neuroplasticity," Wikipedia, (accessed March 3, 2016), http://en.wikipedia.org/wiki/Neuroplasticity.

121 **He furthers that:** Dr. Wayne W. Dyer, *I Can See Clearly Now* (Carlsbad, CA: Hay House, Inc., 2014) Chapter 41, 231–232.

122 **reducing heart attacks:** "Meditation may reduce death, heart attack and stroke in heart patients." *American Heart Association website*, November 2012.

123 **reducing anxiety:** Wake Forest Baptist Medical Center, "Anxious? Activate your anterior cingulate cortex with a little meditation." *ScienceDaily*, www.sciencedaily.com/ releases/2013/06/130604114001.htm, (accessed March 3, 2016).

124 **Daily practices of:** Massachusetts General Hospital. "Meditation appears to produce enduring changes in emotional processing in the brain." *ScienceDaily*, www.sciencedaily.com/ releases/2012/11/121112150339.htm (accessed March 3, 2016).

125 **Regular practice:** S.W. Lazar et al., "Meditation experience is associated with increased cortical thickness," *Neuroreport*, 2005;16(17):1893-1897.

126 **So, a meditation:** "Meditation Might Keep Brains Young, Healthy and Connected," *EMax Health*, July 2011.

127 **And especially important:** Association for Psychological Science. "Meditation helps increase attention span," *ScienceDaily*, www.sciencedaily.com/releases/2010/07/100714121737.htm (accessed March 3, 2016).

128 **This is particularly helpful:** University of California, San Francisco (UCSF), "Wandering minds associated with aging cells: Attentional state linked to length of telomeres," *ScienceDaily*, www. sciencedaily.com/releases/2012/11/121117184551.htm, (accessed March 3, 2016).

129 **Meditation may also help:** Lutz A, Slagter HA, et al., "Mental training enhances attentional stability: Neural and behavioral evidence," *The Journal of neuroscience : the official journal of the Society for Neuroscience,* 2009; 29(42):13418-13427. doi:10.1523/JNEUROSCI.1614-09.2009.

130 **In an 8-week:** Britta K. Hölzel, James Carmody, et al., "Mindfulness practice leads to increases in regional brain gray matter density," *Psychiatry Research: Neuroimaging*, 2011; 191 (1): 36 DOI: 10.1016/j.pscychresns.2010.08.006.

131 **A decrease in blood:** Benson, *The Relaxation Response*, 116.

132 **Such rapid decreases:** Benson, *The Relaxation Response*, 112–113.

133 **Benson later:** Benson, *The Relaxation Response*, 8.

134 **These findings proved:** Benson, *The Relaxation Response*, 6-8.

135 **Centuries prior:** Benson, *The Relaxation Response*, 105.

136 **Through further studies:** Benson, *The Relaxation Response*, 120-121.

137 **Using an electroencephalogram:** Benson, *The Relaxation Response*, 106.

138 **In 2009:** Jim Lagopoulos, Jian Xu, et al., "Increased Theta and Alpha EEG Activity During Nondirective Meditation," *The Journal of Alternative and Complementary Medicine*, November 2009, 15(11): 1187-1192. doi:10.1089/acm.2009.0113.

139 **Here is a list:** Carolyn Gregoire, "The Daily Habit of These Outrageously Successful People," *HuffPost Healthy Living*, July 2013, http://www.huffingtonpost.com/2013/07/05/business-meditation-executives-meditate_n_3528731.html.

140 **Here is a list:** Arianna Huffington, *Thrive: The Third Metric to Redefining Success and Creating a Life of Well-being, Wisdom, and Wonder,* (New York: Harmony Books, 2014), 48.

141 **Here is a list:** Jhaneel Lockhart & Melanie Hicken, "14 Executives Who Swear by Meditation," *Business Insider*, May 2012, http://www.businessinsider.com/ceos-who-meditate-2012-5?op=1.

142 **Sand and water visualization:** Rolf Gates, (author, yoga teacher, national figure) during teacher training taught a similar meditation to our class in 2010.

143 **Don Miguel Ruiz:** don Miguel Ruiz, *The Four Agreements: A Practical Guide to Personal Freedom* (San Rafael, CA: Amber-Allen Publishing, Inc., 1997), Chapter 2: 25–46.

144 **We hold onto:** Gates, *Meditations From the Mat*, 67–68.

Chapter 10—Leaving a Legacy

145 John Mackey: Beth Kowitt, "John Mackey: The conscious capitalist," August 2015, http://fortune. com/2015/08/20/whole-foods-john-mackey/

146 **Among the enlightened:** David Gelles, "At Aetna, a C.E.O.'s Management by Mantra," *The New York Times*, February 2015, http://www.nytimes.com/2015/03/01/business /at-aetna-a-ceos-management-by-mantra.html?_r=0.

Index

Q

R

S